The Power of RTI
and Reading Profiles

The Power of RTI and Reading Profiles

A Blueprint for Solving Reading Problems

by

Louise Spear-Swerling, Ph.D.
Southern Connecticut State University
New Haven

·P·A·U·L·H·
BROOKES
PUBLISHING Cᵒ ®

Baltimore • London • Sydney

Paul H. Brookes Publishing Co.
Post Office Box 10624
Baltimore, Maryland 21285-0624

www.brookespublishing.com

Typeset by Scribe Inc., Philadelphia, Pennsylvania.
Manufactured in the United States of America by
Sheridan Books, Inc., Chelsea, Michigan.

Library of Congress Cataloging-in-Publication Data

The Library of Congress has cataloged the printed edition as follows:

Spear-Swerling, Louise.
  The power of RTI and reading profiles : a blueprint for solving reading problems / Louise
Spear-Swerling.
     pages   cm
     Summary: "The reading problems addressed in the book move beyond those associated with
disabilities such as dyslexia or high-functioning autism. The author addresses experientially based
reading difficulties caused by inadequate instruction or limited exposure to academic language/
literacy. Unlike other books on response to intervention (RTI), this book presents an argument
for using RTI as a method of identification as well as intervention in combination with individual
students' reading profiles. The case studies and practical examples cover a broad range of reading
problems (not only learning disabilities) to help make research findings applicable to a multidisciplinary audience, especially practitioners" —Provided by publisher.
     ISBN 978-1-59857-315-2 (paperback)—ISBN 978-1-59857-793-8 (epub e-book)—ISBN
978-1-59857-796-9 (pdf e-book)
     1. Reading disability.   2. Reading—Remedial teaching.   3. Response to intervention (Learning
disabled children)   I. Title.
     LB1050.5.S637 2014
     371.91'44—dc23   2014022508

British Library Cataloguing in Publication data are available from the British Library.

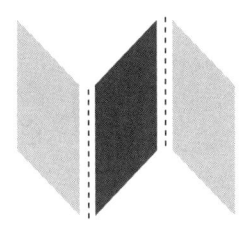

Contents

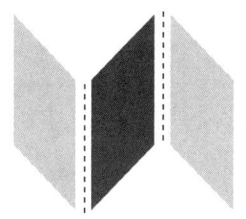 # About the Author

Louise Spear-Swerling, Ph.D., Professor, Department of Special Education, and Reading and Coordinator, Graduate Program in Learning Disabilities, Southern Connecticut State University, 501 Crescent Street, New Haven, Connecticut 06515

Dr. Spear-Swerling's research interests include literacy acquisition, reading difficulties, and teacher education, and she has published many peer-reviewed articles and book chapters on these topics. In addition to consulting for K–12 public schools and state departments of education, she has for more than 3 decades helped prepare both general and special educators to teach reading.

Foreword

In this book, *The Power of RTI and Reading Profiles*, Louise Spear-Swerling has done a masterful, scholarly job of integrating multiple, diverse strands of knowledge. Over the past 2 decades, there have been major developments in the science of reading. We now have strong research evidence on how children learn to read, why some struggle, and most important, how to best teach children to read even if they struggle. In addition, there has been a sustained effort to improve beginning reading instruction that includes early identification and intervention of struggling readers, as well as efforts to improve reading outcomes for all children. As the book makes clear, these efforts include multiple syntheses of research that identify the essential components of learning to read and the importance of explicit instruction for many children. As the education pendulum swings back toward approaches that are demonstrably less effective than explicit and component-based instruction, this book is an effective reminder of why the focus on beginning reading and its components should be areas of accumulating knowledge, not abandoned fads.

In tandem with these efforts, we have seen the development of a new approach to service delivery in schools that focus on instructional response. This approach, known as response to intervention (RTI) and a multi-tiered system of supports (MTTS), was formally codified in federal regulatory language in the reauthorization of the Individuals with Disabilities Education Act in 2004 (IDEA 2004). Again, this approach is not new but it has seen large-scale implementation for many years in states like Iowa and Kansas, as well as large school districts across the country.

As Spear-Swerling outlines in Chapter 1, there are many influences on the development of RTI approaches to service delivery, and they align well with current approaches to effectively teaching children to read, including those who are struggling. RTI methods have their origins in preventative approaches to addressing behavior problems in schools by researchers at the University of Oregon that led to widely implemented schoolwide positive behavior support (PBIS) programs. These programs introduced the screening and multiple tiers of intervention based on public health models that distinguished primary, secondary, and tertiary levels of intervention administered in a hierarchical manner. The goal is to prevent health problems first by introducing systemwide interventions, such as a focus on reducing tobacco consumption in our society in an effort to prevent cancer and other illnesses. Some people will still smoke, in which case they may need to participate in a smoking cessation treatment program. Tertiary interventions involve treatment for an actual illness, such as lung or throat cancer. The PBIS frameworks introduced the concept of problem-solving teams and progress monitoring.

The applications to reading emerged from research focusing on beginning reading instruction at the University of Texas. Researchers there were at the forefront of developing the three-tier framework described by Spear-Swerling. Tier I represents the attempt to enhance reading outcomes for all children by improving general education instruction. If a child struggles, Tier II involves small-group pull-out instruction. If this level of intervention is not sufficient, Tier III involves more intense intervention and may represent special education. Children are screened early and frequently and progress is monitored through repeated probe assessments of oral reading fluency and other types of curriculum-based assessment. In the RTI framework, there is ongoing discussion of the use of problem-solving approaches where, as in the behavior area, a team meets to discuss each child. This approach is contrasted with a standard protocol for delivering reading instruction in the RTI framework. Like Spear-Swerling, I think that reading protocols should be standardized up to the level of Tier III and/or special education because of the need for extensive professional development of teachers and the number of children who struggle with some aspect of reading.

To effectively enhance reading instruction, Spear-Swerling makes a compelling case for the examination of reading profiles. She recognizes that not all reading problems are the same. She also identifies variations in the pattern of reading difficulties that are critical for organizing intervention. Reading has multiple, interconnected pathways to proficiency (Chapter 2). Children vary in their capacity for working at the word level, the comprehension level, or both. Spear-Swerling describes each of these patterns in Chapters 7–9, as well as approaches to intervention in these chapters and Chapter 6. She makes it clear how these different components are connected in typical reading development and what happens when a child fails to develop proficiency in a particular component, including the more general issue of automaticity. Research supports the finding that teachers who are helped to differentiate instructional needs at the word-level versus text-level processes obtain better outcomes than teachers who are not assisted with this differentiation.

The reader of this book will understand the research base for a componential view of reading development, how to identify different components as they develop, and what to do in terms of intervention. Throughout the book, there are clever and well-integrated sections that explain the science under-lying a componential approach to reading and case examples to illustrate what these problems look like in the context of schools. The perspective is developmental (especially Chapter 3), covers preschool to high school, and outlines the role of different school personnel. As such, the book will be espe-cially useful to professionals who work in schools and want to enhance read-ing proficiency for all students, which is the primary goal of an RTI approach to service delivery.

If a child persistently struggles and needs the protection of special edu-cation, Spear-Swerling nicely outlines the type of information that is needed both from a compliance perspective with U.S. federal regulations and for the comprehensive evaluation needed for IDEA (Chapters 5 and 6). She wisely focuses on the assessment of reading strengths and weaknesses and appro-priately identifies assessments that aren't contributory to eligibility and intervention decisions (e.g., IQ tests). As such, the book is a useful addition to the library of the school psychologist and other assessment professionals. As Spear-Swerling documents, it is difficult to see how programming could be adequate if the only information available were the screening and progress monitoring assessments, especially for domains like reading comprehension and written expression. It is important to minimize assessment in favor of earlier and more intense instruction, including fast tracking to special educa-tion if indicated. Of course, fast tracking begs the question of whether out-comes are enhanced with special education placement, which is an issue the field is attempting to address. Part of the problem is we don't know what spe-cial education would look like if instructional casualties were reduced, which Spear-Swerling makes clear.

As a whole, the book shows that the research basis for integrating these approaches to service delivery and reading instruction are strong. Like Spear-Swerling, I also lament the emergence of the term *response to inter-vention* as opposed to *response to instruction*. As a concept for explaining the essential characteristic of a child with a learning disability, *unexpected under-achievement*, intractability, and persistence of difficulties in the face of strong efforts at intervention are compelling markers. These are new perspectives on the nature of a learning disability and are fundamentally dependent on the approaches to service delivery outlined in this book.

The final chapter addresses the most cogent issue presently facing the implementation of effective reading instruction and approaches to service delivery based on instructional support: teacher education. The problems with enhancing reading instruction in all schools are not lack of a scientific basis. As Spear-Swerling documents in Chapter 10, these issues are transla-tional and involve scaling of what is known from research. Teacher education is still not adequate, and too many teachers leave preservice training with-out adequate preparation. Spear-Swerling, an experienced teacher educator, nicely addresses how teacher preparation can be improved—and without the politically laden approaches that incentivize test scores in relation to arbitrary standards.

A key to better reading by our children is enhanced teacher preparation. Ultimately, this lack of preparation reflects a failure to adopt scientific research as a basis for decision making in education. This persistent refusal to accept science as a basis for decision making continues at the peril of our educational system. It requires a coordinated effort at the level of the university and the school in which the teacher works, especially in terms of the need for sustained professional development. Science is not static, and teachers need access to up-to-date information.

If a policy maker, professor of teacher education, teacher, or other professional wants to understand the scientific basis for enhancing reading outcomes in all children, he or she will find it here. Similarly, if the goal is to understand how the science of reading can be linked to service delivery models based on instructional response, this book is excellent. Finally, if a researcher wants to understand the evidence base for the science of reading and for RTI, this book provides that information in a well-organized, coherent fashion. Louise Spear-Swerling has done a masterful job of integrating different pieces of research and distilling them at a practical and scientific level that should be compelling to multiple audiences.

Jack M. Fletcher, Ph.D.
Hugh Roy and Lillie Cranz Cullen
Distinguished University Professor and Chair
Department of Psychology
University of Houston

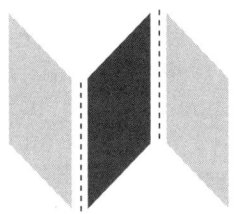# Acknowledgments

Numerous people contributed, directly or indirectly, to my writing of this book. First, many thanks to my editor at Brookes, Astrid Zuckerman, as well as to the entire editorial and production staff involved in producing *The Power of RTI and Reading Profiles*, for all their support and assistance. I also found the initial proposal review process at Brookes, with feedback from six anonymous reviewers, extremely valuable in planning my writing and avoiding several pitfalls I otherwise might not have anticipated. I am grateful to these reviewers as well as to Sarah Shepke, former editor at Brookes, who shepherded me through this initial review process.

I have had some wonderful mentors at various stages of my professional life. At the very beginning of my career, during my own teacher education program, Phyllis Fischer and the late Elizabeth Gallistel provided me with strong preparation for teaching poor readers. More than 30 years ago, this preparation included teaching me (and my fellow classmates) about the role of phonological awareness and other phonological skills in reading acquisition—and having us read the seminal work of Isabelle Liberman and Donald Shankweiler. During and after my doctoral program, Bob Sternberg taught me how to think broadly and critically about important issues in psychology and education, and he mentored me in vital ways as I began to publish my ideas. Later, and at various times, Marilyn Adams, C.K. Leong, Louisa Moats, and Hollis Scarborough all offered warm encouragement and wise counsel from which I benefited and that ultimately contributed to my ability to pursue projects such as this one. (Special thanks go to Louisa for her exceptionally long-standing and gracious support of my work.) I also am greatly indebted to Jack Fletcher for his generosity in writing the foreword to this book and grateful for many other experts in literacy, too numerous to name here but cited throughout this volume, who have influenced my thinking and from whom I continue to learn.

Colleagues and administrators at my institution, Southern Connecticut State University, provided key support by awarding me the sabbatical that enabled me to focus on writing *The Power of RTI and Reading Profiles*.

My department chair Ruth Eren and past and present deans of the School of Education, including Sharon Misasi, Michael Sampson, and Deborah Newton, have consistently supported my scholarly and creative activity, in particular, through their recognition that this activity requires some release from teaching responsibilities. In addition, my students at Southern as well as the many teachers and administrators I have come to know in K–12 schools have helped me to understand the challenges that confront contemporary educators, and they continue to inspire me day after day. I would like to give a special shout-out to my former research assistant Kim Freeman for all her help with the study mentioned in the opening to Chapter 6 and for being a stellar example of the dedicated, caring individuals who choose a career committed to teaching children with learning challenges.

During the semester of my sabbatical, several good friends and colleagues offered specific assistance related to different parts of my manuscript or expressed strong enthusiasm for the project as a whole. These include Tory Callahan, Hannah Dostal, Margie Gillis, Elena Grigorenko, Patricia Major, Jule McCombes-Tolis, Laura Raynolds, and Jamie Zibulsky. Many thanks to you all.

Last but certainly not least, I deeply appreciate the support of my family. My parents, Walter and Georgette Cheetham, always held the unwavering conviction that I could accomplish any educational or professional goal to which I set my mind, and their conviction helped give me the confidence to pursue those goals. My husband Bob has unflaggingly supported my professional endeavors over the many years of our marriage. His understanding of my desire to do meaningful, intellectually engaging work; his interest in learning about it; and his ability to offer perspective and make me laugh on the days when things do not go so well all have been essential to my motivation and ability to write. Likewise, my children Olivia and David offered ongoing support and encouragement throughout my planning and writing of this book. Although they were among the lucky ones who learn to read with ease, they have grown into thoughtful, kind adults with genuine compassion for those who find learning to read difficult or who face other types of adversity. What a joy it is to have you all in my life.

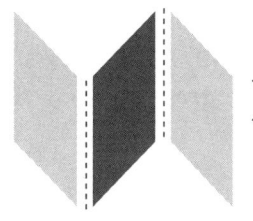 For the Reader

In my descriptions of all the children in this book, I have used pseudonyms and changed details so that actual children would not be recognizable. In addition, all the case examples of students in Chapters 7, 8, and 9 involve composites of real cases, again with identifying details such as names, grades, types of school districts, and parental occupations altered to further disguise the actual children involved. I chose to use composites not only to render real children unidentifiable but also because I wanted to be completely candid—for example, about inadequacies in school practices—in ways that I might avoid if cases were recognizable.

However, all the situations described here are authentic in that I have truly encountered children with literacy problems and from instructional environments very similar to the ones described. I have especially adhered to authenticity in relation to examples of overall patterns of test scores and to certain details that might be very surprising to some readers (especially those without wide experience working in schools). There truly was a child whose school did not have a single fourth-grade student meet the goal on the state-mandated reading test, like Anthony's school in Chapter 1. A student actually received years of tiered interventions without comprehensive evaluation for special education, like Henry in Chapter 7, and I have found numerous schools employing the same problematic approach to universal screening as Kevin's in Chapter 9. Conversely, I have also encountered schools with exemplary core general education reading instruction like Alicia's in Chapter 7 and Daniel's in Chapter 9, as well as many highly effective, dedicated special educators and reading teachers like those described throughout the book, who intervene successfully and make a difference every day in the lives of children.

For the many children who find learning to read
difficult and the educators dedicated to helping them

1 Introduction

Especially when trying to achieve sweeping, ambitious change, policy makers sometimes invoke the maxim "Don't let the perfect be the enemy of the good," usually attributed to Voltaire. This adage suggests that an insistence on perfection can impede meaningful, though imperfect, progress. New social and educational policies can never be perfect, but they surely should be an improvement over what they have replaced, and improvements would seem more likely if scientific evidence and data are used to inform policy changes. Regrettably, with regard to educational practice in reading, policies have sometimes been neither perfect nor good—nor informed by scientific evidence. To illustrate these problems, let us begin with the story of an unhappy little boy: a struggling reader whom I call Anthony.

ANTHONY'S STORY

Anthony was an African American student in a K–6 school in a large urban district. Like Anthony, most children who attended the school were African American children or English language learners (ELLs) from low-income backgrounds. The school had the achievement problems of many large, low-income districts, and the majority of the children there routinely failed to meet the goal for reading on the state-mandated achievement test. Indeed, one year the percentage of fourth graders meeting the goal on the state-mandated reading test was an appalling *zero*.

In hindsight, Anthony's difficulties, which involved problems in learning to sound out printed words, were evident even in kindergarten and early first grade; at the time, however, because he was a quiet, compliant, well-behaved child, and because many of his classmates seemed needier than he did, teachers overlooked his difficulties. Still, by the beginning of second grade, Anthony's reading problems could not be ignored. The only avenues for intervention at Anthony's school involved the goodwill of individual educators, an overburdened remedial reading program, and special education. When the first two avenues failed to improve his reading difficulties, his third-grade teacher referred him for a comprehensive evaluation, a process that involves gathering and interpreting extensive test data and other information to determine if a child is eligible for special education. To be eligible, a child must fit into a disability category such as specific learning disability (LD), intellectual disability (ID), emotional disturbance (ED), or autism spectrum disorder (ASD).

Anthony clearly did not meet criteria for ID, ED, or ASD, but his problems did seem similar to those of many children with LDs. However, Anthony's state required an IQ–achievement discrepancy for a child to be eligible for services in the LD category, meaning that Anthony's IQ had to be substantially higher than his reading achievement for him to obtain services under this category. Anthony's comprehensive evaluation yielded standard scores for word decoding and reading fluency that were quite low—in the mid-70s, around the fifth percentile—demonstrating that his reading problems were severe and certainly warranted intensive intervention. Unfortunately, his IQ—at 84—was not high enough relative to his achievement for him to meet eligibility criteria for LDs in his state. Even worse, because Anthony's IQ was slightly below average, although well above the cutoff for an ID, it led some of his teachers to think that maybe he was, well, not too smart (or phrased more delicately by one examiner, "functioning close to his potential"). His IQ test led many teachers to attribute Anthony's reading failure to limited capacity to learn and to conclude that nothing more could be done for him. Anthony certainly believed that he was not too smart, and his ongoing lack of progress in reading provided further evidence to support that belief. Now somewhat less well behaved and compliant than he had been in first grade, he continued to flounder until his fifth-grade teacher, a determined woman who was not inclined to take Anthony's IQ test score too seriously, finally found him the kind of help that he needed at a nearby university reading clinic.

In fact, Anthony had a genuine disability: He was dyslexic. As a preschooler, he had an important warning sign of future reading difficulties, early language delay, although his language abilities appeared to have caught up by the time he entered kindergarten, and at the time of his comprehensive evaluation, all his oral language scores were well within average range. Low reading achievement was rampant at Anthony's school, but Anthony's difficulties with learning to decode unfamiliar printed words, a central problem in dyslexia, were severe even relative to those of his classmates and required intensive intervention at the university clinic before he began to make progress. His family history also suggested dyslexia: Although Anthony's mother read well, his father had had very serious difficulties learning to read and was illiterate. Yet, despite the fact that dyslexia is the most well-researched reading disability and that much is known about how to identify and help students with dyslexia learn to read, Anthony did not receive the help he needed until he had experienced years of failure. At that point, he was very far behind in reading; his difficulties were influencing his ability to function in all school subjects and were compounded by his embarrassment and his conviction that he was incapable of learning. Now a teenager, Anthony is definitely doing better with appropriate intervention, and he is happier—at least, as happy as the average adolescent. Still, his reading problems could have been addressed much earlier, saving him considerable anguish, making intervention far less complex and difficult, and perhaps leading to better long-term outcomes for him.

Other students at Anthony's school, though not dyslexic, had very similar reading problems to his, revolving around word decoding skills; they could have benefited greatly from some of the same assessments and interventions that might have helped Anthony—had his school only used them. Of course, not all the struggling readers at Anthony's school had problems with decoding: Some learned to decode words with ease but still could not comprehend well what they were reading. Some children's difficulties emerged early in schooling, like Anthony's; other children's reading problems emerged later, in the middle- or upper-elementary grades. However, an existing and continually emerging body of scientific evidence that is mapping the processes involved in typical reading development, as well as the processes implicated in common reading problems, can greatly inform assessment, instruction, and interventions for all these students. The right educational practices could have made a great difference, especially if they had been implemented not only by the occasional, unusually determined or knowledgeable teacher but, rather, on a more systemic basis—in a coordinated effort involving all teachers. Furthermore, the types of assessments, instruction, and interventions that could have helped children at Anthony's school can help children at all schools, regardless of the populations they serve.

THEMES OF THIS BOOK

Anthony's story illustrates two broad themes that form the foundation for this book. The first involves a theoretical model that provides an educationally useful way to conceptualize reading development, as well as a wide array of common reading difficulties, and that is grounded in current scientific evidence about language and literacy. This evidence is both multidisciplinary and interdisciplinary in nature. It includes research and research collaborations involving the fields of not only reading and education (e.g., Allington & McGill-Franzen, 2008; Chall, 1967, 1983; Kuhn, Schwanenflugel, & Meisinger, 2010; Lesaux & Kieffer, 2010; Valencia, 2011) but also special education (e.g., Compton et al., 2010; Fuchs et al., 2012; Siegel, 1988, 1989, 1999), speech and language (e.g., Catts, Adlof, & Weismer, 2006), cognitive psychology (e.g., Cain & Oakhill, 2008; Ehri, 1991, 1997, 2005; Scarborough, 1998, 2005; Stanovich, 2000; Torgesen, Wagner, & Rashotte, 1994), behavioral genetics (e.g., Grigorenko, 2005; Olson & Byrne, 2005), and neuroscience (e.g., Cutting et al., 2013; Pugh & McCardle, 2009). This way of conceptualizing reading problems could have greatly improved reading outcomes for Anthony and his classmates without the risks and potential damages of IQ testing.

The second theme of the book involves a groundbreaking shift in educational policy, termed *response to intervention* (RTI) or *multi-tiered systems of support* (MTSS), with wide implications for serving students in general education as well as for identifying those who need special education. This shift represents both a great challenge and an unparalleled opportunity for contemporary educators. Together, RTI and scientific evidence can greatly advance educators' abilities to identify and effectively teach struggling readers as well as prevent some reading problems altogether.

An Educationally Useful Way to Conceptualize Reading Problems

Evidence suggests that most struggling readers—whether they have actual disabilities or problems stemming primarily from experiential factors such as inadequate instruction, poverty, or limited knowledge of English—exemplify one of several common profiles and patterns of reading difficulties (e.g., Badian, 1999; Catts et al., 2006; Catts, Compton, Tomblin, & Bridges, 2012; Huemer & Mann, 2010; Leach, Scarborough, & Rescorla, 2003; Lesaux & Kieffer, 2010). The profiles and patterns involve sets of strengths and weaknesses in specific reading and language abilities, often with a characteristic underlying dynamic. An understanding of these profiles and patterns is vital to early identification and intervention with struggling readers as well as to effective educational practices for preventing reading problems.

For example, as a kindergartner and first grader, Anthony had a profile involving specific difficulties learning to decode printed words, coupled with average oral vocabulary and comprehension; when not addressed successfully in intervention, those decoding problems inevitably prevented him from developing fluent reading and impaired his reading comprehension despite his ability to comprehend when listening. However, certain screening procedures could have identified Anthony's risk of reading difficulties well before second grade, and research-based interventions could have helped address his reading problems if applied promptly and with sufficient intensity. Even if these steps did not eliminate all of Anthony's reading difficulties, they would have at least kept him from falling so far behind and likely avoided some of the emotional consequences of severe reading failure.

Although the most important assessments for helping Anthony and other struggling readers involve specific reading and language assessments, other types of tests may sometimes be useful, including tests of specific cognitive abilities that can influence reading performance such as working memory and executive function. In specific cases, IQ tests can even sometimes be relevant, for instance, to rule out (or rule in) a genuine ID. However, *routine* IQ testing should not be done, because IQ testing does not provide information needed for planning reading interventions and because this testing involves significant risks, as Anthony's case illustrates. These risks are especially pronounced for low-income and minority students but are certainly not unique to those populations.

Many educators, as well as the public (including most parents), believe that IQ tests measure something fixed, immutable, and of overwhelming importance: a child's broad capacity to learn in the future. In this regard, IQ tests are like no other tests given in education. Most people, including most educators, think that reading difficulties can be improved through intervention and that even specific cognitive weaknesses, such as working memory problems, can be amenable to compensation; however, for limited intelligence, as represented in a child's IQ score, they believe there is no remedy. Despite these widespread beliefs, however, extensive environmental influences on IQ test performance are well documented (Nisbett et al., 2012), and long-standing reading difficulties, circumscribed language or cognitive impairments, and limited knowledge of English may all affect students' performance on IQ measures (Gunderson & Siegel, 2001). The phenomenon of *stereotype threat* (Steele & Aronson, 1995), the tendency of test takers to perform badly when they are aware of negative stereotypes of their intelligence, may also lower some struggling readers' IQ test performance. Researchers have typically studied stereotype threat in relation to racial, gender, or socioeconomic differences (Nisbett et al., 2012; Walton & Spencer, 2009), but negative stereotypes of poor readers' intelligence also exist. If ever there were individuals vulnerable to believing such stereotypes, it is those with a history of repeated failure in reading, such as Anthony. Furthermore, although IQ tests do tap a subset of important cognitive abilities, they are not strong measures of many other important abilities, such as creativity and practical intelligence (Sternberg, 1985) or decision making and judgment (Stanovich, 2009).

Finally, the use of an IQ–achievement discrepancy to identify LDs as required by Anthony's state and others involves not only the potential risks and problems associated with IQ testing but many additional problems as well (to be discussed further in Chapter 2). A different approach to the identification of LDs is possible, one that would have yielded much better results for Anthony and for many of his classmates.

The Opportunities Presented by Response to Intervention

Alternative approaches to using an IQ–achievement discrepancy in identification of LDs are permitted by the Individuals with Disabilities Education Improvement Act of 2004 (IDEIA, popularly termed IDEA 2004), the federal law most pertinent to identification of disabilities for students in K–12 schools. One alternative approach involves RTI. RTI bases provision of intervention simply on need; a child does not have to fit in a category or have a special education label in order to receive extra help. The emphasis is on early identification and prompt intervention, with more intensive intervention for children at greater levels of risk. Advocates of this model tend to conceptualize children with genuine LDs, in part, as those who fail to make adequate progress even when they are provided with intensive, research-based interventions effective for most struggling readers. Other criteria must also be met, but IQ testing is not necessary in order to identify children for extra help or, usually, even for special education.

Had this model been in place at Anthony's school, educators likely would have caught his reading problems early, and he would have received intervention quickly. Even if ultimately he still required special education, with appropriate early intervention, he almost certainly would not have been so far behind by the time he received special education services, which also would not have been yoked to an IQ score that led many adults to lower their expectations for him. Moreover, many other students at the school could have benefited from the interventions provided in RTI as well as RTI's emphasis on ensuring good classroom reading instruction, whether or not those students had actual disabilities. For example, a number of authorities (e.g., Gerber & Durgunoglu, 2004; Gersten et al., 2007; Rivera, Moughamian, Lesaux, & Francis, 2008) have noted the value of RTI models for students who are ELLs. Students with disabilities other than LDs also could have profited from an emphasis on early identification, prompt intervention, and effective general education practices. For instance, students with ASD often are identified for services even before entering kindergarten, and RTI criteria are not relevant to the diagnosis of ASD. Nevertheless, these students would often be included in a general education classroom for part of the school day and could benefit from effective classroom practices in reading as well as other areas such as behavior.

Achieving successful implementation of an RTI model is not easy for school districts, and although most states have some level of RTI implementation, individual states vary greatly in the extent to which they promote and provide guidance to districts on RTI (see, e.g., http://state.rti4success .org). Among other challenges, RTI requires a systemic approach, and therefore, individual teachers, no matter how capable or well intended, cannot implement it on their own. Using RTI to identify LDs entails particular challenges, and RTI should never be the sole criterion for identification. Nevertheless, weighed against the many problems of past identification practices for LDs, as well as the potential to radically improve instruction and intervention for large numbers of children, RTI represents a dramatic advance in educational policy.

Either of the preceding concepts by itself—the use of profiles and patterns to understand reading difficulties *or* the use of RTI models in reading—can be enormously valuable to educators in helping students with reading difficulties. Together, the two concepts provide a powerful approach, a blueprint, for preventing, ameliorating, and addressing reading difficulties on a large scale— not only in some of the nation's most vulnerable schools but in all schools.

OVERVIEW OF RESPONSE TO INTERVENTION/MULTI-TIERED SYSTEMS OF SUPPORT

RTI models grew out of public health approaches to disease prevention, representing a blend of evidence-based educational practices with population-based systems approaches to education (Vaughn, Wanzek, Woodruff, & Thompson, 2007). The systems aspect is why individual teachers cannot implement RTI on their own: RTI requires the involvement of an entire school or school district and, hence, the leadership of administrators and other school officials. An emphasis on systems is essential to ensure that general education is maximally effective for most children and that at-risk students are not overlooked. Without a systemic approach, the gains made with one teacher in one grade may be lost with a far less effective teacher in the next; a child may flounder, as Anthony did, until an unusually determined teacher comes along; or children's instruction may simply lack efficiency and consistency, problems likely to affect the more vulnerable readers the most negatively. The term *multitiered systems of support* (MTSS) sometimes is used in lieu of RTI to emphasize the systemic nature of the approach as well as its use of tiered interventions for children at different levels of risk. Although the focus in this book is on using RTI in the domain of elementary reading, RTI models have been applied to a wide range of domains, including mathematics (e.g., Gersten et al., 2009) and preschool education (e.g., Coleman, Buysse, & Neitzel, 2006). Furthermore, virtually all RTI models address behavior as well as academics (e.g., Sugai & Horner, 2005) in recognition of the interplay between behavior and academic achievement.

Common Features and Assumptions of Response to Intervention

Approaches to implementation of RTI vary, but in the following list are some features central to all RTI models (e.g., Brown-Chidsey & Steege, 2005), described here in relation to reading:

- *Universal screening and progress monitoring.* RTI involves screening the entire school population for potential risks in reading, with children's progress monitored regularly and with additional diagnostic testing of at-risk children as needed.

- *Provision of intervention for children determined to be at risk, with more intensive or individualized intervention for children at greater levels of risk.* Children determined to be at risk based on screening and progress-monitoring procedures (or sometimes based on other data) receive intervention promptly, with no need for a special education label. Educators closely monitor the progress of children receiving intervention. Students failing to respond to initial levels of intervention may receive more intensive or individualized help—for example, more frequent time in intervention with a smaller teacher–student ratio.

- *A focus on effective and systemic core general education reading instruction.* Lack of good core instruction provides a perpetual stream of children requiring intervention simply because they were improperly taught. Not only is this situation bad for the children, but it also will overburden any system for providing intervention. Hence ensuring effective core instruction is an essential initial emphasis in the implementation of RTI. Good core instruction cannot prevent all reading difficulties, but it will result in fewer difficulties and permit interventionists to focus on a relatively small number of students who truly require additional help. Core curriculum and instruction must also be systemic—that is, consistent across teachers within a grade and coherent across grades—so that educators work in an efficient, coordinated effort and so that individual children's exposure to appropriate instruction does not hinge on which teacher they happen to have.

- *Attention to fidelity of implementation.* Educators recognize the importance of implementing core instruction and interventions as intended, with adherence to features such as time requirements, use of proper materials, and necessary professional development of classroom teachers and interventionists.

- *Systemic data collection and data analysis, with clear decision rules.* Within a grade, teachers use the same screening and progress-monitoring procedures as well as the same rules for deciding which children they consider for interventions. For instance, if the cutpoint for intervention on screening assessments used for the fall of first grade is the 25th percentile, then every first-grade teacher would consider all students below the 25th percentile (i.e., in the bottom quarter of their classes) for possible intervention. Some of these children might not end up receiving intervention; for example, intervention might be deemed unnecessary for a child whose low screening performance seems due to illness and who performs well on other reading assessments. However, educators at least examine the performance of all children scoring below the cutpoint.

- *Use of data to inform educational practice in relation to not only individual children but also core general education and intervention systems.* Educators employ screening, progress monitoring, and other data to inform systemic educational practices as well as instruction and intervention for individual students. For example, if second-grade screening data reveal that a majority of second graders require intervention in decoding, then decoding instruction in kindergarten and first grade is obviously problematic and must be improved. If progress-monitoring assessments from children receiving intervention show that most children do not respond to intervention, then educators should attempt to improve the system of interventions by considering factors such as whether choices of interventions, amount of intervention time, and expertise of interventionists are generally appropriate.

As these features suggest, some key assumptions undergird RTI. One assumption is that scientific research should inform educational practice and that educators should base important decisions on data, including data gathered for a particular school and group of students as well as data gathered in scientific studies. In addition, prevention and early intervention are better, in both human and practical terms, than waiting until children's reading difficulties become severe, entrenched, and greatly compounded by behavioral or social-emotional factors. Finally, RTI involves a belief in the power of education to help children succeed. Although individual children vary widely in the ease with which they learn to read, effective educational practices can make a tremendous difference in children's reading outcomes.

The Three-Tiered Model

Descriptions of RTI/MTSS approaches to general education instruction and intervention sometimes employ a three-tiered model to convey the overall organization of the system (see Figure 1.1). Typically, this model represents the general education system as a triangle divided into three tiers. Tier I (sometimes termed *primary prevention*) is the largest, base part of the triangle, whereas Tier II (or *secondary prevention*) is the middle part, and Tier III (or *tertiary prevention*) is the smallest part, the apex of the triangle.

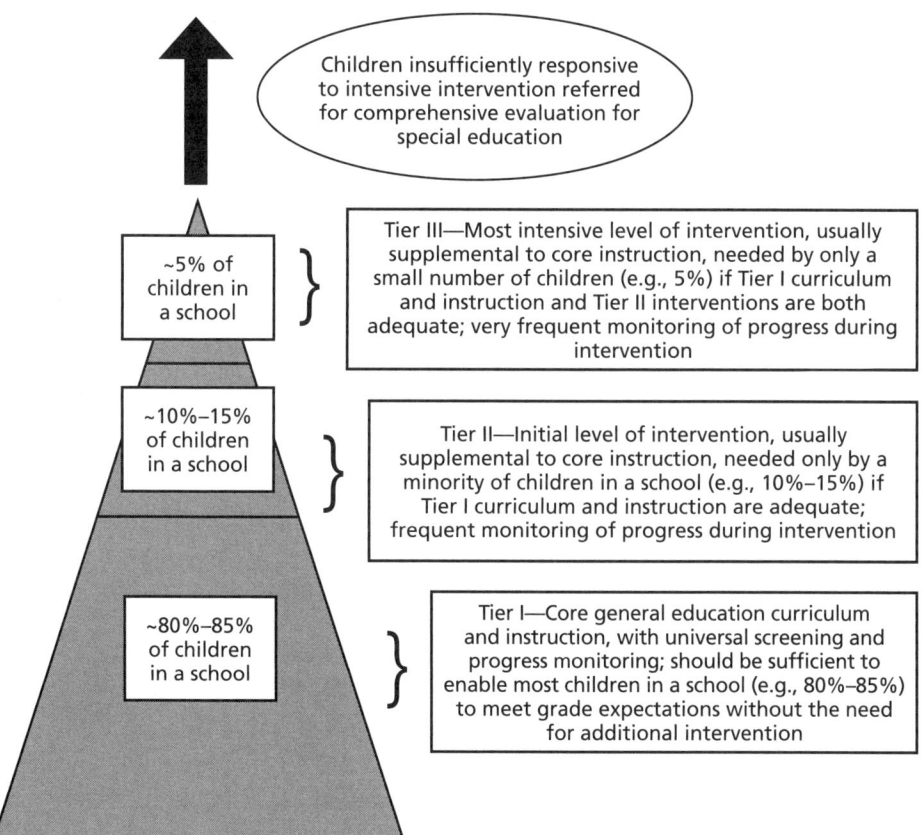

Figure 1.1. Example of a three-tiered response to intervention model.

Tier I represents core general education practices in reading for all students, including the general education reading curriculum, instructional activities and materials, and the use of universal screening and progress-monitoring procedures in reading. Core curriculum and instruction should be comprehensive and research based; for example, in the primary grades, core instruction should explicitly and systematically address important components of reading such as those outlined by the National Reading Panel (NRP; 2000). The initial screening usually is done in the fall; additional progress monitoring assessments often are done once in the winter and then again in the spring. Effective Tier I practices should permit the majority of students (e.g., 80%–85%) in a school to meet important grade-level benchmarks and goals—such as progress-monitoring benchmarks and goals on the state-mandated reading assessment—without the need for supplemental intervention or special education.

Tier II involves initial interventions for students who struggle in Tier I (e.g., 10%–15%), including children not meeting benchmarks on screening or progress-monitoring assessments, despite the use of good core practices that are effective for most students. Tier II interventions usually are conceptualized as supplemental, short-term interventions, lasting months as opposed to years. There is no single standard for frequency, duration, or group size of Tier II interventions, but, as an example, a school might deliver Tier II interventions four times per week, for half an hour at a time, in small groups of one teacher with three or four students. Students must be homogeneously grouped; for instance, those with similar decoding needs are in a different group than those with comprehension needs. A general educator or a specialist such as a special educator, remedial reading teacher, or other literacy specialist may deliver interventions. The interventionist monitors students' progress in intervention frequently, perhaps every couple of weeks, and when students are assessed as meeting grade expectations, the intervention is discontinued.

Tier III interventions target students who are not showing adequate progress in Tier II interventions (e.g., 5%). Tier III involves intensification or individualization of interventions through more frequent intervention time or smaller group size; through a different, more intensive intervention approach; or both. For example, nonresponsive students who have been receiving a phonics intervention 4 times per week, for half an hour at a time, in a small group of 1 teacher to 4 students, might receive an intervention intensified to 45 minutes per session, 5 times per week, in a group of 1 teacher with 2 students. Tier III also often involves more frequent progress monitoring as well as interventionists with more specialized expertise than does Tier II.

Tier III is an especially variable aspect of RTI models (Fuchs, Fuchs, & Compton, 2012). Some RTI models conceptualize Tier III as special education, whereas others do not. Whatever the most intensive level of intervention provided within general education, general educators typically refer students who do not respond sufficiently to that level for comprehensive evaluation for special education. If a student is eligible for special education, then he or she would receive services in the appropriate disability category. Students who are not eligible for special education can still continue to receive tiered interventions.

If Tier I practices are effective, then only a minority of students in a school should require Tier II interventions. For example, Foorman, Francis, Fletcher, Schatschneider, and Mehta (1998) found that explicit, systematic phonemic awareness and phonics instruction, coupled with a print-rich classroom environment, enabled 75% of low-achieving first-grade readers in high-poverty schools to attain average levels in word reading without any additional intervention at all. Likewise, if Tier II interventions are generally effective, then an even smaller percentage of students should require Tier III intervention (Foorman, 2003; Torgesen, 2004). It also bears emphasizing that RTI approaches view interventions as part of the general education system. To put it another way, in this view, general education has a responsibility to provide options for extra help for struggling students. Special education is vital, but it should not be the *only* avenue for students to receive extra help; otherwise, many students without disabilities who do not truly require special education may end up there.

THE ROLE OF SPECIAL EDUCATION

Virtually all studies involving implementations of RTI find some struggling readers who fail to respond even to the most intensive levels of intervention (e.g., Al Otaiba, 2001; Denton, Fletcher, Anthony, & Francis, 2006; Denton et al., 2010; Simmons et al., 2011; Speece, Case, & Malloy, 2003; Vellutino & Scanlon, 2002). The percentage of nonresponders varies across studies depending on variables such as the duration and frequency of interventions, the length of a particular study, and the ages of participants. However, studies such as the preceding ones suggest that, although well-implemented RTI approaches can greatly improve core general education reading instruction and help many struggling readers through prompt interventions, they definitely cannot be expected to address *all* poor readers' needs successfully. In other words, even the best implementations of RTI will not eliminate the need for special education.

Furthermore, as previously noted, although use of an RTI process may be required for identification of LDs, not all children with disabilities have LDs. Some children, such as those whose disabilities manifest in very early childhood or at birth (e.g., Down syndrome, many ASDs, many sensory impairments), will not undergo an RTI process prior to a comprehensive evaluation for special education. Nevertheless, for all students with disabilities, not only LDs, as well as for struggling students in general, RTI approaches can help ensure that children receive good instruction and that the difficulties of children undergoing comprehensive evaluation are not mainly due to inadequate general education practices.

Fuchs, Fuchs, and Stecker (2010) point out that, in the early years of special education, special educators were often the "go-to" experts in a school for general educators seeking help with their most challenging students. However, in recent decades, the identity of special education has weakened, despite the fact that difficult-to-teach students still abound, and schools' records of accomplishment for helping these students—in both general and special education—are not reassuring. Fuchs and colleagues (2010) suggest experimental teaching, an approach with a long tradition in special education research (e.g., Deno, 1985; Fuchs, Deno, & Mirkin, 1984), as an alternative for helping students with the most serious learning difficulties. In this approach, an expert teacher works with students individually or in small groups to implement very intensive intervention, with systematic application of effective teaching strategies, continuous monitoring of children's progress toward benchmarks, data-based decision making, and very frequent, ongoing adjustment of intervention based on the results of progress-monitoring assessment. Experimental teaching instantiates many key principles of RTI, applied in a particularly intensive and systematic way.

With or without RTI, special education has an essential role to play in addressing the needs of not only students with identified disabilities but also those who fail to respond to evidence-based interventions implemented in general education, whether or not the children actually meet eligibility criteria for a disability. This role should include serving as expert interventionists as well as consulting and collaborating with general education colleagues and other specialists such as remedial reading teachers, school psychologists, and speech-language pathologists. In order to fulfill their roles well, all these specialist groups—and of course, general educators, too—need appropriate preservice preparation and professional development. The need for effective preparation and professional development is one key challenge, although far from the only challenge, involved in implementation of RTI.

CHALLENGES OF RESPONSE TO INTERVENTION

Since the implementation of RTI in our state (Connecticut), some of my colleagues and I have used an anonymous questionnaire to elicit practitioners' opinions about RTI. Practitioners' responses to this questionnaire suggest that most who are familiar with RTI believe that RTI practices benefit their students, especially through early identification and early intervention for learning problems. However, there is a relationship between practitioners' opinions and their experience implementing RTI. Respondents' opinions tend to be more uniformly positive when they lack actual experience with RTI and somewhat more mixed—mentioning both positives and negatives about RTI—when they say they have had experience implementing it. (It is rare for respondents' opinions to be uniformly negative.) These mixed responses from experienced practitioners likely reflect a realistic understanding of the challenges of RTI, in relation to both implementation of the models in general education and identification of LDs.

Implementation Challenges

Screening of entire school populations—with early identification of at-risk readers—is fundamental to all RTI models. However, although factors that tend to presage reading difficulties are well known, accurate identification of *individual* at-risk students on a large scale involves many problems. Early identification practices must avoid false negatives (truly at-risk students missed by screening) as well as false positives (not-at-risk students inappropriately identified for intervention); the latter group will stress available resources, making fewer resources available for the students who genuinely require them. If schools employ a one-stage universal screen, as appears to be true in most current implementations of RTI, then identifying the majority of truly at-risk students on currently used screening measures involves casting a wide net that will also falsely identify many not-at-risk students (Fuchs, Compton, et al., 2012; Fuchs & Vaughn, 2012; Johnson, Jenkins, Petscher, & Catts, 2009). Furthermore, it appears possible to identify highly at-risk students who should be "fast-tracked" to the most intensive level of intervention (e.g., Tier III or special education) rather than being required to demonstrate unresponsiveness in earlier levels first. Yet most schools implement RTI in a rigid fashion that requires students to progress through levels of intervention in a more lockstep manner: first Tier I, then Tier II, then Tier III (Fuchs, Compton, et al., 2012).

Another issue in RTI implementation involves the fact that decisions about intervention responsiveness may vary depending on choices of progress-monitoring measures as well as specific decision rules. For example, several studies (e.g., Denton et al., 2010; Mathes et al., 2005) have found that when decisions about adequacy of children's progress during intervention are based on word-reading accuracy, more children meet the criterion (i.e., their progress is considered adequate) than when oral reading fluency (ORF) criteria that include rate are employed. Hence, with an ORF measure, children are more likely to have their progress evaluated as inadequate as well as to experience intensification of intervention and perhaps referral to special education.

Successful implementation of RTI practices requires that both general and special educators have a strong knowledge base about reading. Although the use of appropriate curricula and programs is very important, meeting the needs of at-risk students in reading requires both research-based methods and knowledgeable teachers (Piasta, Connor, Fishman, & Morrison, 2009). Unfortunately, research on teacher knowledge raises significant concerns about the knowledge base of many elementary-level teachers, including special as well as general educators, for implementing RTI. Many teachers appear to lack knowledge important for effective reading assessment and instruction—and especially for meeting the needs of the most vulnerable readers in a classroom (e.g., Brady et al., 2009; Cunningham, Perry, Stanovich, & Stanovich, 2004; Moats, 1999; Moats & Foorman, 2003; Spear-Swerling, Brucker, & Alfano, 2005). Moreover, many educators may be unfamiliar with specific research-based interventions that could serve as vital resources for them in implementing RTI (Spear-Swerling & Cheesman, 2012). Of course, educators also need adequate access to effective curricula and interventions, a particular problem for many low-income districts such as the one that Anthony attended.

Two models exist for selecting interventions in RTI: standard-protocol approaches and problem-solving approaches (Fuchs et al., 2010). Standard-protocol approaches use one standardized, research-based intervention for all children with a particular type of difficulty. For instance, an elementary school might decide to use one particular multisensory-structured language program, such as the Wilson program (Wilson, 1988), for all students who require intervention in decoding. Problem-solving approaches have been described in a variety of ways, but generally, they eschew the use of one standardized intervention in favor of consultation and collaboration to select individualized interventions based on specific student needs. Hybrids of these two approaches are also possible; a school might adopt a standard-protocol approach for Tier II and a problem-solving approach for Tier III. Each approach to selecting interventions has distinct advantages and limitations. For example, the use of a standard-protocol approach has some obvious advantages in relation to resources and teacher professional development, because it involves purchasing materials and training teachers on a relatively small number of interventions. This approach also provides consistency in choice and delivery of interventions, and it makes selection of reading interventions a straightforward process that does not require much time for discussion or decision making. However, even in the relatively well-researched domain of reading, standard protocols are not available for all areas, such as vocabulary and comprehension. In addition, no intervention program, even one that is generally highly effective, can be expected to work for all struggling students.

Another important challenge in implementing RTI, and one often mentioned by respondents to the anonymous questionnaire mentioned previously, is time—for educators to meet to discuss implementation issues, to determine the needs of individual students, to evaluate the results of progress-monitoring assessments, and of course, to implement the interventions. As Torgesen (2006) has noted, implementing RTI in a school or district is a bit like making major repairs to an airplane while the plane is in flight; the day-to-day business of schools does not stop while educators are learning about this new policy and trying to implement it successfully.

All the preceding challenges tend to be especially problematic at the middle and secondary levels at which there are fewer progress-monitoring tools and fewer well-researched interventions for certain reading problems that tend to be especially common at these levels (e.g., in comprehension). A research base on using RTI in reading with adolescents is certainly emerging (e.g., Vaughn et al., 2011), but at upper grade levels, at-risk students may be very far behind in reading with very entrenched reading difficulties. Children also have multiple teachers for different classes, making scheduling of interventions, consistency of programming, and achievement of a systemic approach particularly daunting for educators.

At all grade levels, effective leadership is critical to implementation of RTI because of its systemic nature. Among other decisions, those involving screening practices, selection of curricula, purchasing of materials and interventions, and school schedules are ordinarily the purview of principals and other administrators, not individual teachers. Poor choices in these areas may scuttle RTI efforts before they even begin. Knowledgeable consultants can sometimes serve a valuable function in both advising districts on implementation of RTI and planning interventions for individual students. Still, to fulfill their roles well, both school leaders and consultants must have a knowledge base about research-based practices in reading.

Challenges in Using Response to Intervention to Identify Learning Disabilities

With the use of RTI criteria, all the issues discussed in the preceding section can potentially influence identification of LDs. If a school implements flawed practices for early identification and interventions, not only will these problems undermine the overall effectiveness of the RTI model, but they also will undermine the use of RTI criteria in identification of LDs. For example, if a school's approach to selection or delivery of interventions is inadequate, then special educators cannot be confident in ruling out inappropriate reading instruction as a factor in the reading problems of a student under consideration for an LD classification. If a child has a genuine disability, poorly chosen or poorly implemented interventions, or a rigid implementation of RTI that does not allow for appropriate "fast tracking" of the most at-risk children, may unduly delay the child's entry into special education.

Other challenges in using RTI to identify LDs revolve around inconsistent identification practices and the fact that standardized decision rules, standardized early identification and progress-monitoring practices, as well as standardized procedures for selection of interventions do not yet exist. Not only do states vary in the criteria they have adopted for identification of LDs, with some states not employing RTI at all, but many states have chosen to leave decision making about overall criteria for LDs to local districts, meaning that even within states there may be great variability in identification practices (Zirkel, 2011; Zirkel & Thomas, 2010). Inconsistency in LD identification practices is nothing new (see, e.g., Moats & Lyon, 1993), but the use of RTI criteria to identify LDs will likely worsen this situation, at least for the near term.

Perhaps most seriously, RTI is a relatively new approach with a limited empirical base, especially in relation to its use as an approach to identifying LDs. Many critics of RTI (e.g., Hale et al., 2010; Kavale, Kauffman, Bachmeier, & LeFever, 2008) have pointed out the inadequacies of using RTI criteria *alone* to identify LDs. Moreover, the use of RTI criteria alone would not be in keeping with IDEA 2004, which requires multiple criteria for identification of LDs (as well as other disabilities). Hale and colleagues (2010) suggest that perhaps the most important problem with using RTI approaches to identification of LDs is that they lack a true positive; RTI criteria define LDs by default, by children's failure to respond to intervention, a failure that in reality can have many causes. However, this problem of defining LDs by default—by what they are not rather than what they are—has a long-standing history (see, e.g., Spear-Swerling & Sternberg, 1996) and is certainly not unique to RTI criteria. Indeed, the same criticism can be made of IQ–achievement discrepancy methods; the fact that individual children's achievement does not match up with their IQs also can have many causes.

WHY CONTINUE TO PURSUE RESPONSE TO INTERVENTION POLICY?

Despite all these challenges, there are compelling reasons to continue to pursue RTI policy in education. First, as a model for general education, RTI makes effective prevention and early intervention for children's reading difficulties much more likely than do traditional educational practices (Algozzine et al., 2012; Al Otaiba, 2001; Denton et al., 2010; Foorman, 2003; Speece et al., 2003; Torgesen, 2004; Vellutino & Scanlon, 2002). Not only do RTI practices provide help to at-risk readers more promptly, but the use of data to inform core general education reading instruction can avoid perpetuating practices that inadvertently contribute to children's reading difficulties. In an RTI model, the fact that few children at Anthony's school met the goal on the state-mandated reading test would be seen as a giant, waving red flag that general education reading instruction needed improvement, not an excuse for writing off children with economic disadvantages as incapable of learning. Making the necessary changes to core instruction might not be easy, but at least educators would recognize the need to make those changes, and they would use data to determine whether the resulting changes were effective or whether additional changes were needed. Also, RTI practices involving clear decision rules and cutpoints for intervention may help to avoid referral bias, the tendency for teachers to refer (or to not refer) students for help based on criteria other than their reading achievement. For example, although serious reading difficulties occur roughly as often in girls as in boys, boys are much more likely to be referred for extra services by their teachers because they are more likely to be perceived as having behavior problems (Shaywitz, 2003). With universal screening and progress monitoring, children do not need to act out behaviorally in order for their reading problems to be noticed promptly.

Furthermore, RTI practices help to avoid potential harms associated with IQ testing, such as those seen in Anthony's case, as well as the costs and time burdens of administering such tests, because IQ testing is unnecessary for children to obtain intervention. IQ is not a strong predictor of reading achievement in the early- to middle-elementary grades, nor does IQ predict responsiveness to intervention in reading, especially in relation to decoding (Gresham & Vellutino, 2010). Other measures, particularly specific reading and language measures, are much more relevant to educational planning, and they lack the risks of IQ testing.

Finally, the use of RTI helps to orient educators toward instructionally relevant questions. Since my own state began implementing RTI and requiring RTI criteria in identification of LDs, I hear the following kinds of questions from both general and special educators much more often: Are we using good core practices in teaching reading, and if not, how should those practices be improved? How do we identify at-risk readers early? What is the best intervention for a particular child? Is the child making adequate progress in the intervention? Is there a way to accelerate progress? These are important questions to ask, even if their answers might not always be clear or easy to implement.

HOW RESEARCH ON READING PROFILES CAN ENHANCE RESPONSE TO INTERVENTION PRACTICES

Information about poor reader profiles and patterns can greatly enhance the systemic approaches to early identification and intervention characteristic of RTI. For instance, most struggling readers in the primary grades have reading problems associated at least partly with phonological difficulties and poor decoding skills, as did Anthony. Therefore, ensuring effective Tier I decoding instruction in these grades, as well as additional decoding interventions for children who need them, is vital to preventing reading failure.

Nevertheless, nonphonological weaknesses in vocabulary and other language abilities also play an important role in reading difficulties, especially beyond third grade (Leach et al., 2003; Scarborough, 2005). Furthermore, certain types of language weaknesses, such as limitations in vocabulary, are much more prevalent in some populations, such as low-income children or ELLs (August, Carlo, Dressler, & Snow, 2005; Hart & Risley, 1995; Lesaux & Kieffer, 2010). Educators who are aware of research on common poor reader profiles can shape Tier I instruction and screening accordingly—for example, by including nonphonological language measures in screening for reading problems (Scarborough, 2005) and by emphasizing early vocabulary and language development in vulnerable populations of students (Biemiller, 1999). These steps might substantially improve prevention, early identification, and early intervention efforts.

Knowledge about common profiles and patterns of reading difficulties also is essential for understanding the types of assessments most helpful in planning instruction for struggling readers as well as the types of interventions those readers will need. High-functioning students with ASD often have a profile of specific reading comprehension difficulties (SRCD); they may learn to decode relatively easily but have specific cognitive-linguistic weaknesses that influence their comprehension. Such weaknesses include, for example, pragmatic language, or use of language in a social context (Huemer & Mann, 2010), and theory of mind or mentalizing, the ability to understand the mental states of others (Frith, 2012). An emphasis on these cognitive-linguistic abilities in assessment and intervention is often especially important for students with ASD. The broader point is that research on reading development in typical students, and on common profiles of reading difficulties, can be used to understand the kinds of reading problems seen in ASD and other disabilities (Norbury & Nation, 2011) as well as in students with experientially caused reading problems.

Without an understanding of reading development and common poor reader profiles, implementation of RTI lacks the theoretical foundation needed for effectively addressing a wide range of reading difficulties. Without the use of RTI practices, educators may overlook many children's reading difficulties, fail to address them properly, or even inadvertently exacerbate them by faulty instruction. Using RTI practices in combination with the kind of theoretical model to be described here will certainly not be perfect policy, but it will be far better than traditional practices for identifying and serving struggling readers. Ongoing research to improve RTI practices (e.g., Fuchs, Compton, et al., 2012) is critical. However, the challenges of RTI should not lead to abandonment of these models any more than problems in multilevel systems of health care (e.g., Gawande, 2011) should lead health care providers to abandon practices such as vaccination, appropriate preventive health screenings, or intensive health care options for a subset of the population.

Even outspoken critics of RTI criteria for identification of LDs (e.g., Hale et al., 2010; Kavale et al., 2008) have generally recognized the value of RTI for improving prevention efforts and helping many struggling readers. It is the use of RTI in identification of LDs, especially the *sole* use of RTI criteria, which they most strongly oppose. The next chapter considers which criteria should be used to identify LDs in reading as well as the types of abilities that should be examined in diagnostic assessment of at-risk readers—for not only children with LDs but struggling readers in general.

2

A Componential View
of Reading Abilities and
Reading Problems

F
ew endeavors in the lives of parents are more nerve jangling than teaching their teenage child how to drive a car. Of course, the ultimate goal of
driving instruction is to produce highly skilled drivers who can operate
a car safely under a wide range of road conditions. However, no parent would
commence their teenager's driving instruction on an unfamiliar highway
interchange or in a blinding snowstorm when the child cannot yet reliably
distinguish the brake pedal from the accelerator or keep the car safely on
the road under optimal conditions. By comparison, although there is virtually universal consensus that the ultimate goal of reading instruction is good
reading comprehension, reading educators have disagreed about whether
instruction should emphasize comprehension over other abilities right from
the start, or whether initial instruction should emphasize skills foundational
to reading comprehension, particularly word decoding or phonics (e.g., Chall,
1967). The scientific evidence, for anyone who refers to it, has long settled this
debate; the development of foundational reading abilities is necessary, though
definitely not sufficient, for good reading comprehension (e.g., Adams, 1990;
Chall, 1967; National Research Council, 1998; National Reading Panel [NRP],
2000)—just as development of basic driving skills is necessary, though not
sufficient, for highly skilled driving.

An understanding of the distinct abilities underlying reading comprehension, how these abilities tend to influence one another, and how the
importance of different abilities may shift across the course of development
is fundamental to both scientific progress in reading and educational practice. These distinct abilities are often termed *components* of reading. Formally
defined, a component is an ability that can have an independent influence on
performance and growth in reading comprehension (Aaron, Joshi, Gooden, &
Bentum, 2008; Gough & Tunmer, 1986; Hoover & Gough, 1990). Despite this
capacity for independently influencing reading comprehension, however,
many components of reading tend to be interrelated; scientific investigators
have often grouped interrelated components into two broad types of abilities

that contribute to skilled reading comprehension—word recognition and language comprehension—sometimes termed the *simple view of reading* (Hoover & Gough, 1990). In this chapter, various component abilities are discussed individually, but becoming a skilled reader involves developing fluid execution and coordination of these abilities over the course of years, as illustrated in Scarborough's (2002) well-known rope model (see Figure 2.1).

I begin this chapter by explaining important component abilities in reading that scientific investigators have identified as well as the value of a componential view to practitioners. Next, I briefly review research on factors that influence the development of different component abilities (i.e., genetic inheritance, experience, and instruction). The final sections of the chapter consider some implications of this research for identification of LDs, with conclusions about the most appropriate ways to identify LDs in reading.

A COMPONENTIAL VIEW OF READING

At the elementary level, the most influential source for important components of reading has been the NRP (2000) report and its five components of reading—a report that generated a firestorm of debate at the time of its release.

Five Components of Reading

In its systematic review of research on reading instruction, the NRP identified five abilities especially important to learning to read in the primary

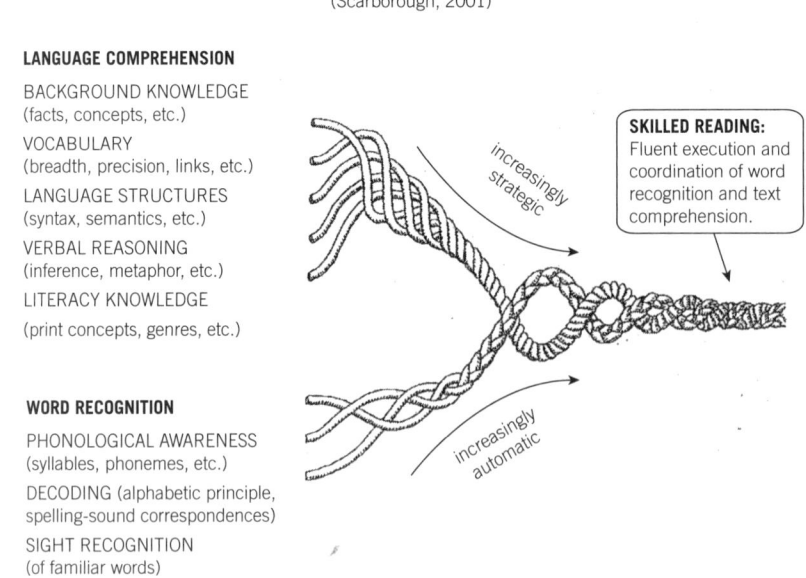

The Many Strands that Are Woven into Skilled Reading
(Scarborough, 2001)

LANGUAGE COMPREHENSION

BACKGROUND KNOWLEDGE
(facts, concepts, etc.)

VOCABULARY
(breadth, precision, links, etc.)

LANGUAGE STRUCTURES
(syntax, semantics, etc.)

VERBAL REASONING
(inference, metaphor, etc.)

LITERACY KNOWLEDGE
(print concepts, genres, etc.)

WORD RECOGNITION

PHONOLOGICAL AWARENESS
(syllables, phonemes, etc.)

DECODING (alphabetic principle,
spelling-sound correspondences)

SIGHT RECOGNITION
(of familiar words)

increasingly strategic

SKILLED READING:
Fluent execution and
coordination of word
recognition and text
comprehension.

increasingly automatic

Figure 2.1. Scarborough's rope model of reading development. (From Scarborough, H.S. [2001]. Connecting early language and literacy to later reading [dis]abilities: Evidence, theory, and practice. In S.B. Neuman & D.K. Dickinson [Eds.], *Handbook of early literacy research* [pp. 97–125]. New York, NY: Guilford Press; reprinted by permission.)

grades: phonemic awareness, phonics, fluency, vocabulary, and comprehension. Criticisms of the report quickly emerged (e.g., Garan, 2001; Pressley, Dolezal, Roehrig, & Hilden, 2002; Yatvin, 2000), with most critiques focusing on the report's omission of certain reading-related abilities, topics, and studies. The NRP took a conservative approach to its meta-analysis of studies, one that might have led the panel to overlook some important abilities, but that makes it highly unlikely that the five abilities identified were in error (Shanahan, 2004). Indeed, even critics of the NRP report have acknowledged the importance of all five components to reading acquisition (e.g., Pressley et al., 2002). Table 2.1 summarizes the five components, with examples of tasks commonly used to assess them.

Phonemic awareness involves sensitivity to sounds in spoken words as well as the ability to manipulate those sounds, for example, in oral blending

Table 2.1. Five components of reading

Component	Definition	Examples of assessment tasks
Phonemic awareness	Awareness of, sensitivity to, and ability to manipulate individual phonemes (sounds) in spoken words	Students are asked to blend orally presented phonemes into a spoken word (e.g., "What's this word? /m/ /a/ /sh/") or segment a spoken word into individual phonemes (e.g., "Tell me all the sounds you hear in *mash*.").
Phonics (also called word decoding or word attack)	Knowledge of letter sounds and the ability to apply that knowledge when reading unfamiliar printed words	Students are asked to read unfamiliar words presented out of context (e.g., in a list), with at least some nonsense words (e.g., *strab, gloon*) included.
Fluency	The ability to read grade-appropriate text (passages) accurately, with ease, and with reasonable speed; fluent oral reading also has good intonation and appropriate phrasing (prosody)	Students are asked to read a passage aloud, with the main score of interest the number of words read correctly within a certain time frame, usually 1 minute; a rubric may be used to evaluate prosody.
Vocabulary	Knowledge of the meanings of individual words	Students are asked to point to an appropriate picture from a set of options when the examiner says a word aloud (receptive vocabulary) or to name a pictured object (expressive vocabulary).
Comprehension	The ability to understand language that has been read (reading comprehension) or heard (listening comprehension)	Common formats for assessing broad (overall) comprehension include 1) answering questions about a passage that has been read or listened to; 2) cloze or maze, reading/listening to a passage containing blanks and providing a contextually appropriate word to fit in each blank; and 3) retelling the content of a passage that has been read or heard.

or segmentation tasks. Phonemic awareness, which requires full awareness of every speech sound in a word, is the most advanced level of *phonological awareness*, a broad umbrella term that also encompasses rudimentary levels of awareness. For instance, oral rhyming tasks—"What rhymes with *boat*?"—represent a rudimentary level of phonological awareness. In contrast, completing the task—"Tell me all the sounds you hear in the word *boat*"—requires phonemic awareness, full awareness of each sound in the word. Phonological and phonemic awareness are especially important in the earliest stages of learning to read, because (among other reasons) they help children grasp the alphabetic principle—that printed letters represent speech sounds in spoken words.

Phonics involves knowledge of letter sounds and the ability to apply that knowledge in decoding unfamiliar printed words. Decoding many English words requires attention to letter patterns such as the *igh* in *night* or the *ee* in *free*, so in order to decode many words successfully, children require knowledge about sounds for common letter patterns as well as for individual letters. Children also need to be able to recognize common roots and affixes (prefixes and suffixes) in words, such as the *un-, -ly,* and *-est* in *unwise, unwisely, wisest, gladly, gladdest, unfair,* and *unfairly*, a skill that informs their spelling and vocabulary knowledge as well as their decoding. Phonics skills develop most rapidly in typical readers in the early- to middle-elementary grades, although struggling readers of any age can have phonics-based difficulties.

Perhaps in part because of their common *phon-* root, phonological awareness, phonemic awareness, and phonics are frequently confused in education (Scarborough & Brady, 2002). Phonological and phonemic awareness are abilities involving oral language; phonics skills involve print. However, phonics knowledge and phonemic awareness interact in critical ways in early reading development. For example, a child who can sound out the letters in the printed word *cap* but cannot blend the sounds /k/, /a/, /p/ together to form the spoken word "cap" will have difficulty reading unfamiliar words (although he or she might be able to memorize specific printed words). Likewise, a child with good phoneme blending skills who does not know sounds for letters such as *c, a,* and *p* will not be able to decode despite his or her capable blending. The former child has a phonemic awareness problem and the latter a phonics problem.

Fluency is the ability to read grade-appropriate text with not only accuracy but also ease, appropriate speed, and prosody in oral reading. Prosody involves reading aloud with appropriate phrasing and intonation—for example, a rising intonation at the end of a question. Lack of fluency often creates a drain on reading comprehension; for instance, dysfluent readers with problems based in decoding may struggle so much to decode individual words that they lose track of meaning, especially in relatively challenging texts. Poor fluency also may reduce motivation to read, as people rarely want to perform for enjoyment tasks that they perceive as laborious and difficult—hence the often-heard comments from poor readers such as, "I'd rather have a root canal / clean the toilet / eat spinach than read." In typical readers, fluency develops most rapidly from late first grade through third grade, but additional fluency development continues into the later grades.

Vocabulary involves knowledge of word meanings and understanding the meaning of words (receptive vocabulary), as well as having the ability to retrieve words and use them appropriately (expressive vocabulary). Vocabulary knowledge is important to success in reading at all grade levels, but it becomes especially important beyond third grade because of increases in the vocabulary demands of the texts used at later grade levels.

Comprehension involves the ability to understand what has been read or heard—not only individual sentences but also longer discourse such as passages and lengthy texts. Discussions of the five components from the NRP report typically include reading comprehension as well as oral language comprehension under the comprehension component, but technically, only oral language comprehension is a component ability because reading comprehension cannot be a component of itself. As with vocabulary, oral comprehension of sentences and longer discourse is important to reading success at all grade levels, but it becomes increasingly critical beyond third grade due to the escalating comprehension demands of texts used at later grade levels.

The Value of a Componential View in Prevention and Intervention

Effective educational practices depend heavily on a componential view of reading. First, knowledge about important components of reading has implications for the design of successful core reading curricula and general education instruction. Most components develop in tandem with each other, and at all grade levels, reading instruction must address multiple component areas. However, core classroom instruction that gives short shrift to a component vital at a particular grade level—such as phonemic awareness in kindergarten and early first grade, or phonics in kindergarten through Grade 3—is likely to manufacture reading problems in a subset of students. A componential view of reading also greatly facilitates early identification of reading problems. For instance, poor phonemic awareness in kindergarten tends to presage first-grade reading difficulties, and limitations in oral vocabulary tend to forecast later reading comprehension problems (Biemiller, 1999; Scarborough, 2005). Without an understanding of important components of reading, educators may overlook at-risk readers until their reading problems are severe and less amenable to intervention.

In addition, effective diagnostic assessment and intervention require a componential understanding of reading. Children can have relatively selective weaknesses in specific components, as in the earlier example involving one child with a phonemic awareness difficulty and another with a phonics difficulty; effective interventions in these two cases would require different emphases, the former on blending skills and the latter on learning letter sounds. Moreover, children may perform quite differently on abilities directly involved in word recognition (e.g., phonemic awareness, phonics) and those more directly involved in comprehension (e.g., oral vocabulary, listening comprehension), especially in the elementary grades (e.g., Catts et al., 2006). Two students might obtain the same score on a reading comprehension measure yet have completely different underlying reading problems, one revolving heavily around phonological skills and decoding and the other around language comprehension.

Different components of reading certainly influence each other, with strengths or weaknesses in one component often contributing to strengths or weaknesses in other components. For example, vocabulary knowledge influences children's oral comprehension of sentences and longer discourse as well as their reading comprehension. Children also may use strengths in some component areas to try to compensate for weaknesses in other areas, as when poor decoders use good oral language abilities and context cues to compensate for their decoding weaknesses in reading passages. The existence of interactions among components does not eliminate the need for a componential understanding of reading any more than the interplay of ingredients in a cake eliminates the need for a recipe. Rather, this complex interaction is one reason a componential understanding of reading, with the use of focused assessments of component skills, is essential to pinpoint the nature of individual children's reading problems, provide successful intervention, and troubleshoot potential future difficulties.

A Closer Look at Comprehension

Close consideration of the abilities involved in comprehension is especially important to two types of readers: those beyond the primary grades, who must meet increasingly sophisticated comprehension demands to achieve grade expectations in reading, and those whose reading difficulties center heavily on comprehension as opposed to decoding. Investigators with an interest in comprehension and comprehension-based reading difficulties (e.g., Cain & Oakhill, 2008; Hulme & Snowling, 2011; Nation, 2005; Rand Reading Study Group, 2002) have described certain concepts important to understanding reading comprehension and have studied specific language abilities contributing to good comprehension.

The Surface Code, the Text Base, and the Mental Model As they read a text, readers mentally construct representations of what they are reading. These representations have been termed the *surface code,* the *text base,* and the *mental model* (Rand Reading Study Group, 2002). The surface code involves the literal words of the text. The text base involves individual ideas from the text, including inferences. Comprehending any text also requires constructing a broader mental model, influenced by schemas and background knowledge, about the meaning of the text. For example, consider the following

paragraph from the opening of *Parallel Journeys* (Ayer, Waterford, & Heck, 1995), the true story of a Jewish woman and a German soldier who both survived World War II and eventually became friends:

> It was a terrific time to be young in Germany. If you were a healthy teenager, if you were a patriotic German, if you came from an Aryan (non-Jewish) family, a glorious future was yours. The Nazis promised it. You were one of Adolf Hitler's chosen people. You were part of his Master Race whom he considered the highest class of human beings on earth. (p. 1)

In the previous passage, the surface code involves the actual words and their meanings (e.g., *patriotic* means devoted to one's country), whereas the text base includes the basic idea units: At this time (the 1930s), life was promising for certain groups—young Germans, healthy people, non-Jews—but by implication, not for other groups, including Jewish people. In constructing a mental model of the text, most readers would employ background knowledge about the events of World War II that would give them a sense of irony in reading this passage. However, readers also can have background "knowledge" that is false or misleading: Someone who is a Holocaust denier might miss the irony or reach a different interpretation of the passage.

Language-Related Abilities Contributing to Good Comprehension   The kinds of studies mentioned in the section "A Closer Look at Comprehension" have identified numerous language-related abilities that contribute to readers' construction of meaning. Some key abilities, listed in Table 2.2, are described next.

One set of abilities involves a *strategic approach to reading comprehension.* Good comprehenders tend to be active and strategic when they read, whereas poor comprehenders are often passive. For example, good comprehenders recognize when something they have just read does not make sense to them, and they have ways to remedy comprehension failure such as rereading or looking up a word in a dictionary; poor comprehenders may simply keep reading without understanding. Examples of specific comprehension strategies include comprehension monitoring (keeping track of meaning during actual reading), summarizing what one has read, generating and answering questions, and using context to infer the meaning of a word (NRP, 2000; Rand Reading Study Group, 2002).

Inferencing requires the ability to "read between the lines" as opposed to understanding the literal content of a text. Even very simple texts require inferencing, but inferencing demands increase beyond the early grades as texts become more sophisticated. Prediction questions (e.g., *What do you think will happen next?*) always entail inferencing. Questions about theme, main idea, characters' motivations and feelings, as well as cause and effect usually also call for inferencing. Many of the more sophisticated comprehension abilities addressed in both literary and informational texts beyond the early grades—such as analyzing the author's craft, evaluating how point of

Table 2.2. Examples of specific abilities and knowledge important to comprehension

Ability/knowledge	Definition	Examples of the ability/knowledge
Strategic approach to reading comprehension	Use of an active approach to understanding while reading or listening	Students think about meaning as they read and try to correct problems in word reading or comprehension (e.g., by looking more carefully at a word to decode it or by rereading a difficult passage).
Inferencing	Ability to "read between the lines," to draw conclusions about information that is not explicitly stated in a text	Students can predict what is likely to happen next in a story; they can grasp the moral or theme of a story—or key points of an informational text—when the theme, moral, and key points are not explicitly stated.
Background (prior) knowledge	Relatively broad knowledge that contributes to understanding a text but that is not explicitly stated in a text	Students have prior knowledge about the Underground Railroad that facilitates their understanding of a narrative set in the Civil War era.
Syntactic and grammatical competence	Ability to understand grammar and word order in sentences	Students can understand long sentences with multiple prepositional phrases or dependent clauses; students can resolve anaphora by relating words such as *he*, *she*, and *it* to their appropriate nouns.
Knowledge about text structure, genre, and discourse	Knowledge about the ways that different paragraphs or longer texts tend to be organized	Students know that a narrative involves a setting, plot, and characters; students understand the importance of attending to subheadings in an informational text; students understand important cohesive words in a text such as *however, therefore, in contrast,* and *because*.
Pragmatic language	Ability to use language appropriately in a social context	Students can infer characters' feelings from dialogue or can appreciate subtle humor in a text.

view shapes the content of a text, and integrating knowledge across a variety of texts—depend heavily on higher-level inferencing.

Background (or prior) knowledge involves knowledge important to understanding a specific text that is not actually stated in the text. This kind of knowledge comes heavily into play in both narrative and informational types of texts. For instance, a child who already has some background knowledge about snakes is likely to have an advantage in comprehending a science text about snakes, and narratives frequently involve specific routines or situations—going to the movies, eating at a restaurant, visiting the dentist—that also assume prior knowledge and experience. Background knowledge often contributes to the reader's ability to make inferences. For example, after reading the sentence *Joe was terrified when he saw the funnel cloud approaching,* a reader who does not know that tornadoes are violent storms with a funnel shape will probably be unable to infer why Joe was terrified.

Syntactic and grammatical competence involves the ability to understand sentences with a variety of grammatical structures and word order, including the more complex, dense sentence types that are typical of texts used in upper grades. Certain sentence structures are more difficult for all readers to understand (Rand Reading Study Group, 2002). For instance, sentences with left-embedded syntax, which pack many clauses, qualifiers, and phrases before the main verb, such as the following, can be hard to comprehend: *The fluffy-tailed black cat that went after the butter on the countertop and that Monica chased with the broom scampered under the bed.* As another example, garden path sentences are worded in a way that often leads readers to an incorrect initial interpretation, requiring reinterpretation later: *John wrote the nasty review off after he realized it had been done by his angry ex-wife* or *Mary gave the interminable speech her lowest rating.* Initially, readers are likely to misunderstand the first sentence as a sentence about John writing rather than dismissing a review, and the second as about Mary giving rather than rating a speech. Other grammatical structures known to make comprehension difficult include those with a high density of complex Boolean expressions, such as numerous *and, or, not,* and *if/then* statements. (For an example of a text with complex Boolean expressions, remember the last legal document you read.) All readers tend to find these complex or ambiguous sentence types relatively difficult to understand, but their impact will be even greater on certain readers, such as those with limitations in language (e.g., ELLs) or poor reading fluency.

In grammar, one particularly important class of words is *anaphora:* pronouns or other words used to refer back (or sometimes, forward) to another word or phrase. Examples of anaphoric reference include the word *she* in the sentence *Before she died, Aunt Gertrude gave Rebecca the family heirloom* or the word *one* in the sentence *Separation of powers is an important principle, one that is sometimes ignored.* Readers who cannot correctly interpret anaphora might not comprehend who died in the first sentence or what is ignored in the second; because lengthy texts require readers to track many different anaphoric references, problems in this area can create serious comprehension difficulties.

Knowledge about text structure, genre, and discourse entails the understanding that different types of texts are organized differently. For instance, narratives have characters, a setting, and a plot line, whereas expository texts usually lack these features. Paragraphs in expository or informational texts often have a main idea in the first or last sentence with related details in the remaining sentences, a paragraph structure less common in narratives. Chapter and section headings carry important information in informational or expository texts because they tend to outline key points, whereas in a fiction book, readers can often ignore chapter titles completely without sacrificing much in the way of comprehension. Furthermore, especially beyond the earliest grades, readers' abilities to recognize texts with different logical structures—comparison, sequencing, cause and effect—greatly facilitate comprehension. And at all grade levels, readers' understanding of common connecting or cohesive words in text—such as *because, and, so, but, then, however, in addition, also*—play a key role in comprehension because these words tend to signal important relationships among the ideas in a text. In the sentence *George embezzled money because his wife needed expensive cancer treatment*, substituting *and then* for *because* would signal very different logical and temporal relationships between George's embezzlement and his wife's cancer treatment.

Pragmatic language involves the use of language in a social context, such as turn-taking in conversation, use of polite language (e.g., *please* and *thank you*), understanding humor, and providing sufficient information for the listener to understand. Pragmatic abilities can influence both listening and reading comprehension in numerous ways, including children's abilities to understand the motivations and interactions of characters in a narrative, to appreciate humor in a story, and to grasp literary devices or themes. Children with impairments in pragmatic language, such as those with ASD, often have particular difficulties with these aspects of comprehension. In one third-grade class that I observed, children read a short text that included the sentence *After he saw the movie, Alfred was afraid to go to sleep*. The passage provided no specific details about why Alfred might have been afraid, but most children easily generated plausible reasons for Alfred's fear, such as that the movie had been a scary one. However, one child, a boy with high-functioning autism (HFA) who read the words in the text effortlessly, had great difficulty generating these kinds of interpretations, probably because of his weaknesses in pragmatic language and perspective-taking.

Other Important Cognitive-Linguistic Abilities that Influence Reading

In addition to the aforementioned abilities, other important cognitive-linguistic abilities can influence reading performance, including word retrieval, rapid automatic naming, verbal working memory, and executive function. *Word retrieval* involves the ability to retrieve a known word quickly from memory. Word retrieval (and other) processes are implicated in *rapid automatic naming* (RAN) tasks, which require rapid naming of a set of visually presented stimuli, usually single digits, letters, pictured objects, or colors. Everyone experiences occasional problems in word retrieval, such as the sensation that a word is on the tip of one's tongue but cannot be immediately recalled; however, some children have unusual difficulties with word retrieval or rapid naming that appear to be linked to problems with reading, especially with reading fluency (Norton & Wolf, 2012). This evidence suggests an individual difference variable that may limit some children's reading speed even when those children can read accurately. Some investigators (e.g., Kirby, Parrila, & Pfeiffer, 2003; Wolf & Bowers, 1999) also have found that children with a double impairment in both phonemic awareness and rapid naming tend to have particularly severe reading problems. Although theoretical interpretations of RAN and its role in reading problems remain matters of dispute (see, e.g., Vukovic & Siegel, 2006), RAN is an important predictor of reading, independent of other known predictors such as phonological awareness; thus there is good evidence for its inclusion in screening and early identification batteries (Kirby, Georgiou, Martinussen, & Parrila, 2010).

Verbal working memory has been defined as the ability to maintain a set of items in memory while processing an additional task (Daneman & Carpenter, 1980; Just & Carpenter, 1992). Phonological processes influence working memory and comprehension in both listening and reading; for example, whether reading a text or listening to it, readers must maintain individual words in memory while integrating meaning across phrases, sentences, and passages. Limitations in working memory may cause difficulties in comprehending syntactically complex sentences, understanding anaphora, and many other aspects of comprehension. Without good working memory abilities, by the time a reader reaches the end of a sentence such as *The fluffy-tailed black cat that went after the butter on the countertop and that Monica chased with the broom scampered under the bed*, he or she is likely to have forgotten the subject *cat*. Working memory also appears to play a role in decoding, especially of complex, multisyllabic words (Catts et al., 2012), which may tax readers' abilities to hold sounds and word parts in memory while decoding.

Executive function is a broad term for cognitive processes that oversee, manage, and control other cognitive processes. A number of the abilities discussed in the previous section, including working memory, inferencing, comprehension monitoring, and the use of a strategic approach to comprehension, have been conceptualized under the rubric of executive function (Denckla, 1989; Sesma, Mahone, Levine, Eason, & Cutting, 2009). Sesma and colleagues (2009) found that executive function contributed significantly to reading comprehension even after controlling for word reading, fluency, attention, and vocabulary. Furthermore, some evidence (e.g., Eason, Goldberg, Young, Geist, & Cutting, 2012) indicates that executive function may play an especially important role in comprehension of expository text (as opposed to narratives) and in answering inferential (as opposed to literal) questions. Other evidence (e.g., Cutting, Materek, Cole, Levine, & Mahone, 2009) has implicated executive function in the comprehension difficulties of children who decode adequately but have difficulty with reading comprehension.

Oral Language, Reading, and Written Expression: Similarities and Differences

Many of the specific comprehension abilities described in the two preceding sections of this chapter directly influence both oral language comprehension and reading comprehension. Readers who have difficulties with inferencing, syntax, background knowledge, pragmatic language, or working memory, for example, will likely have comprehension difficulties whether they are reading a text or listening to it. However, there also are some key differences between listening and reading, which can make the latter more challenging than the former. Many complex language structures are much more common in written than in oral language; thankfully, only the rare individual speaks heavily in Boolean expressions or sentences with left-embedded syntax. In addition, if readers have inaccurate or dysfluent word reading, these problems will create further challenges for reading comprehension as opposed to oral comprehension. Conversely, reading does have some advantages over listening; for instance, many strategies for repairing comprehension failure tend to be more feasible in reading, during which readers can choose to reread, than in listening, during which (at least under ordinary conditions) listeners cannot control the input.

Finally, virtually all the aforementioned abilities influence writing as well as reading, and limitations in any of these abilities will likely impair specific aspects of written expression. Children with weak phonemic awareness and phonics skills will be poor spellers as well as poor decoders. Limitations in background knowledge, an impoverished vocabulary, and poor understanding of text structure all will likely be evident in text generation aspects of a child's writing, which involve the ability to translate one's thoughts into language (Berninger et al., 2006). Poor executive function may influence students' abilities to plan, organize, and revise a piece of writing, as well as to comprehend in reading. Although a detailed discussion of written expression is beyond the scope of this book, a basic understanding of how various reading-related component abilities also affect writing can enhance educators' capacities to recognize and intervene successfully with children who have different types of literacy difficulties.

Which Abilities Should Be Assessed?

Research on all the preceding abilities—the five components of reading, specific language and reading comprehension abilities, as well as other cognitive-linguistic abilities such as executive function or working memory—has added greatly to scientific knowledge about reading development and reading problems and continues to do so. Obviously, however, it is not feasible for teachers to assess each struggling reader's performance in every one of these areas. In educational practice, the time requirements and expense of assessments as well as the educational value of the information they provide beyond other assessments that already are available are key considerations in choosing which abilities to assess for planning instruction. For educational purposes, the most vital areas to assess are component reading and language abilities with direct relationships to reading as well as clear implications for intervention (Fletcher, Lyon, Fuchs, & Barnes, 2007)—such as the five components from the NRP (2000) report, with more in-depth assessment of language abilities as warranted. For example, a struggling reader whose problems clearly center on word decoding but whose broad listening comprehension and vocabulary are strong probably does not require in-depth assessment of language comprehension; however, children whose difficulties revolve around comprehension might well benefit from closer assessment of specific language comprehension abilities. Likewise, children diagnosed with ASD or specific language impairments often have problems with oral language comprehension, so assessment of specific language abilities would be important for these types of students.

Assessment of other cognitive-linguistic abilities, such as working memory, executive function, and RAN, may also sometimes provide insights into certain struggling readers' performance, especially for those with poor fluency or reading comprehension. In addition, educators should strongly consider RAN for inclusion in assessments whose purpose involves screening or prediction (Kirby et al., 2010). Nevertheless, children's performance on any of these educational, cognitive, or linguistic assessments, by itself, cannot be used to distinguish genuine disabilities as opposed to more experientially based reading problems, as will be discussed next.

UNDERLYING CAUSES OF READING DIFFICULTIES

All the abilities discussed in the preceding section are at the level of psychological description, and a variety of underlying causes can influence performance on measures of these abilities in individual cases. A child's low score on a vocabulary measure might be due to language impairment or limited exposure to vocabulary. Poor understanding of text structure might be due to underlying cognitive-linguistic weaknesses or lack of exposure to different text types. Poor performance on measures of executive function could involve an intrinsic disability, such as attention-deficit/hyperactivity disorder (ADHD), or be shaped primarily by dysfunctional experiences, such as repeated failure in reading. Thus practitioners must always consider the nature of children's experiences, including the type of instruction they have received, when evaluating them for a possible disability. Still, regardless of underlying causation, appropriate measures of component reading and language abilities are extremely valuable for early identification and for planning instruction. For example, whether a child's vocabulary weaknesses are due to language impairment or limited exposure to English, he or she needs an emphasis on vocabulary development in intervention and, without intervention, is at risk for future comprehension problems.

Both intrinsic (e.g., genetic and neurobiological) and extrinsic (e.g., experiential and instructional) factors influence reading development. Next, I summarize some research findings in these areas. For a much more detailed discussion of genetic and neurobiological influences on reading, as well as their interplay with environmental influences, please see sources such as Byrne and colleagues (2007); Grigorenko (2005); Hensler, Schatschneider, Taylor, and Wagner (2010); Olson and Byrne (2005); Olson and colleagues (2011); Pugh and McCardle (2009); and Wolf (2007).

Genetic and Neurobiological Influences on Reading Development and Reading Difficulties

Behavior-genetic studies of children's reading development have found substantial genetic influences on both word recognition and oral language comprehension (Byrne et al., 2007; Olson et al. 2011), suggesting that genetic factors contribute to the ease with which individual children learn to read. Studies of specific disabilities also demonstrate the existence of intrinsic problems in learning to read. For example, research on developmental dyslexia—generally conceptualized as an intrinsic reading disorder characterized by core difficulties with phonological skills, word decoding, and spelling that are not caused mainly by poor instruction, another disability, or lack of opportunity to learn (e.g., Fletcher, 2009; Fletcher et al., 2007; Lyon, Shaywitz, & Shaywitz, 2003)—indicates a significant role for genetic factors in dyslexia (Grigorenko, 2005; Willcutt et al., 2010). Converging evidence from functional brain imaging and anatomic studies further suggests a neurobiological basis for at least some cases of dyslexia (Eckert et al., 2003; Lyon et al., 2003; Richlan, Kronbichler, & Wimmer, 2009). Many other disabilities, such as hearing impairment, ASD, and specific language impairments, affect oral language acquisition; children with these kinds of disabilities can be expected to have problems in learning to read simply by virtue of their language difficulties.

Behavior-genetic studies are frequently misunderstood to mean that a genetically influenced trait is immutable; however, the fact that a trait is highly heritable does not mean that it cannot be improved through intervention (Hensler et al., 2010). For example, an individual might have a completely inherited yet correctable hearing impairment and hear normally after surgery or with a hearing aid. Likewise, studies showing neurobiological differences in some poor readers do not imply that it is impossible for children with these differences to learn to read; in fact, some studies (e.g., Shaywitz et al., 2004) indicate that research-based educational interventions can actually alter such neurobiological patterns to be more like those of typical readers. Nevertheless, results of behavioral-genetic and neurobiological studies do suggest that some children have an intrinsic vulnerability in reading and may struggle even when provided with excellent instruction and intervention—findings that support a continued role for special education in serving students with persistent or severe reading difficulties. Furthermore, as explained by Wolf (2007), genetic and neuroscientific studies demonstrate that there is no single reading gene or reading center of the brain; every child who learns to read must establish new circuits that connect various parts of the brain originally programmed for other tasks, such as language and visual pattern recognition. Hence learning to read is not natural, not simply a function of everyday exposure, as is learning to talk for most children. Even for typical children, learning to read requires instruction; failure to provide appropriate instruction can manufacture reading problems in children with no intrinsic disabilities at all.

Experiential and Environmental Influences on Reading and Language

Children's early exposure to literacy, especially through adults reading to them, is one important influence on their reading-related abilities. However, reading to children appears to influence their oral language development more than their word-reading skills (Scarborough, 2005; Scarborough & Dobrich, 1994; Whitehurst & Lonigan, 2002); most children do not spontaneously begin reading in the conventional sense merely because adults read to them. The influence of read-alouds on children's oral language stems in part from the fact that books tend to use unusual vocabulary and language structures not typically employed in everyday conversation, even the conversation of well-educated adults (Hayes & Ahrens, 1988). Most adults who have been driven to distraction by a small child's request to hear the same book repeatedly can recall words or phrases that the child subsequently imported into his or her oral language from that book. In addition, in terms of sheer volume of vocabulary, children from poverty backgrounds are exposed to dramatically fewer words than are children from more affluent backgrounds (Hart & Risley, 1995). Furthermore, children who are ELLs by definition have limitations in their familiarity with spoken English; the tendency of ELLs to come disproportionately from low-income backgrounds is an additional, and important, factor in these children's reading difficulties (Lesaux & Kieffer, 2010). All these experiential factors can influence the ease with which individual children learn to read.

Formal schooling, classroom instruction, and intervention are especially important influences on children's reading development. Numerous studies (e.g., Al Otaiba, 2001; Denton et al., 2006; Denton et al., 2010; Simmons et al., 2011; Speece et al., 2003; Vellutino & Scanlon, 2002) suggest that early intervention in reading is effective in ameliorating or preventing many children's reading difficulties, with more intensive, longer-duration interventions producing higher percentages of intervention responders. No intervention is effective with all children, and children can sometimes appear to catch up in reading at one grade level, only to fall behind again later. Nevertheless, research-based interventions can make a great difference in children's reading outcomes. Furthermore, other studies focused on teacher professional development (e.g., McCutchen, Green, Abbott, & Sanders, 2009; Piasta et al., 2009; Podhajski, Mather, Nathan, & Sammons, 2009; Spear-Swerling & Brucker, 2004) suggest that providing research-based professional development to teachers also has the potential to improve their students' reading outcomes. In one review of evidence on professional development in reading and math, Yoon, Duncan, Lee, Scarloss, and Shapley (2007) conclude that, on average, control group students would have increased their reading performance by 21 percentile points had their teachers received professional development.

Another line of research (e.g., Chetty, Friedman, & Rockoff, 2011; Hanushek & Rivkin, 2010; Heck, 2009) has focused on teacher effectiveness using value-added measures (VAM) of teacher quality. These studies have tried to separate specific teachers' effects on student achievement growth from other important variables such as students' demographic background or prior achievement. Although there are legitimate concerns about the use of VAM in high-stakes evaluations of individual teachers (e.g., Darling-Hammond, Amrein-Beardsley, Haertel, & Rothstein, 2011), this line of work indicates that teachers are a key influence on student growth in reading and in other domains. Furthermore, studies such as Heck (2009) highlight the collective importance of teachers. For example, a *series* of highly effective teachers across successive grades can have a particularly positive impact on student achievement; and relatively stronger (or weaker) teachers may tend to cluster within specific schools. Cumulatively, such effects may provide a substantial advantage (or disadvantage) to the students at a particular school.

Taken as a whole, these kinds of studies demonstrate that good teachers matter. One teacher can certainly make a difference in students' reading achievement. However, highly skilled teachers can have an especially powerful collective impact as part of a well-conceived, well-designed educational system—as in successful RTI models. The next section of this chapter considers some of the history behind the development of these models.

HISTORICAL CONTEXT OF RESPONSE TO INTERVENTION/MULTI-TIERED SYSTEMS OF SUPPORT APPROACHES

RTI (or MTSS) models developed in the context of concerns about the lack of evidence-based practices in reading instruction in the 1990s. The NRP (2000) report certainly gave further attention to concerns about problems in elementary reading instruction, but such concerns existed well before the advent of the NRP (e.g., Anderson, Hiebert, Scott, & Wilkinson, 1985; Liberman & Liberman, 1990; Moats, 1994; Nolen, McCutchen, & Berninger, 1990). For example, as discussed at length by Liberman and Liberman (1990), in many American schools, the predominant approach to reading instruction in the early 1990s involved whole language. This instructional approach completely shuns explicit, systematic teaching of phonics, despite long-standing scientific findings (e.g., Chall, 1967) that beginning readers in general—especially those with a vulnerability to reading difficulties—benefit greatly from explicit phonics teaching.

The development of RTI models also grew, in part, out of concerns about the use of an IQ–achievement discrepancy to identify LDs, particularly in reading. In the mid-1970s, the revolutionary federal law PL 94-142, the Education for All Handicapped Children Act, established an ability–achievement discrepancy, operationalized in most states as an IQ–achievement discrepancy, as one requirement for identification of LDs. This law also required the use of exclusionary criteria in LD identification—that is, the learning problems of a student classified with LDs could not be primarily due to another disability (e.g., hearing impairment, IDs, EDs) or to factors involving lack of opportunity to learn (e.g., cultural difference, economic disadvantage). The definition of LD in PL 94-142 involved ideas long central to most conceptualizations of LDs. These involved the ideas that LDs are intrinsic to the individual and are not caused by environmental factors or poor teaching; are relatively specific types of learning difficulties, distinct from intellectual or broad cognitive-developmental disabilities; and involve *unexpected* learning failure that cannot be explained by other factors commonly associated with low achievement, such as poverty, limited knowledge of English, or low intelligence (e.g., Stanovich, 1991).

By the mid-1990s, scientific investigators had clearly established problems in word decoding as central to many cases of reading disabilities (e.g., Rack, Snowling, & Olson, 1992; Torgesen, Wagner, & Rashotte, 1994). It was evident that whole language practices provided a disastrous instructional context for children with any vulnerability to decoding problems, raising concerns about not only these students' future reading outcomes but also their classification with disabilities (e.g., Spear-Swerling & Sternberg, 1996). If students with decoding difficulties had never received appropriate instruction in decoding, then their eligibility in relation to exclusionary criteria for LDs was seriously in question. In addition, by this time, a flood of studies—especially the early work of Siegel (1988, 1989)—followed by many other investigations (e.g., Fletcher et al., 1994; Stanovich, 1991; Stanovich & Siegel, 1994; Vellutino et al., 1996) suggested that an IQ–achievement discrepancy was not an educationally useful way to distinguish different subgroups of poor readers. Whether or not they had an IQ–achievement discrepancy, poor readers at the elementary level tended to have similar types of reading difficulties, revolving around phonology and decoding, and they tended to benefit from similar types of interventions, involving explicit, systematic phonics teaching. There was no sound educational reason for excluding nondiscrepant poor readers—those who did not meet IQ–achievement discrepancy criteria—from educational services. Other problems with IQ–achievement discrepancy criteria included their dependence on the use of IQ tests, problematic for the reasons detailed in Chapter 1 as well as because discrepancy methods made it difficult to identify struggling readers early (Fletcher et al., 2007). Moreover, as noted by Stanovich (1991), a history of reading problems might tend to undermine students' performance on IQ tests, because reading, especially wide independent reading, influences the development of many cognitive and linguistic abilities tapped by IQ tests (e.g., vocabulary). Evidence about the possible influence of reading on IQ test performance thus contradicts the notion that IQ tests are pure measures of innate potential for learning as well as the assumption of specificity central to virtually all conceptualizations of LDs.

Stanovich (1991) discussed some alternative ways to operationalize an ability–achievement discrepancy that did not involve IQ, such as the use of a listening comprehension–reading comprehension (LC–RC) discrepancy. This approach would require students with LDs to have reading comprehension significantly below their level of listening comprehension (instead of below their IQ score). This idea does avoid the myriad problems associated with IQ tests, and it is a more educationally useful way to think about reading problems than is an IQ–achievement discrepancy, because of the strong relevance of broad language comprehension to reading. However, use of an LC–RC discrepancy would not avoid other problems associated with the use of discrepancy criteria, such as problems with the assumption of specificity; over time, problems in reading may undermine the development of higher-level language comprehension as well as IQ test performance. Furthermore, use of an LC–RC discrepancy would tend to exclude from LD services children with language disabilities or comprehension-based reading disabilities—that is, children whose problems revolve partly or entirely around core comprehension abilities as opposed to decoding alone (Spear-Swerling, 2011a). Many of these children's language abilities are weak enough to impair their reading significantly but are still not low enough for them to be eligible for speech-language services (Nation, 2005). Again, there is little justification for excluding such children from LD services based solely on the lack of an LC–RC discrepancy.

Innumerable problems with the use of discrepancy criteria led to proposals (e.g., Berninger & Abbott, 1994; Vellutino et al., 1996) to redefine LDs in relation to intervention responsiveness. Such proposals did not abandon the idea of LDs as intrinsic, relatively specific types of disabilities involving unexpected reading failure, but they redefined unexpectedness in relation to typical progress during intervention rather than in relation to IQ (Fletcher et al., 2007), generally retaining exclusionary criteria in their definitions of LDs. IDEA 2004 is currently the most important federal law for the identification of LDs in school-age children. This law requires states to allow the use of RTI criteria in the identification of LDs. IDEA 2004 also permits alternative research-based procedures such as the diagnosis of a pattern of strengths and weaknesses in cognitive-linguistic abilities or academic performance, a concept long associated with LDs (Hallahan & Mock, 2003). The law and its ensuing regulations prohibited states from requiring the use of IQ tests or an IQ–achievement discrepancy in the identification of LDs (Fletcher et al., 2007).

IDEA 2004 maintained the use of exclusionary criteria in the identification of LDs as well as requiring other criteria such as low achievement relative to age or grade norms. Thus the use of RTI alone to identify LDs would clearly conflict with federal requirements. IDEA 2004 also indicated that, for all students being considered for special education—in all disability categories, not only LDs—identification was not appropriate if children's learning problems were mainly due to inadequate reading (or math) instruction or to language minority status (Fletcher et al., 2007).

HOW SHOULD WE IDENTIFY LEARNING DISABILITIES?

The multiple identification options for LDs in IDEA 2004 and its regulations are confusing, to say the least. For example, although states can no longer *require* the use of a discrepancy method—in fact, they can ban its use out-right if they wish—they can allow individual districts the *option* to use a discrepancy. Many states do appear to be leaving decisions about specific identification criteria for LDs—ability–achievement discrepancy, RTI, and/or a pattern of strengths and weaknesses—to individual districts (Zirkel & Thomas, 2010). Although inconsistent identification practices for LDs have long been common (e.g., Moats & Lyon, 1993), past inconsistencies have usually involved issues such as different cutoffs for severe discrepancy or different methods for calculating discrepancy. The current situation involves using some entirely different *criteria* to identify LDs—potentially in neighboring school districts. This is not like having one group of physicians use 140/90 as the cutoff for high blood pressure and another group use 130/80; it is more like having some doctors use blood pressure cuffs to diagnose high blood pressure, and others, in the office next door, using thermometers instead. What is the way out of this morass, and how should educators identify LDs?

Some authorities have argued strongly in favor of using both an ability–achievement discrepancy and RTI criteria as part of an overall process for LD identification (e.g., Kavale et al., 2008). Others (Hale et al., 2010) have suggested the use of the third option permitted by IDEA 2004: identifying a pattern of strengths and weaknesses in cognitive-linguistic abilities with accompanying academic impairments. However, the use of an ability–achievement discrepancy combined with RTI criteria would not avoid either the challenges of RTI or the many problems with discrepancy methods detailed earlier; it would seem to be the worst of both worlds. In addition, the "third option" approach involving a pattern of strengths and weaknesses can be problematic for children with the most severe LDs, who are less likely to show this pattern (Fletcher et al., 2007). Furthermore, although appropriate measures of cognitive and linguistic functioning can sometimes be useful, they are at the level of psychological description, and as discussed previously, they do not permit educators to distinguish genuine disabilities in reading from more experientially based types of reading problems. Excessive testing that is time-consuming and costly but that does not add educationally useful information is another potential hazard of this approach, especially if cognitive or linguistic measures are not well chosen.

RTI skeptics in the LD community have sometimes raised concerns about "twice exceptional" students (Baum, 1984): those with strong cognitive-linguistic abilities who may be able to compensate to some degree for their reading problems and who may have difficulty qualifying with RTI approaches to identification, especially when low achievement is required, as is typically the case. Individuals with LDs do vary in their broad cognitive-linguistic abilities, and those with strengths in certain areas may indeed be able to compensate in reading to some degree. However, if educators consider important components of reading, such as word decoding and reading fluency, someone with a genuine reading disability should have below-average achievement in at least one of these components (Siegel, 1999). If a student is solidly average in *all* components of reading, it makes little sense to identify that student as having a disability merely because of his or her high IQ (or above-average language comprehension). For example, as Gunderson and Siegel (2001) point out, the relationship between IQ and reading achievement in the elementary grades is about as strong as the relationship between parental income and reading achievement. Should we then identify average achievers from affluent backgrounds as having disabilities because they are not living up to their "socioeconomic potential"? Of course not, and neither should we use IQ tests in this way.

Virtually all authorities on LDs, whether they are RTI advocates or skeptics, recognize the value of RTI in prevention and early intervention as well as the need for all poor readers to receive educational help promptly. Moreover, virtually all authorities on LDs recognize the need for multiple identification criteria as well as the role of comprehensive evaluations in identification of LDs—requirements that have been part of federal legislation for decades. Clearly, research on RTI must continue to inform educational practice, with future changes to practice as warranted; just as clearly, however, practitioners cannot await the results of future studies to decide how to serve struggling readers and identify LDs in the present.

Here is what the field should advocate and how individual states and school districts should identify LDs. The IQ–achievement discrepancy should be dispatched for good, and we should not require routine IQ testing for the identification of LDs, although IQ tests remain potentially relevant in certain specific situations, such as to rule out IDs in children with limitations in adaptive behavior or to obtain information about the nonverbal abilities of children with serious language disabilities. Educators should employ RTI criteria, including both low achievement and inadequate response to intervention combined with exclusionary criteria, to identify LDs. Identification must occur as part of a comprehensive evaluation that includes standardized, technically adequate assessments of important component abilities, especially in reading and language, and that examines other key information such as the student's developmental and educational history. We should not task educators with providing special education to completely average readers, but we should avoid overly stringent cutoffs for low achievement (e.g., standard score below 85) in favor of somewhat more liberal cutoffs (e.g., standard score below 90) that permit identification of students with milder types of difficulties, when appropriate. Additional research-based criteria must also be considered; for example, preschool language delay is a known risk factor for reading disabilities (Catts et al., 2006; Scarborough, 2005), so the presence of this factor should be weighed strongly in comprehensive evaluations for LDs in reading. There is simply no way to avoid the consideration of multiple factors, students' performance patterns over time, and the nature of instruction and intervention that students have received in identification of LDs.

Although, in my view, this approach is most defensible both educationally and scientifically, relative to ability–achievement discrepancy approaches to identification of LDs, it would likely identify not only students with dyslexia but also a greater proportion of students with comprehension-based reading disabilities. Thus it would likely result in some changes to the population of students identified with LDs relative to the use of discrepancy methods, as suggested by Waesche, Schatschneider, Maner, Ahmed, and Wagner (2011).

To interpret students' performance patterns and the meaning of specific component weaknesses, understanding the role of different component abilities in the broader process of reading development, including how different component abilities may interact and how the importance of various abilities tends to shift with development, is critical. Moreover, knowledge about typical reading development has implications extending far beyond identification of LDs; it is essential professional knowledge for both general and special educators, and it remains a highly active area of research. A theoretical model for understanding typical reading development, based on research that has mapped the key processes involved in learning to read, is the subject of the next chapter.

3

The Path to Proficient Reading

Even for typical children, reading development is a long process spanning many years. Although the abilities discussed in the previous chapter all play a role in learning to read, these abilities are not equally important at all points in this process. In particular, abilities related to reading words, especially phonological types of skills such as phonemic awareness and word decoding, tend to be especially crucial in the early phases of learning to read, when children are first learning to crack the alphabetic code. Phonemic awareness, phonics knowledge, and decoding skills are relatively less important in later phases of development, not because the ability to use phonology in reading words ever becomes unimportant, but because typical children in later phases have already mastered all or most phonological reading skills. Therefore, there is not much room for further growth in phonemic awareness and phonics to drive overall growth in reading. Returning to the driving example from the previous chapter, differentiating the brake pedal from the accelerator is necessary at all phases of driving but probably does not contribute much to growth in driving skill beyond the initial phases of learning to drive, simply because experienced drivers can already make this differentiation automatically.

Conversely, abilities related to comprehension, especially advanced comprehension abilities such as higher order inferencing, pragmatics, or discourse knowledge, tend to be particularly important in later phases of reading development, when the comprehension demands of schooling dramatically increase. Good comprehension is essential in all phases of reading, of course, and teachers should always address comprehension instructionally. However, because of the increasing demands of schooling across grades, comprehension abilities are relatively more critical to reading success in the later grades than in the earliest ones.

Escalation in comprehension demands from the elementary level to the high school level is apparent in the requirements of many state-mandated reading comprehension assessments. At the elementary level, students frequently have to read passages and answer questions about them, including both multiple-choice and open-ended questions that require composing answers. Some comprehension questions at this level certainly do call for relatively sophisticated inferencing or other higher-level comprehension abilities. Still, compare these kinds of elementary requirements to one version of a 10th-grade reading comprehension assessment that I recently encountered. This assessment required 10th graders first to read three different selections on the merits (pro and con) of having a national health care database, then to convey their own opinions in a persuasive essay with reference to evidence from each of the three selections—obviously a far more challenging literacy task than answering questions about individual passages. Successfully negotiating the leap from the elementary to secondary level requires students to develop many advanced comprehension abilities, such as the ability to evaluate evidence and integrate information across texts, not to mention more advanced levels of word recognition and vocabulary knowledge (e.g., reading and understanding the term *national health care database*).

This chapter focuses on understanding how the abilities described in the previous chapter fit into the overall course of typical students' reading development, from prekindergarten through adulthood. I begin by addressing several important background topics: the role of context cues in learning to read, changes in the relationship between listening and reading comprehension across development, and vocabulary and morphological development. This background is important for understanding the theoretical model of typical reading development that is the heart of the chapter. The chapter concludes with a discussion of relationships among the model, the Common Core State Standards (CCSS), and RTI/MTSS approaches.

THE ROLE OF CONTEXT CUES IN READING DEVELOPMENT

Understanding the role of context in reading development requires a central distinction between the use of context to aid word reading and the use of context to aid comprehension. Let us consider the former use of context first. Some theoretical models of reading (e.g., Goodman, 1976) have emphasized the role of picture and sentence context in word reading. These models have maintained that skilled reading involves the ability to use context cues in conjunction with partial letter cues, such as the first and last letters of a word, to read unfamiliar words. This viewpoint has some intuitive appeal because children do sometimes use pictures or the part of a sentence that they have read successfully to guess an unknown word. For instance, suppose a beginning reader struggles to read the word *flapjacks* in the sentence *Joe saw a big platter of flapjacks on the table* with a picture of hot buttered flapjacks next to the text. In this situation, assuming the child had the word *flapjacks* in his or her oral vocabulary, he or she might indeed be able to use the first few letters of the word, along with the picture, to guess it.

However, especially if children are not disposed to look carefully at words after having guessed them based on context cues, then they are unlikely to retain the word in memory, and they would have to repeat this guessing process every time they encountered the word. Furthermore, as children advance beyond the early phases of reading, books often do not have pictures or the kind of sentence context helpful for predicting words successfully; also, the effort that such prediction requires may deplete mental resources needed for comprehension. Research on reading development (e.g., Adams, 1998; Stanovich, 2000) has convincingly demonstrated that heavy reliance on context to decode unfamiliar words is associated with *unskilled* reading, such as that typical of young novice readers or older struggling readers. Skilled readers do not rely heavily on context to aid decoding because they have highly accurate and automatic decoding skills that enable them to identify most printed words quickly. Progress in reading is characterized by increasingly accurate, automatic decoding skills, not by an increasing ability to use context cues in decoding.

The use of context to aid comprehension is a different issue entirely and does characterize skilled reading (Adams, 1998). In relation to the previous example, a child who is using context as an aid to comprehension might employ the picture to figure out what the word *flapjacks* means—that is, they are the same thing as *pancakes*. Other examples of using context to aid comprehension include employing information stated in the text to interpret characters' motivations or feelings, to understand figurative language such as metaphors or similes, or to disambiguate multiple meanings of a word (e.g., *fly*, the insect, versus *fly* in an airplane). Context cues are not always readily available to readers in every situation; without a picture or additional supportive sentence context, a child reading the sentence *Joe saw a big platter of flapjacks on the table* might only infer that *flapjacks* are some kind of food. Nevertheless, research suggests that, where possible, teachers certainly should encourage children to use context to aid comprehension. When it comes to children's reading of words, teachers should emphasize close attention to the print and application of decoding skills, not guessing at words based on pictures or sentence context; for instruction, they should use texts that are a reasonable match to children's decoding skills—otherwise, children have little option but to guess.

LISTENING AND READING COMPREHENSION ACROSS DEVELOPMENT

As suggested by the discussion of component reading abilities in the previous chapter, and as illustrated in Figure 1.1, language abilities have a consistent, central role in reading development. Indeed, despite the fact that vision is necessary to read print, phonological and nonphonological language abilities are much more central to reading development than are visual abilities (Stanovich, 2000; Vellutino, 1979). Comparisons of children who are born deaf with those born blind underscore this point. Most congenitally deaf children experience great difficulty in learning oral language as well as reading, whereas (other than needing to use Braille) most blind children have much less difficulty with reading acquisition because their oral language development is much less affected by their disability than is true for deaf children. When blind children do have reading difficulties, these problems often involve the same weaknesses found in sighted children, such as poor phonemic awareness (Elbro, 2004).

Listening comprehension develops well before reading and continues to develop as children become literate. Throughout development, reading comprehension and listening comprehension interact and are mutually facilitative, with experience in one influencing the other (Perfetti, Landi, & Oakhill, 2005). For instance, exposure to rich oral language and vocabulary (including through adults' read-alouds) facilitates children's learning to read, but children's own reading experience (e.g., through independent reading) also develops their vocabularies and cognitive-linguistic abilities (Cunningham & Stanovich, 1997; Mol & Bus, 2011). Many reading-related abilities involve this kind of reciprocal causation, with causality running in both directions; as another example, a threshold level of phonological awareness appears necessary to crack the alphabetic code, but learning to decode yields further refinements in phonemic awareness (Ehri, 2005).

However, relationships between listening and reading change greatly during the course of reading development. In early reading acquisition, correlations between reading comprehension and listening comprehension are low, because word-reading skill sets a limit on reading comprehension; children cannot read words well enough even to approach their listening level. As children's word-reading skills develop, correlations between reading comprehension and listening comprehension increase, with correlations for college students as high as .90 (Gernsbacher, 1990). Also, the acquisition process is quite different for speaking than for reading: All typical children, and even most of those with disabilities, learn their first language naturally, simply through exposure and everyday interaction. In contrast, most children require instruction in order to learn how to read.

VOCABULARY AND MORPHOLOGICAL DEVELOPMENT

Vocabulary knowledge is a strong predictor of both oral and reading comprehension, although the causal relationship between vocabulary and comprehension is complex and reciprocal (Beck, McKeown, & Kucan, 2002; Nagy & Scott, 2000; NRP, 2000; Pearson, Hiebert, & Kamil, 2007; Rand Reading Study Group, 2002). Vocabulary is critical to reading comprehension at all points in development, but the vocabulary demands of the texts used in schooling increase sharply in the middle- to upper-elementary grades, so students with significant vocabulary weaknesses are especially likely to begin having difficulty with comprehension in these grades.

Investigators interested in vocabulary have emphasized the multifaceted nature of vocabulary knowledge as well as the depth and breadth of word learning. Knowledge of word meanings is not "all or nothing"; rather, initial encounters with a word may lead to a vague understanding of what it means, with subsequent encounters in a variety of contexts leading to deeper understanding of the word, its connotations, and its related words. For example, the words *segregate* and *sequester* both mean to set apart or to separate, but *sequester* is much more likely to be used in the context of words like *jury* and *deliberations*, whereas *segregate* is more likely to be used in the context of words like *race* or *religion*. The words *candid* and *blunt* have similar meanings—to speak honestly—but whereas people might be charmed by someone's candor, they are not usually charmed by his or her bluntness. A superficial understanding of a word might be sufficient for comprehension in some contexts, but in more challenging contexts, or for use in expressive language or written expression, a deeper understanding of words is particularly important. Vocabulary researchers (e.g., Anderson & Nagy, 1992; Beck et al., 2002; Graves, 2006; Stahl & Nagy, 2006) have also emphasized the role of word consciousness in vocabulary learning. Word consciousness involves appreciation of the power of language, an interest in word learning, and an understanding of the importance of word choice.

Vocabulary knowledge is important to children's development of word-recognition skills as well as to their comprehension. In preschoolers, growth in oral vocabulary appears to be a precursor of phonological and phonemic awareness (Walley, Metsala, & Garlock, 2003). As children learn to decode in English, they begin to encounter many words with more than one pronunciation that is consistent with phonics generalizations. For example, *cabin* can be pronounced with a long or short *a*, the *ow* in *glow* can be pronounced to rhyme with *snow* or *how*, and the *oo* in *stood* can be pronounced to rhyme with *good* or *food*. Furthermore, the proportion of such words increases greatly as children advance beyond the initial phases of reading and begin to encounter long, complex words. Children who have such words in their oral vocabularies are more likely to be able to read them correctly and quickly.

An aspect of vocabulary that has received increasing attention in recent years is morphological development (e.g., Carlisle, 2010; Carlisle & Stone, 2005; Goodwin, Gilbert, & Cho, 2013). Morphemes are the smallest units of meaning in a language. They include both free morphemes, words that can stand alone (e.g., *bag, wish, speak*), and bound morphemes, affixes that are always part of a longer word (e.g., the *-s* in *bags*, the *-ful* in *wishful*, the *un-* and *-able* in *unspeakable*). Morphemic knowledge greatly expands children's vocabularies because familiarity with common morphemes facilitates understanding of many interrelated words. For instance, if a child understands the meaning of morphemes like *-ful, -ly, -less -ing*, and *un-* as well as the base word *care,* then he or she can generate the meanings of *careful, carefully, careless, carelessly, caring,* and *uncaring*, as well as many other words for which the base word is known.

Children learn morphemes orally from early childhood, well before they learn to read, but just as phonological awareness plays a role in reading development, so does *morphological awareness,* defined by Carlisle (2010) as "the ability to reflect on, analyze, and manipulate the morphemic elements in words" (p. 466). Morphological awareness and knowledge can be improved with instruction, and they influence not only vocabulary knowledge and word reading but also spelling, because morphemic knowledge is necessary for correct spelling of many words in English (Goodwin & Ahn, 2013). Without morphemic information about the spelling of common roots and affixes, a pure encoding process based strictly on common letter–sound relationships might yield *nolijabul* for *knowledgeable* or *futogriffer* for *photographer.* Likewise, it is impossible for children to hear that the second vowel in *colonist* should be spelled with an *o,* because that vowel sound is a schwa that can be represented with any vowel; however, children can use their knowledge of morphemically related words, such as *colonial* and *colony,* to help them spell *colonist* correctly.

Even beginning readers have some morphological awareness. A typical first grader understands that the final /z/ in the word *dogs* should be represented with *-s,* not *-z,* because *-s* denotes plurality. However, morphological awareness appears to develop especially rapidly as children begin reading complex multisyllabic words in the middle- and upper-elementary grades (Carlisle, 2010; Goodwin et al., 2013; Seymour, 1997).

A MODEL FOR UNDERSTANDING DEVELOPMENT IN TYPICAL READERS

The model outlined in Table 3.1 conceptualizes typical reading development for children learning to read English as involving a series of six phases. Learning to read in other alphabetic languages involves many of the same processes involved in English, including the components of reading outlined in the previous chapter. However, there are also significant differences between English and other alphabetic languages, particularly in that English is an unusually opaque language with complex letter–sound mappings, which may make reading development in English unrepresentative in some important respects (Share, 2008).

This model is based on a previous version (Spear-Swerling, 2004a; Spear-Swerling & Sternberg, 1996), which has been updated and revised to reflect ongoing research on reading development. It owes much to the work of many investigators in reading, including (to name but a few) Adams (1990), Carlisle (2010), Chall (1983), Cutting and colleagues (2009), Ehri (1991, 2005), Frith (1985), Gough and Tunmer (1986), Perfetti and colleagues (2005), Seymour (1997), Scarborough (2005), Stanovich (2000), and Vellutino (1979). Some discussion of spelling is included, because spelling and reading draw on many of the same underlying abilities, and observations of children's spelling can often provide useful information about their word reading. For a more detailed discussion of spelling, readers may wish to consult sources such as Cassar and Treiman (2004); Ehri (1997); Joshi, Treiman, Carreker, and Moats (2008–2009); and Templeton and Morris (2000).

Table 3.1. Phases of reading development in typically developing children

Phase	Key features	Approximate grades	Examples of related Common Core State Standards (CCSS)[1]
Visual-cue (prealphabetic) word recognition	Little grasp of alphabetic principle; use mainly of visual cues in word recognition; limited letter knowledge and phonological awareness	Prekindergarten	None
Phonetic-cue (partial alphabetic) word recognition	Grasp of alphabetic principle; some use of phonetic cues to recognize words; more advanced levels of letter knowledge and phonological awareness than in previous phase; reading comprehension far below listening level	Kindergarten to about middle of first grade	RF.K.1b: Recognize that spoken words are represented in written language by specific sequences of letters. RF.K.2e: Add or substitute individual sounds in simple, one-syllable words to make new words.
Controlled (full alphabetic) word recognition	Full use of phonetic cues in word recognition; full phonemic awareness; word recognition of common words is generally accurate but not highly automatic; decoding of unusual, complex, or multisyllabic words still limited; reading comprehension still well below listening level	Later first grade to second grade	RF.1.2d: Segment spoken single-syllable words into their complete sequence of individual sounds (phonemes). RF.1.3b: Decode regularly spelled one-syllable words. RF.1.3e: Decode two-syllable words following basic patterns by breaking the words into syllables.
Automatic (consolidated alphabetic) word recognition	Recognition of common words quickly and effortlessly as well as accurately; better reading of multisyllabic words; automatic word reading integrated with comprehension processes for fluent text reading at grade level; reading still below listening level	Later second grade to third grade	RF.2.3e: Identify words with inconsistent but common letter–sound correspondences. RF.3.3c: Decode multisyllabic words. RF.3.4b: Read grade-level prose and poetry orally with accuracy, appropriate rate, and expression on successive readings.

(continued)

47

Table 3.1. *(continued)*

Phase	Key features	Approximate grades	Examples of related Common Core State Standards (CCSS)[1]
Strategic reading	Increasing morphological knowledge and awareness; increasing ability to read complex or unusual words; highly accurate, automatic recognition of most words, with fluent text reading at grade level; routine use of at least some strategies to aid comprehension; reading used as a tool for gathering information; gap between reading comprehension and listening comprehension starting to close	About third grade to sixth grade	RI.3.5: Use text features and search tools (e.g., key words, sidebars, hyperlinks) to locate information relevant to a specific topic efficiently. RL.5.4: Determine the meaning of words or phrases as they are used in a text, including figurative language. RI.5.2: Determine two or more main ideas of a text, and explain how they are supported by key details; summarize the text.
Proficient reading	Increasing higher order comprehension abilities, with the ability to read critically as well as evaluate and integrate information across multiple sources; highly accurate, automatic recognition of most words, with fluent text reading at grade level; reading comprehension comparable to listening comprehension and may even exceed listening comprehension for certain types of texts	About seventh grade to eighth grade through adulthood	RL.7.9: Compare and contrast a fictional portrayal of a time, place, or character and a historical account of the same period as a means of understanding how authors of fiction use or alter history. RI.7.8: Trace and evaluate the argument and specific claims in a text, assessing whether the reasoning is sound and the evidence is relevant and sufficient to support the claims. RI.8.9: Analyze a case in which two or more texts provide conflicting information on the same topic and identify where the texts disagree on matters of fact or interpretation.

[1]. This displays only a few examples of relevant CCSS; to see the full set of K–12 English Language Arts standards, go to http://www.corestandards.org/ELA-Literacy/RH/introduction.

Source: Spear-Swerling (2004a).

Visual-Cue Word Recognition

During this first phase of reading, also termed *prealphabetic* (Ehri, 1991, 2005), children do not yet fully grasp the alphabetic principle: the understanding that written English is a code in which letters represent speech sounds. Children generally have only limited knowledge of letter sounds (e.g., knowing the letters in their first name) as well as limited phonological awareness. Instead of attempting to decode words systematically, they rely primarily on visual cues, such as word configuration, an accompanying logo, or pictures to recognize words. For example, a child in this phase of reading might recognize the word *stop* on a stop sign or the word *Coca-Cola* written in the characteristic flowing font but would not be able to read those words if they were printed on a page in ordinary font. Children's spelling in this phase reveals little understanding of the alphabetic principle as well as limitations in phonological awareness and letter knowledge; for instance, a very young child might scribble on a page without writing any recognizable words or letters and then tell her mother, "This says 'I love you.'" Children in this phase may understand some fundamental print concepts, such as the idea that print and writing convey meaning, but they are not yet reading and writing in the conventional sense. They are highly dependent on context to identify words, and their oral comprehension of language far exceeds their very limited reading skill. Visual-cue word recognition is typical of many preschoolers.

Phonetic-Cue Word Recognition

Also termed *partial alphabetic* reading (Ehri, 1991, 2005), this phase of reading characterizes many children in kindergarten and the first half of first grade. Phonetic-cue readers grasp the alphabetic principle, and they have more advanced levels of phonological awareness and letter knowledge than do visual-cue readers. These children make use of partial phonetic cues, such as the first and last letters of words, to try to decode, but they do not make consistent use of all letter information in a word. For example, a phonetic-cue reader might be able to decode very simple consonant-vowel-consonant (cvc) words such as *mat* and *fun* but incorrectly decode words such as *boot, boat,* and *blush* because of limitations in his or her knowledge of sounds for letter patterns like *oo, oa,* or *sh.* Likewise, in spelling, children can often spell simple cvc words or the first and last letters of a word correctly, but they still misspell most one-syllable words, especially those with many phonemes (e.g., *scraps*) or those requiring knowledge of letter patterns (e.g., *night*). Children in this phase remain quite dependent on context to identify words because of their limitations in decoding, and their listening comprehension continues to greatly exceed their reading comprehension.

Controlled Word Recognition

In this phase, also termed *full alphabetic* (Ehri, 2005), children make use of all phonetic cues in a word. They have full phoneme awareness as well as knowledge of not only single letter sounds but also many common letter patterns (e.g., *oo, ar, igh, sh, th*). Therefore, they are able to decode correctly a wide range of words, especially common, phonetically regular one-syllable (e.g., *boot, snake, meet, shark, crunch*) and two-syllable (e.g., *rabbit, lantern, mistake*) words. In spelling, they can represent all sounds in a word so that even in misspellings the intended word is usually obvious (e.g., *garbij* for *garbage*), and they can often apply some spelling generalizations, such as those involving adding common inflectional endings to a known base word (e.g., *fan, fanned, take, taking*). However, although they can make use of some letter patterns in spelling, they may lack word-specific spelling knowledge (e.g., *shirt* is spelled with an *ir*, not an *er* or *ur*), and they can usually read many more words than they can spell correctly. Moreover, their ability to decode or spell multisyllabic words, those of three syllables or more, is limited, and their decoding is not yet highly automatic. Thus they remain somewhat dependent on context to facilitate or speed word recognition, and their text reading may not be fluent, especially when they are reading relatively challenging texts. In this phase, children's listening comprehension still exceeds their reading comprehension. Controlled word recognition is characteristic of children in the latter half of first grade and second grade.

Automatic Word Recognition

This phase, typical of children later in Grade 2 through Grade 3, has sometimes been termed *consolidated alphabetic* (Ehri, 2005), because children in this phase consolidate common letter patterns within words, such as common prefixes, suffixes, and rimes (e.g., *-ear, -ance*), to make word recognition faster and more automatic. This phase is one of rapid fluency development, which requires not only skilled, automatic word recognition but also integration of word-identification processes with comprehension processes (Kuhn et al., 2010; Wolf, 2007). Children in this phase recognize most common words automatically as well as accurately, and they can read with better prosody than in previous phases. They can also decode a wide range of multisyllabic words, especially those in their oral vocabularies (e.g., *animal, impossible, television*), although they continue to have difficulty with unusual or complex multisyllabic words (e.g., *boutique, psychological, negotiate*), and their skills for reading such words continue to develop well beyond this phase. In spelling, children have knowledge of many common orthographic patterns (e.g., *igh, ow, ear*) as well as greater levels of word-specific knowledge than in the controlled word-recognition phase. Children can also apply some morphemic knowledge in spelling (e.g., *wood, wooden, gold, golden*), and they can spell some multisyllabic words, such as those with common prefixes and suffixes (e.g., *invention*).

In this phase, children's listening comprehension still substantially exceeds their reading comprehension, but because they have automatic recognition of most common words, children are much less dependent on context to aid decoding than in previous phases. Limitations on children's reading comprehension now begin to revolve more around background knowledge and language factors (e.g., vocabulary or syntactic competence) than around decoding processes. Likewise, limitations in reading fluency may begin to revolve more around vocabulary and language comprehension than word reading (Tilstra, McMaster, van den Broek, Kendeou, & Rapp, 2009), especially when children read challenging texts. For instance, a third grader might read the words in a passage about ocean life accurately but still have halting prosody because of lack of understanding of vocabulary or concepts in the passage.

Strategic Reading

In this phase, characteristic for about Grades 3–6, children have attained the ability to read strategically—that is, to make routine use of numerous strategies to aid comprehension. Examples of such strategies include summarization, using context to determine the meanings of words, employing strategies to repair comprehension failure (e.g., rereading), and using knowledge about text structure to assist comprehension. Children certainly may employ some comprehension strategies in listening well before Grade 3, and their development of strategy knowledge will continue after Grade 6. However, during this phase, typical readers first begin to read strategically on a consistent basis because their word identification skills are sufficiently well developed and automatic and their text reading is sufficiently fluent that they can focus most of their mental resources on comprehension. This phase also involves greatly increasing morphological knowledge and awareness, which contributes to not only children's ability to read complex, multisyllabic words but also their vocabulary and spelling knowledge for such words. An increasing volume of exposure to words in print (e.g., through independent reading) contributes to further growth in children's orthographic and word-specific spelling knowledge. At this point, children can use reading as a tool for gathering information, and the long-standing gap between listening comprehension and reading comprehension closes by the end of this phase (Carlisle & Rice, 2002).

Proficient Reading

Development of higher order comprehension abilities is the primary focus of this phase, beginning around Grade 7 or 8 and continuing throughout adulthood. Readers can now read more reflectively and critically. In reading literature, they can achieve a deeper appreciation of the author's craft and of literary themes as well as recognize literary allusions to texts with which they are familiar; in reading informational texts, they can evaluate the quality of evidence or arguments, integrate information across multiple sources, and resolve conflicting information across texts. Perfetti and colleagues (2005) suggest that attaining higher order comprehension abilities requires readers to adopt a high standard for coherence—that is, a high standard for caring that a text makes sense, at least most of the time. This high standard motivates them to make inferences, resolve inconsistencies, read with greater interest, and read more effectively. The views of Perfetti and colleagues (2005) are consistent with research demonstrating significant linkages among reading motivation, reading comprehension, and amount of reading (Guthrie et al., 2004; Guthrie, Wigfield, Metsala, & Cox, 1999).

For proficient readers, reading comprehension is generally on a par with listening comprehension (Biemiller, 1999; Carlisle & Rice, 2002), with reading sometimes exceeding listening for certain kinds of texts (e.g., a dense narrative or an informational text with highly technical information). The superiority of reading over listening for these texts stems from the fact that readers can often be more strategic when reading than when listening; for example, if comprehending material is difficult, they can choose to read more slowly, to reread, or to look up the meaning of an unknown vocabulary word. Some development in word-recognition skills, especially for unusual or complex multisyllabic words (e.g., words of foreign derivation such as *rendezvous* or *siesta*, technical words such as *pneumonia* or *mitochondria*), continues in this phase, as do additional refinements in text reading fluency. However, typical readers can read the vast majority of words they encounter with ease and automaticity. By the phase of proficient reading, students can spell complex multisyllabic words with Latin and Greek roots and affixes (e.g., *photographer, telephone, thermostat*); however, further development in spelling—as well as in vocabulary, background knowledge, and other comprehension-related abilities—continues throughout this phase. The cumulative effects of reading volume and experience are greatest in this final phase of reading development, with avid reading contributing to further growth in a wide variety of reading-related and cognitive-linguistic abilities (Cunningham & Stanovich, 1997; Mol & Bus, 2011; Stanovich, 2000).

Caveats and Conclusions

Phases of reading development do not simply unfold spontaneously; instruction and experience are key influences on children's reading acquisition. The grade ranges outlined in Table 3.1 are approximate and reflect the development of typical children who have had home exposure to literacy, ample access to books, and appropriate instruction. Transitions among phases in the model should be conceptualized as gradual rather than abrupt. Furthermore, descriptions of children's performance within a phase reflect their approach to most, but not necessarily all, reading tasks during that phase. For example, preschoolers who have knowledge of letter names may sometimes apply this knowledge in word recognition rather than relying solely on visual cues (Bowman & Treiman, 2008); a strategic or proficient reader will recognize most words automatically but may rely on a phonological decoding process for the occasional unusual word, such as a technical word or an unfamiliar name (e.g., *Bosnia-Herzegovina* or *General Shalikashvili*). Moreover, as noted in the description of the phases, development of many reading-related abilities is not confined to a single phase, and the extent of development is especially wide in the final phase of proficient reading; there are certainly substantial differences between the reading development of a typical seventh or eighth grader and that of a highly literate adult.

In the last couple of decades, many scientific investigators of reading, especially those in cognitive psychology, have emphasized connectionist models of reading. Instead of focusing on the underlying abilities involved in learning to read, connectionist models emphasize the number and quality of mental representations of words as well as the networks between them (see, e.g., Perfetti, 1992; Seidenberg, 2005; Stanovich, 2000). These models usually conceptualize automatization of word recognition in relation to modularity (Fodor, 1983) rather than in relation to limited mental resources; in this view, the key feature of automatic word recognition is that it is modular—that is, encapsulated and not dependent on higher-level processes or background knowledge. Connectionist models have contributed a great deal to our current understanding of reading. One example, discussed by Seidenberg (2005), involves the recognition that there is a continuum of phonetic regularity in printed English words rather than an absolute division between completely irregular and completely regular words. For example, although the word *pretty* is usually taught as irregular, the only irregularity in the word involves the vowel *e*, with all other letters having their expected sounds. An implication of this observation is that children's knowledge about letter–sound correspondences can facilitate their learning of not only phonetically regular words but also words traditionally considered irregular.

Despite these caveats, there are good reasons why so many investigators have conceptualized reading acquisition as involving a series of phases or stages and why many retain the concept of automaticity in explaining reading development. With the kinds of qualifications discussed previously—that phases do not involve all-or-nothing transitions and children's performance can sometimes vary within a phase for specific words—phase models provide an educationally useful way to conceptualize children's learning to read. Reading development does not merely involve growth in individual component abilities. It involves qualitative changes in how children tend to approach reading tasks, shifts in the abilities most important to driving further growth in reading, and changes in the interrelationships among component reading abilities, all of which a phase model captures well.

Utility of the Model for Practitioners

The research and model described earlier have important practical implications. First, they suggest the abilities most important to address instructionally for children at various phases of reading development as well as ways to differentiate typical difficulties in reading from more worrisome ones. Beginning first graders who find it challenging to decode more difficult types of one-syllable words, such as those with vowel-*r* patterns, but who can identify all letter sounds, decode simple cvc words, and have good phonemic awareness are likely doing well. However, educators should be quite concerned about beginning first graders who cannot identify sounds for many letters, who lack even a rudimentary level of phonological awareness, or who appear to have no grasp of the alphabetic principle. Understanding phases of reading development also is valuable for general educators in differentiating instruction, because at any grade level, there inevitably will be readers with a range of abilities. Fourth-grade teachers will have many students in the phase of strategic reading who need instructional emphases on developing morphological knowledge, with application to reading and spelling multisyllabic words and to vocabulary, as well as on developing and applying comprehension strategies in reading. However, a few children will enter fourth grade as highly advanced readers, functioning at the proficient phase, and will need an emphasis on building higher order comprehension abilities. Yet other children will be functioning below grade expectations and will have the needs of children at previous phases of reading.

For educators who teach primarily at-risk children or those with disabilities, knowledge about phases of reading development is helpful in understanding individual children's intervention needs as well as the kinds of goals that must be set for students to narrow or close gaps with their grade peers. Development of decoding skills provides one good example. Typical readers make remarkable growth in decoding in the first few grades of school. Although some development in word recognition continues into the upper grades, especially in relation to complex or unusual words, typical children can easily decode a wide variety of words, including many multisyllabic words, by the end of Grade 3. Bringing struggling decoders to grade expectations therefore requires setting and achieving appropriately ambitious goals for decoding. The phase model also conveys the importance of developing foundational reading abilities. Children cannot leapfrog from partial alphabetic reading to automatic word recognition; they must develop accuracy as a prerequisite for automaticity. Thus struggling middle- or upper-grade readers who are functioning well below grade expectations in word decoding accuracy must have those skills addressed through intervention, even though such skills are not part of the general education curriculum at the student's grade placement.

THE MODEL AND THE COMMON CORE STATE STANDARDS

The CCSS were the outcome of a collaboration sponsored by the National Governors' Association and the Council of Chief State School Officers to provide a consistent set of educational standards for all states that would lead to better college and career readiness for American students. As of this writing, all but a few U.S. states have adopted the CCSS, and the standards are having a strong influence in education. (See http://www.corestandards.org/ELA-Literacy to view the complete set of standards for English Language Arts.)

A central motivation for the development of the CCSS involved evidence that many entering college students are not prepared to do college-level work and that high school students are required to do significantly less challenging reading than was the case in the 1970s (Adams, 2012; Moats, 2012; Williamson, Fitzgerald, & Stenner, 2013). Moreover, quality of education appears especially important to the economic growth of a country (Adams, 2012; Hanushek & Woessman, 2009). Whether or not students go on to college, if they lack advanced literacy (or mathematics) skills, they will not be prepared to compete in an increasingly global economy, with serious consequences for the United States as a whole, as well as, obviously, for the students themselves. Data from the National Assessment of Educational Progress, currently showing a full third of American students scoring at the lowest, below-basic level in reading, indicate that poor reading achievement often begins long before high school (Moats, 2012).

The CCSS and the theoretical model of reading development described in this chapter align in many ways. The information in the "Examples of related Common Core State Standards" section of Table 3.1 gives examples of standards relevant to various phases of reading acquisition in the model. Individual standards constitute specific achievements that students should attain in order to be progressing well in reading from one grade to the next, with the model describing the underlying reading-related and cognitive-linguistic abilities important to reading development—as well as their interrelationships and shifts—in broader terms across grades. The CCSS for Reading: Foundational Skills are especially relevant to the early phases of the model, whereas those for Reading: Literature and Reading: Informational Text are especially relevant to the later phases.

Additional parts of the CCSS certainly are also relevant to the model, including Speaking and Listening as well as Language (see, for example, standards for Vocabulary Acquisition and Use). As discussed previously, oral language comprehension is important to, and interacts with, reading comprehension throughout reading development. However, the model emphasizes the reading-related abilities most critical to driving growth in reading at different points in development; in the early phases of the model, these abilities are principally those related to word-reading processes, whereas in later phases, those related to comprehension processes become more crucial. This kind of componential view of reading is not obvious from perusing even the best set of standards, in which it is easy to lose sight of the forest for the trees. Indeed, in the absence of an appropriate theoretical model of reading development, the CCSS are quite vulnerable to misinterpretation, in part, because of certain perplexing aspects of the standards' organization. For instance, although decades of research have demonstrated the importance of phonological and word-reading processes to driving growth in early reading, in the CCSS, these standards are set apart in a separate section from other reading standards, in which case educators may overlook them or incorrectly infer that they are not central to children's primary-grade reading progress (Brady, 2012). Likewise, standards for spelling are under Language instead of under Reading or Writing and, considering the ample research on spelling development and its relation to reading, are often vague, especially beyond Grade 3 (e.g., "Spell grade-appropriate words correctly").

One aspect of the CCSS that has received considerable attention involves their recommendations for increasing text complexity across grades in order for students to achieve college and career readiness. The standards do allow educators some flexibility in text complexity levels within grades, and alternative pathways for reaching the ultimate Grade 12 text complexity goal exist; for example, higher levels of complexity could start immediately in Grade 1, or greater levels of complexity could be more heavily focused toward the later grades and older students (Williamson et al., 2013). Determinations of text complexity must take into account many factors, including vocabulary and linguistic complexity as well as word-reading demands of a text (Mesmer, Cunningham, & Hiebert, 2012); furthermore, as Williamson and colleagues (2013) point out, the impact of specific changes in text complexity will likely differ for students at different levels of reading development. Making such changes effectively requires an understanding of the processes and shifts involved in reading acquisition. For instance, if increases in text complexity in the early grades make it more difficult for beginning readers to develop accurate, automatic decoding skills, such changes could seriously undermine children's development of the foundational reading skills crucial to long-term reading success (Hiebert, 2012a; Hiebert & Mesmer, 2013). Also, problems with declining challenge in reading material seem mainly to afflict later levels of schooling; Gamson, Lu, and Eckert (2013) as well as Hiebert and Mesmer (2013) showed that typical *elementary*-level reading has not declined in difficulty in recent decades.

With regard to RTI and MTSS, both the model and the CCSS provide indicators of important abilities to address in Tier I reading instruction across grades as well as possible benchmark goals for students receiving Tier II or III interventions. If students are far behind in reading, educators may need to sustain intensive interventions for long periods, perhaps throughout some students' school years, in order for them to meet or even approach these goals (Haager & Vaughn, 2013). Effective interventions must be based on an accurate understanding of the nature of individual students' reading problems. The next chapter extends the model of reading development discussed here to understanding common types of reading difficulties, with implications for educational practice, including the use of the CCSS in reading.

4

Common Profiles and Patterns of Reading Difficulties

Anyone who has ever tried to teach large groups of children to read knows that struggling readers are not all exactly alike. As detailed in previous chapters, numerous abilities are involved in learning to read, and children with reading problems can vary greatly with regard to their individual strengths and weaknesses in these abilities. Nevertheless, three broad profiles of reading difficulties tend to recur repeatedly. Rachel, Cameron, and Tamisha, all beginning fifth graders at different schools, provide examples of these common profiles of reading problems.

THREE FIFTH-GRADE STRUGGLING READERS

Rachel attends a middle-class suburban district with a Tier I reading curriculum that educators describe as "literature based." The curriculum emphasizes teacher read-alouds of authentic children's literature, development of oral vocabulary and oral language, and independent reading and writing activities; teaching of word-recognition skills such as phonemic awareness, phonics, and structural analysis is not systematic. Rachel is the daughter of two lawyers. Although there is a family history of reading problems on her mother's side, Rachel's early language and literacy development were typical; routine literacy assessments given during Rachel's kindergarten, first-, and second-grade years—including assessments of out-of-context word decoding—did not suggest problems in reading. Mild difficulties first appeared in third grade, with marked worsening in fourth. These difficulties revolved mainly around decoding multisyllabic words and reading fluency. Rachel reads slowly and struggles to decode many of the complex words that are common in fourth- and fifth-grade text. With above-average oral vocabulary and listening comprehension, she has always done very well in verbal activities in her classroom, but she is now beginning to show weaknesses in reading comprehension that were not evident in previous grades, and she does not like to read. Although she still enjoys her teacher's and parents' read-alouds and understands grade-appropriate books very well when adults read those books aloud to her, she finds independent reading laborious and totally unappealing.

Cameron attends an urban school district that has a strong, comprehensive Tier I reading curriculum, providing children with explicit, systematic instruction in important reading abilities and good access to books. Like Rachel, he comes from a relatively affluent and highly literate family. As a preschooler, Cameron displayed a few mild language weaknesses as well as some more worrisome behavior difficulties, including tantrums; poor social interaction for his age; and unusual, obsessive interests. For example, the paint section at the local home-improvement store utterly fascinated him; he quickly learned the names of different paint colors (e.g., "Eggshell," "Linen," "Alabaster") and had tantrums when his parents wanted to leave the store. At age 3, Cameron was identified as having an ASD. Since that time, he has received extensive therapy and special education services as well as substantial inclusion in general education settings with the help of an instructional aide. Early reading development was an area of strength for Cameron. He acquired decoding skills easily; showed no signs of phonological problems; and developed fluent, automatic word reading as expected for his grade. However, last year, in fourth grade, he began to show evidence of significant difficulties with reading comprehension, especially with inferential types of questions. Understanding characters' feelings in narratives or identifying key points in informational texts are particular problem areas for him. The comprehension demands of reading often seem to overwhelm him, and he tends to give up rather than try to figure out the meaning of a passage. Also, Cameron's fluency is sometimes weak, especially in relation to prosody of oral reading. He can usually read the individual words in grade-appropriate texts easily and automatically; however, particularly when he is having difficulty comprehending, he reads in a monotone or with inappropriate phrasing, which sometimes affects his rate of reading in text.

Tamisha is an African American fifth grader who attends the same urban school district as Anthony in Chapter 1. Unlike Anthony, Tamisha has no history of early language delay, and although her parents' formal education is limited, there is no history of severe reading difficulties in the family; all Tamisha's close family members have basic literacy. Tamisha's reading difficulties began early, in Grade 1, and similar to Anthony's, these difficulties involved phonological skills and decoding. However, Tamisha's reading problems have always extended beyond decoding to include broader weaknesses in vocabulary and academic background knowledge. Even when she can decode the words in a text, lack of vocabulary knowledge often affects her understanding of what she has read, and her vocabulary limitations are having an even greater impact on her reading now in fifth grade than they did in earlier grades. Tamisha's comprehension difficulties sometimes are apparent in listening, such as in class discussions, but reading comprehension is even more difficult for her because of the additional impact of her continuing decoding problems on comprehension; Tamisha's decoding skills, even for many one- or two-syllable words, remain weak. Furthermore, her reading fluency is poor because both her decoding and her comprehension difficulties affect her ability to read text accurately, effortlessly, and with good prosody. All these problems affect Tamisha's ability to focus on meaning when she reads and to read strategically.

A MODEL FOR UNDERSTANDING READING DIFFICULTIES

The part of the theoretical model that is the focus of this chapter is an extension and revision of a previous model (Spear-Swerling & Sternberg, 1994, 1996) for understanding classical reading disabilities (e.g., dyslexia). As is true for the portion of the model involving typical reading development described in the previous chapter, this part of the model owes a great deal to the work of many scientific investigators, such as those referenced later. Table 4.1 displays the common profiles and patterns of reading difficulties in the model, and Figure 4.1 shows a way of conceptualizing the relationship between this part of the model and the model of typical development from the previous chapter.

Common Profiles of Reading Difficulties

Research on different types of reading difficulties suggests that three broad profiles of reading problems are common in children learning to read English: specific word-recognition difficulties (SWRD), specific reading comprehension difficulties (SRCD), and mixed reading difficulties (MRD) (Badian, 1999; Catts et al., 2006, 2012; Compton, Fuchs, Fuchs, Lambert, & Hamlett, 2011; Huemer & Mann, 2010; Kieffer, 2010; Leach et al., 2003; Lesaux & Kieffer, 2010; Lipka, Lesaux, & Siegel, 2006; Nation, 2005; Nation & Snowling, 1997; Norbury & Nation, 2011; Spear-Swerling, 2004b; Valencia, 2011; Yuill & Oakhill, 1991). SWRD involve problems specific to learning word-recognition skills, often linked to phonological weaknesses; however, children with this profile have at least average oral vocabularies and oral language comprehension. Therefore, their difficulties with reading comprehension are entirely attributable to poor word reading involving accuracy or automaticity of word recognition. Rachel's case, as well as Anthony's from Chapter 1, exemplifies the SWRD profile.

SRCD involve the opposite pattern: difficulties specific to reading comprehension despite the presence of at least average phonological and word-recognition abilities. Often, children with this profile have weaknesses in oral vocabulary or other aspects of oral language comprehension, although these weaknesses may be mild and not sufficient for the child to qualify for speech-language services (Nation, 2005). Cameron exemplifies an SRCD profile,

Table 4.1. Common profiles and patterns of reading difficulties

Profile	Pattern	Word recognition and phonological skills	Text reading fluency	Oral language comprehension and oral vocabulary	Reading comprehension	Key intervention needs
Specific word-recognition difficulties (SWRD)	Nonalphabetic word reader	Below average, usually because of phonological and decoding weaknesses	Usually below average due to poor word recognition	Average or better	Below average	Systematic phonemic awareness and phonics instruction
	Inaccurate word reader	Below average, usually because of phonological and decoding weaknesses	Usually below average due to poor word recognition	Average or better	Usually below average; may perform adequately in easy texts or in situations in which compensation is feasible	Systematic phonics instruction (with phonemic awareness instruction if phonemic awareness is weak, and fluency intervention if fluency is low relative to reading level)
	Nonautomatic word reader	Below average, especially in automaticity of word reading and sometimes also in decoding of multisyllabic or complex words	Usually below average due to poor word recognition	Average or better	Usually below average; may perform adequately in easy texts or situations in which compensation is feasible	Instruction focused on automaticity of word recognition and fluency building as well as structural analysis and decoding of multisyllabic words if needed

Specific reading comprehension difficulties (SRCD)	Nonstrategic comprehender	Average or better, with no history of word-recognition or phonological difficulties	Varies, but may be below average because of language or reading comprehension limitations	Varies, but often somewhat below average	Below average; lacks a strategic approach to comprehension	Explicit instruction in comprehension strategies and other specific areas of comprehension weakness
	Suboptimal comprehender	Average or better, with no history of word-recognition or phonological difficulties	Varies, but may be below average because of language or reading comprehension limitations	Varies, but may be somewhat below average	Below average; lacks higher order comprehension abilities	Explicit instruction in higher order comprehension abilities such as evaluating and synthesizing information
Mixed reading difficulties (MRD)	Varies depending on the pattern of word-recognition difficulties and types of comprehension difficulties	Difficulties with word recognition: nonalphabetic, inaccurate, or nonautomatic word reading	Usually below average because of limitations in both word recognition and language/comprehension	Varies, but often somewhat below average	Below average because of a combination of weaknesses in word recognition and core comprehension abilities or knowledge	Explicit instruction in word-recognition skills depending on pattern (see earlier), coupled with explicit instruction in specific areas of comprehension in which student is weak

Sources: Spear-Swerling (2011a, 2013).

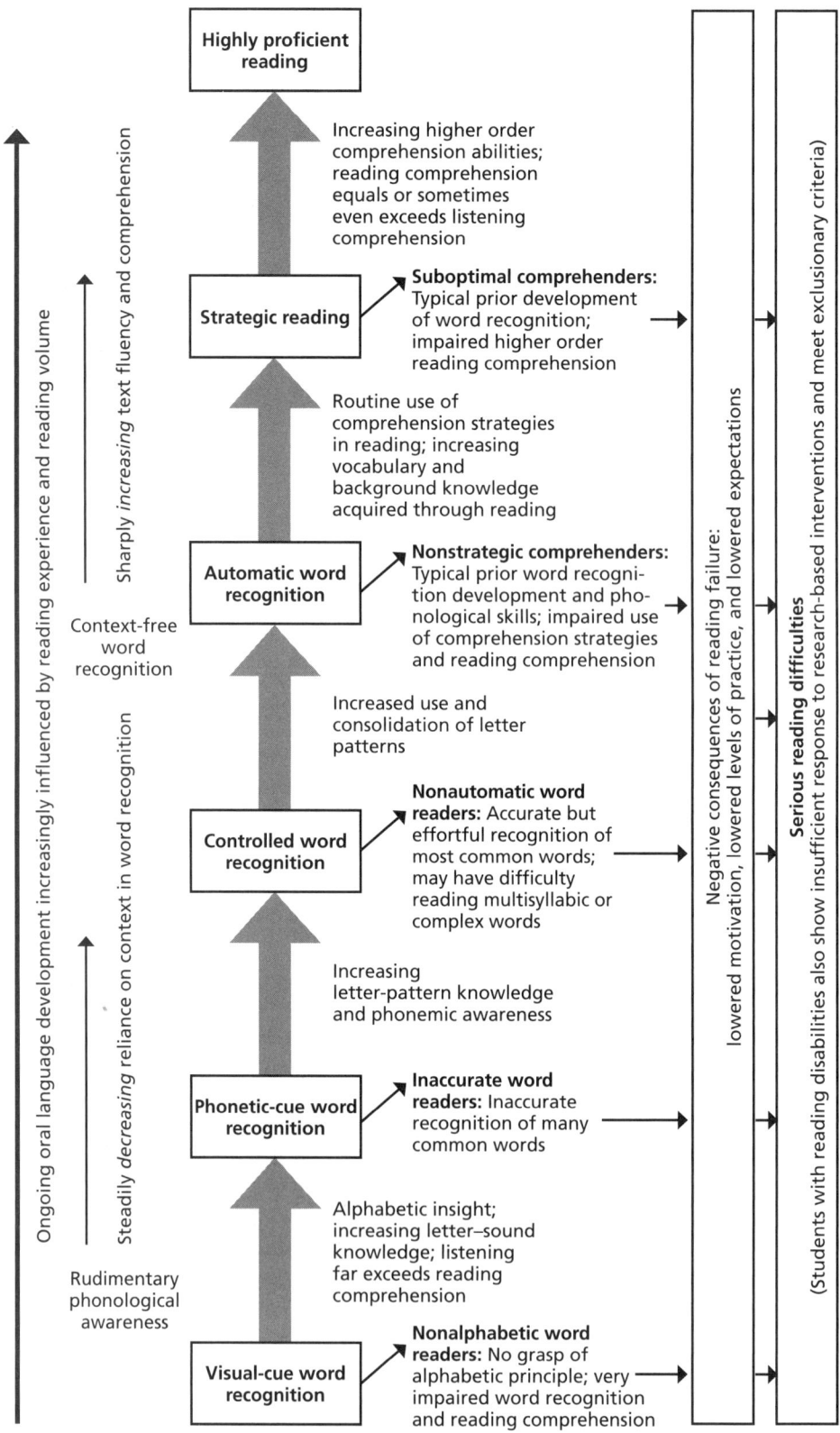

Figure 4.1. Road map model for understanding reading difficulties. (From Spear-Swerling, L., & Sternberg, R.J. [1996]. *Off track: When poor readers become "learning disabled."* Boulder, CO: Westview Press; adapted by permission of Perseus Books Group.)

because his phonological and word-recognition development were grade appropriate, but his reading comprehension was nevertheless weak due to cognitive and linguistic weaknesses associated with ASD. Not all children with ASD have a profile of SRCD, and most children with SRCD do not have autism. The defining aspect of this profile involves reading comprehension weaknesses despite average or better word decoding and phonological skills, and many factors can cause comprehension weaknesses.

MRD, experienced by Tamisha, involve a combination of word-recognition difficulties and comprehension problems. Like children with SWRD, children with MRD have trouble decoding words; however, unlike children with SWRD, those with MRD often have trouble with comprehension even when they read texts at their instructional levels, and those comprehension problems may be evident in listening as well as reading. The defining aspect of this profile is that children have both poor word reading and core comprehension difficulties—that is, some comprehension difficulties that are *not* caused by word-recognition problems. Put another way, children with MRD have problems in reading comprehension that exceed what can be accounted for by poor word reading (e.g., as evidenced even when the child is reading material that he or she can decode well, as in Tamisha's case).

Fluency difficulties can accompany any of the three profiles, but the dynamic underlying the fluency problem may differ depending on the profile. For example, in SWRD, poor text fluency often relates to inaccurate or non-automatic word decoding, whereas in SRCD, it may relate primarily to oral language or comprehension weaknesses (Eason, Sabatini, Goldberg, Bruce, & Cutting, 2013). In MRD, fluency difficulties can relate to impairments in both decoding and language comprehension.

Early-Emerging and Late-Emerging Reading Difficulties

Any of the aforementioned profiles can be early emerging (e.g., manifesting in kindergarten or Grade 1) or late emerging (often defined as emerging after Grade 3). However, the prevalence of each profile varies substantially depending on the age and characteristics (e.g., socioeconomic status [SES]) of the sample studied as well as other factors such as the assessments used to measure word reading and comprehension. In general, an SWRD profile is relatively more common in poor reader samples from the early grades, and an SRCD profile is more common in samples of older struggling readers. For example, Leach and colleagues (2003) found that only about 6% of reading problems identified in third grade or earlier involved the SRCD profile, whereas approximately 49% involved SWRD and 46% involved MRD. In contrast, proportions of SWRD, MRD, and SRCD were similar for cases identified after Grade 3, with each profile constituting roughly a third of poor readers. Catts and colleagues (2012) also found late-emerging poor readers to be heterogeneous, with 52% of late-emerging poor readers in their study having the SRCD profile, 36% the SWRD profile, and 12% the MRD profile.

Spear-Swerling

It bears emphasizing that late-emerging reading problems are not merely early-emerging difficulties that educators failed to identify until children grew older. Although samples of children followed longitudinally for late-emerging reading problems often show early linguistic or nonverbal impairments (e.g., Catts et al., 2012), these children's actual *reading* skills are grade appropriate early on. Shifts in the prevalence of different profiles across grades can be understood, at least in part, in relation to changing reading expectations across grades. For instance, an SWRD profile is likely especially prevalent in the early grades, because in these grades the central reading task for children is learning to decode words. Late-emerging SWRD appear to manifest in most cases by Grade 4 and may sometimes involve relatively mild phonological or working memory weaknesses for which children could compensate when reading simple words but not the more complex, multisyllabic words used in the middle-elementary grades and later (Catts et al., 2012; Lipka et al., 2006). Rachel's story represents late-emerging SWRD; Anthony, from Chapter 1, shows early-emerging SWRD.

Likewise, the SRCD profile is probably relatively more common in older poor readers because of the escalation in comprehension demands at upper grade levels. Children with SRCD may have mild oral language weaknesses from the early grades, but those weaknesses may not strongly influence reading until the comprehension demands of the texts used in schooling increase after Grade 3 (as in Cameron's case). Young poor readers also can evidence an SRCD (or MRD) profile if their comprehension weaknesses are serious enough to influence reading comprehension significantly in the early grades, as for Tamisha, who had early emerging MRD.

Another important factor in the prevalence of different profiles involves the nature of the sample studied, especially the SES of the sample and the proportion of language-minority children in the sample. Relative to middle- or upper-SES children, low-SES children often have limited exposure to vocabulary (Hart & Risley, 1995), and by definition, ELLs have limited experience with English vocabulary as compared with monolingual English-speaking children. Limited exposure to vocabulary will have an impact on children's comprehension over and above any other reading-related weaknesses that children may have, which will tend to yield higher proportions of struggling readers with an SRCD or MRD, as opposed to SWRD, profile. For instance, one sample studied by Lesaux and Kieffer (2010) involved primarily low-SES, sixth-grade struggling readers and included a large number of ELLs. These investigators classified about 79% of struggling readers in their sample with SRCD, about 21% with MRD, and essentially none with SWRD. However, vocabulary weaknesses were extremely widespread in this sample and likely accounted for the absence of students identified with SWRD; about a fifth of struggling sixth-grade readers in this sample did have problems with word reading, but because virtually all also had vocabulary limitations, they had an MRD rather than SWRD profile.

By itself, information about reading profiles is not sufficient for planning instructional programs. For example, as Valencia (2011) points out, two struggling readers could both have an SWRD profile but nevertheless be functioning at very different instructional levels, with one child at an early decoding level and the other requiring work on reading multisyllabic words. Similarly, two students with SRCD might have very different underlying comprehension needs, such as vocabulary limitations versus problems with inferencing. Beyond individual students' specific reading profiles, their other strengths and weaknesses in reading-related abilities—for instance, in vocabulary, background knowledge, or executive function—will interact with the basic features of their profile and certainly must be considered in educational planning. Furthermore, many other important factors, such as motivation, behavior, presence or absence of specific disabilities such as ASD or ADHD, and quality and promptness of educational intervention, also influence individual children's reading outcomes.

So why should educators care about poor reader profiles? For one thing, poor reader profiles provide an essential *starting point* for understanding reading problems and for educational planning. Students with SWRD will not need intervention in comprehension and are likely to benefit from some type of phonics or structural analysis intervention, whereas those with SRCD will require interventions focused somewhere in the domain of comprehension. The former will probably not require extensive, in-depth evaluation of abilities related to comprehension, whereas the latter will probably not require extensive, in-depth evaluation of abilities related to word decoding. Obviously, teachers cannot effectively group these two sets of students together for intervention, although they might be grouped successfully for other parts of their literacy instruction—for instance, during teacher read-alouds or writing activities. Information about a child's reading profile is only a beginning for planning instruction, but it is a fundamental one.

Common Patterns of Difficulties within Each Profile

Within each profile—SWRD, SRCD, or MRD—specific patterns of reading difficulty tend to occur. Consideration of these specific patterns can further inform evaluation, educational planning, and intervention efforts. In addition to studies on common profiles of reading difficulties cited previously, many other investigations of children with reading problems have contributed to knowledge about common patterns of reading difficulties (e.g., Aaron et al., 2008; Cain & Oakhill, 2008; Fletcher et al., 2007; Frith, 1985; Hulme & Snowling, 2011; Norton & Wolf, 2012; Perfetti et al., 2005; Scarborough, 2005; Shankweiler, Crain, Brady, & Macaruso, 1992; Siegel, 1988; Stanovich & Siegel, 1994; Vellutino & Scanlon, 2002; Torgesen et al., 1994, 2001; Wolf, 2007; Wolf & Bowers, 1999).

The "Pattern" section of Table 4.1 displays the common patterns of difficulties within each profile (see also Spear-Swerling, 2004a, 2013), with the first three patterns characteristic of SWRD and the second two patterns characteristic of SRCD. MRD is dependent on the previous patterns, as will be discussed further later, in the section "Understanding Mixed Reading Difficulties." As shown in Figure 4.1, the model conceptualizes children with reading difficulties as straying from the path to proficient reading at different points in reading development. In general, children with patterns involving SWRD tend to go astray relatively early in schooling, at the elementary level, although not necessarily in kindergarten or Grade 1, whereas those with patterns involving SRCD often go astray somewhat later in schooling, at the middle-elementary level or beyond.

Nonalphabetic Word Readers   These struggling readers, who have a profile of SWRD, lose their way very early in reading development in the phase of visual-cue word recognition before grasping the alphabetic principle. Like typical readers in this phase, they generally have limited phonological awareness and limited knowledge of letter sounds with no ability to decode unfamiliar words; thus they are almost entirely dependent on nonalphabetic cues such as word shape or context (e.g., an accompanying logo). Although they might be able to memorize a few specific words, it is almost impossible to advance far in an alphabetic language such as English without a grasp of the alphabetic principle or some ability to decode unknown words; with such weak word-recognition skills, nonalphabetic word readers' reading comprehension is also very poor. Therefore, these children function at extremely low reading levels, in terms of both word reading and reading comprehension, although their oral language comprehension is age appropriate.

Inaccurate Word Readers   These children with SWRD have reading difficulties in the phase of phonetic-cue word recognition; they have grasped the alphabetic principle and started to crack the alphabetic code but have not developed fully accurate decoding skills. Like typically developing readers in the phase of phonetic-cue word recognition, they have some letter–sound knowledge and at least some phonological awareness; however, they do not make full use of all the phonetic cues in a word. Their difficulties in word recognition may relate to limitations in phonemic awareness (e.g., poor phoneme blending skills), poor letter knowledge (e.g., lack of knowledge of sounds for common letter patterns such as *ar, sh, igh*), or difficulties in both areas. Inaccurate word readers will always evidence word-recognition difficulties on out-of-context measures of word reading, especially measures that are sensitive to decoding unfamiliar words such as those involving nonsense words. When reading passages, however, these readers may sometimes be able to use context cues to compensate for weak decoding, and their reading comprehension may be near or even within average range. For instance, a child who cannot decode the word *cupful* in isolation might be able to read this word correctly in a sentence such as *She drank a cupful of tea* and might have good comprehension of the sentence. Nevertheless, the effort required to compensate by using context tends to create a drain on reading comprehension (Stanovich, 2000), especially when children are reading challenging types of materials. Thus, even for children skilled at compensation, inaccurate reading eventually creates problems as they progress beyond the early grades of school.

Nonautomatic Word Readers Nonautomatic word readers, who also have a profile of SWRD, experience trouble reading in the phase of controlled word recognition; they have developed skills for reading most common words accurately, but they lack automatic word recognition. Like Rachel in the opening to this chapter, they may also have difficulties decoding complex multisyllabic words, and their text reading fluency is impaired. The difficulties of nonautomatic word readers may sometimes relate to underlying weaknesses in rapid automatized naming (Norton & Wolf, 2012); to relatively mild phonological difficulties that do not interfere with children's ability to decode simple words but that do affect decoding of multisyllabic words (Lipka et al., 2006); or to other weaknesses, such as limitations in working memory or morphemic knowledge. Like inaccurate word readers, nonautomatic word readers may sometimes be able to compensate for their word-reading weaknesses by using context and may therefore sometimes achieve average scores on measures of reading comprehension; however, their need to compensate exacts a price, especially as they move into the middle- and upper-elementary grades. In these later grades, nonautomatic word readers will often have difficulty keeping up with homework demands because of slow reading, and their reading comprehension may deteriorate because of poor multisyllabic word reading or because effortful word recognition consumes mental resources needed for comprehension, especially in challenging texts.

Nonstrategic Comprehenders As shown in Table 4.1, nonstrategic comprehenders have an SRCD profile, with typical phonological skills and word-recognition development in the beginning phases of reading; they have developed generally context-free word recognition but lack a strategic approach to reading. Unless their comprehension difficulties are relatively serious, their reading problems may not manifest before the middle-elementary grades. Cameron, described previously in terms of his tendency to give up when he failed to understand what he had read, provides an example of a nonstrategic comprehender. Cameron's difficulties with developing a strategic approach to reading comprehension related to problems associated with his autism, such as difficulties with perspective-taking and mentalizing, which overwhelmed him when he was reading challenging types of texts. Different factors might account for the failure of other nonstrategic comprehenders to develop reading comprehension strategies, including limited vocabulary or background knowledge, impoverished reading experiences, or inadequate instruction.

Like Cameron, nonstrategic comprehenders may have difficulties with text reading fluency as well as reading comprehension, but weaknesses in language or reading comprehension tend to drive these fluency problems, not impaired or nonautomatic word recognition (e.g., Eason et al., 2013).

Suboptimal Comprehenders　Similar to nonstrategic comprehenders, suboptimal comprehenders with a profile of SRCD progress typically in the early phases of reading acquisition, with at least average phonological skills and word-recognition development in the early phases of reading. Suboptimal comprehenders also develop strategic reading; their difficulties revolve mainly around higher order comprehension abilities such as evaluating and synthesizing information, although they may also have reading fluency difficulties associated with their comprehension weaknesses. Thus the primary difference between nonstrategic and suboptimal comprehenders is the severity of the reading comprehension problem, with the latter having relatively milder difficulties than the former. However, despite the fact that the reading impairments of suboptimal comprehenders are relatively mild, these problems still warrant attention and intervention because they may influence students' abilities to function well in high school, college, or adult life.

Understanding Mixed Reading Difficulties

As indicated in Table 4.1, children with MRD have the word-recognition problems associated with nonalphabetic, inaccurate, or nonautomatic word reading combined with core comprehension weaknesses that exert an additional negative effect on reading comprehension. These core comprehension weaknesses often involve specific cognitive-linguistic abilities or types of knowledge (e.g., vocabulary, background knowledge) that may affect reading comprehension even in the early grades, before children would be expected to read strategically, or that may lead to nonstrategic or suboptimal comprehension in Grade 3 or later. Tamisha, one of the three students described at the beginning of this chapter, has inaccurate word reading combined with nonstrategic comprehension primarily related to her limited vocabulary and academic background knowledge. Other children with MRD may show evidence of different combinations of patterns. A first-grade ELL might have inaccurate word reading coupled with core comprehension weaknesses due to lack of knowledge of spoken English; a poor ninth-grade reader might have nonautomatic word reading combined with suboptimal comprehension due to limited background knowledge and poor executive function. In any case, all children with MRD will need intervention involving both word recognition and comprehension. Unlike students with SWRD, their reading comprehension problems are not attributable solely to impairments in word reading. Targeting intervention appropriately for individual children with MRD requires determining their specific areas of comprehension weakness as well as their specific word-recognition needs.

Importance of Matthew Effects

Children with reading difficulties are not simply frozen at a particular stage of reading development; they also experience negative consequences of reading failure, such as lowered expectations for achievement, loss of motivation in reading, and less practice reading. Over time, in the absence of effective intervention, these negative consequences may make it increasingly difficult for children to find their way back to the path to proficient reading and achieve success in reading. This phenomenon, captured by the road map model, is shown on the right-hand side of Figure 4.1. Stanovich (1986) proposed and explained in detail the idea that initial failure in reading tends to bring about a chain of negative consequences and that initial success leads to positive consequences, a phenomenon he termed *Matthew effects,* from the biblical phrase about the rich getting richer and the poor getting poorer, after Walberg and Tsai (1983). For example, as compared with those who struggle in reading, children who get off to a good start in reading are likely to have larger reading volumes and wider experience in reading, important assets for future reading growth. Indeed, in a cohort of children they followed longitudinally from first grade through high school, Cunningham and Stanovich (1997) found that the most important predictor of avid reading in Grade 11 was speed of learning to read in Grade 1. (In contrast, first-grade IQ did not uniquely predict reading volume in 11th grade.) Even with individual differences in IQ and reading comprehension accounted for, reading volume and experience are important contributors to the development of many reading-related abilities, including vocabulary knowledge, background knowledge, spelling, and fluency (Cipielewski & Stanovich, 1992; Cunningham & Stanovich, 1991, 1997; Hayes & Ahrens, 1988; Mol & Bus, 2011). That is, reading skill and reading volume have a reciprocal relationship; better readers typically read more than weaker readers do, but reading volume also contributes independently to further growth in reading achievement, with these effects growing stronger across development (Mol & Bus, 2011). Individual differences in reading volume, related to differences in reading skill, are massive. Based on their study of fifth graders' independent reading habits, Anderson, Wilson, and Fielding (1988) estimated that fifth graders at the mean of reading achievement (50th percentile) read 250,000 words more than low achievers at the 10th percentile; very high-achieving readers, at the 98th percentile, read 4,000,000 words more than the average readers!

Differences in reading volume and experience are important side effects, but not the only side effects, of initial failure or success in reading. Repeated failure is not rewarding, so children who struggle in reading may lose motivation and self-confidence, whereas early success in reading tends to have the opposite effect. Moreover, reading failure appears to have more generalized negative effects on young children's socioemotional adjustment than does failure in mathematics (Morgan, Farkas, & Wu, 2012), effects that may influence future reading achievement as well as functioning in domains beyond reading. Children's initial success or failure in reading may also alter the expectations of adults in ways that can contribute to continued success or failure. For example, some teachers have low expectations for struggling readers, as I have occasionally experienced when setting goals for students in special education. Certain teachers express strong doubt that struggling readers—even those with average or better cognitive and broad language abilities—are capable of making more than 1 year's progress in a year in reading, which is essential for narrowing the gap between poor readers and their grade peers. Instead, these teachers want to aim for 1 year's growth, or sometimes even for *less* than 1 year's progress in a year; so, in effect, the "goal" is for the student to fall even further behind grade expectations.

Interactive Perspective of the Model

Here are several additional points about the road map model. First, individual children's patterns of poor reading may change over time. For instance, a young child with inaccurate or nonautomatic word reading may respond well to phonics or fluency intervention, appearing to meet grade expectations, only to fall behind again after several years, becoming a nonstrategic or suboptimal comprehender in later grades, because of underlying, subtle language problems that influence reading comprehension in advanced texts. Determining a child's pattern of reading difficulty is very informative at a specific point in time and can suggest possible difficulties the child may have in the future, but patterns can shift, so periodic reassessment is necessary.

Second, many variables can influence individual children's reading achievement, including intrinsic abilities and knowledge (e.g., vocabulary), other intrinsic qualities such as self-regulation (Smith, Borkowski, & Whitman, 2008), as well as extrinsic factors such as the quality of instruction or experience. Thus, within a given pattern, reading performance may vary somewhat based on the specific strengths and weaknesses that a particular child brings to reading. For instance, an exceptionally strong vocabulary and background knowledge, or unusual motivation and persistence, in a child with SWRD may help him or her compensate for inaccurate word reading (though only to a point).

Third, the fact that a child demonstrates a particular pattern of poor reading, by itself, does not necessarily mean that the child has a disability. For example, in the heyday of whole language, around the late 1980s and 1990s, many children who evidenced inaccurate word reading did not have dyslexia or other LDs; per the tenets of whole language, their teachers simply had not explicitly taught them to decode! Similarly, recent concerns about relative declines in the reading achievement of U.S. high school and college students in international comparisons, which helped lead to the CCSS's emphasis on increasing text complexity (Williamson et al., 2013), involve many students who are suboptimal comprehenders. Most of these students do not have disabilities; rather, their comprehension problems likely involve experiential and instructional factors such as a progressive simplification in high school read-ing materials in recent years (Adams, 2012). Other students, perhaps similar to Rachel in the opening to this chapter, may have a vulnerability to read-ing problems that would never have manifested, or would have manifested more mildly, with appropriate classroom instruction (e.g., systematic teach-ing of word-recognition skills). In all these situations, the use of RTI criteria can greatly increase the odds that poor readers undergoing comprehensive evaluation for special education have had appropriate instruction prior to consideration for a disability classification.

Of course, some children do have genuine disabilities, and the nature of their disabilities—such as the phonological impairments typical of dyslexia or the theory of mind and pragmatic impairments typical of ASD—must inform the design of their reading interventions. Still, even for children with disabilities, extrinsic factors such as quality of instruction and experience, as well as intrinsic variables beyond the disability, play a vital role in out-comes. For instance, self-regulatory characteristics such as the ability to tol-erate some frustration and to cope well with stress seem to promote good outcomes in at-risk readers, whether they are at risk because of environmen-tal and socioeconomic factors (Smith et al., 2008) or because they have LDs (Goldberg, Higgins, Raskind, & Herman, 2003). Like certain other models (e.g., Lipson & Wixson, 1986; Valencia, 2011), the model described here has an interactive perspective on reading development and reading difficulties; individual reading outcomes always involve a complex interaction of intrinsic and extrinsic factors.

More Caveats

Just as transitions among phases of typical reading development should not be conceptualized rigidly, as discussed at the end of Chapter 3, distinctions between different profiles and patterns of reading difficulties also should not be too rigidly drawn. For example, although children with SRCD generally show typical phonological and word-reading skills, Cutting and colleagues (2013) found evidence that these children may have subtle difficulties in their ability to read *low-frequency* real words (as opposed to common words or nonsense words)—for example, difficulties reading words such as *caste*. The investigators hypothesized that these subtle word-reading problems in SRCD might relate to difficulties accessing semantic representations of words—that is, a nonphonological language weakness. Likewise, as Cutting and Scarbor-ough (2006) point out, researchers have generally viewed word-reading skills and language comprehension abilities as mostly separate skill sets. However, research on assessment of reading comprehension (e.g., Cutting & Scarbor-ough, 2006; Keenan, Betjemann, & Olson, 2008), to be reviewed in Chapter 5, reveals that word-reading skills and language-comprehension abilities not only account for unique variance in children's reading comprehension perfor-mance but also share a great deal of common variance in predicting reading comprehension. This latter finding, though not yet well investigated, suggests interrelationships between word reading and language comprehension in reading comprehension, and it is consistent with the idea of multiple, complex influences on children's reading difficulties.

In addition, because achievement in all components of reading and language involves a continuum of functioning, and because any cutoff for low achievement (whether below 90, below 85, or below some other cutoff) is somewhat arbitrary, some children will inevitably fall near the cutoff in achievement. Research on profiles of reading difficulty usually has focused on children whose overall performance falls clearly into the various profiles; however, educators will certainly encounter children whose performance is less clear-cut. Suppose, for example, educators use a standard-score cutoff of 90 to determine low achievement, and Student A has scores of 89 for word recognition and decoding, with scores of 91 for all other components of reading and language. Conversely, Student B has scores of 89 for vocabulary and reading comprehension but scores of 91 for all other reading-related areas, including word recognition and decoding. Obviously, it would not make sense to think of these two students as having completely distinct patterns of reading difficulty involving SWRD and SRCD; rather, both students have comparable performance, hovering around the lower limit of the average range in all component abilities.

With the preceding caveats kept in mind, research on common profiles and patterns of reading difficulties remains extremely useful for practitioners. Many poor readers do exemplify these profiles and patterns, which capture important distinctions among different types of reading problems (e.g., phonologically based versus not phonologically based, lack of accuracy versus lack of automaticity). Moreover, these distinctions are highly relevant educationally.

Finally, a few reading problems are not well addressed by the road map model. One such problem involves children with severe, early-emerging SRCD. These children, who show typical phonological and early word-recognition development but who have severe reading comprehension problems from the earliest grades, usually due to severe language or other cognitive weaknesses, account for only a small number of struggling readers (Catts et al., 2012; Leach et al., 2003). An example of severe, early-emerging SRCD involves some children with autism who learn to decode easily but who have very serious sentence-level language comprehension difficulties that cause extremely impaired reading comprehension. In a sense, these children veer off track in reading even *before* the earliest phase of the model, during early language acquisition, yet they are able to develop grade-appropriate word-reading skills, at least in the early grades, including phonological decoding skills. Likewise, children who are deaf from birth have great difficulty developing oral language, although they may learn to communicate through sign language with ease; children with significant IDs, such as most of those with Down syndrome, have serious, broad delays in language and cognition.

Although scientific research on reading, including the research reviewed in this book, certainly can help inform education for all these children, the road map model is not intended to encompass them. In contrast, most types of reading difficulties, including those involving HFA or Asperger syndrome—experienced by Cameron in the introduction to this chapter—as well as reading problems related to poverty, lack of familiarity with English, dyslexia, and other learning and language disabilities, can be understood in relation to the road map model.

IMPLICATIONS OF THE MODEL

The theoretical model detailed in this and the previous chapter has practical implications for general educators, various specialists involved in reading, and administrators, including specific implications for implementing the CCSS with students who have reading problems. There are implications for researchers as well.

Implications for Practitioners and Use of the Common Core State Standards

The "Key Intervention Needs" part of Table 4.1 gives those needs of children with various patterns of reading difficulties. For instance, both nonalphabetic and inaccurate word readers often require interventions involving phonological and phonemic awareness, which should be included with systematic phonics instruction, another key need for these readers. Nonautomatic readers usually have developed requisite levels of phonemic awareness for decoding unfamiliar words; however, in addition to fluency-building interventions, they may require interventions focused on decoding of multisyllabic or complex words. Nonstrategic comprehenders need an emphasis on becoming strategic in reading—for instance, applying effective comprehension strategies such as questioning and summarization—whereas suboptimal comprehenders need an emphasis on higher order comprehension abilities, such as evaluating claims and evidence presented in a text. As explained at the outset of this chapter, information about common profiles and patterns of reading difficulties is not sufficient for planning interventions, but it is surely necessary. For example, if educators fail to distinguish nonautomatic from inaccurate word readers, then they may emphasize fluency-building interventions with children who still decode inaccurately, which will likely render fluency intervention unsuccessful because accurate decoding is a prerequisite for fluency. If educators do not distinguish students with SWRD who are inaccurate word readers from students with MRD who are inaccurate word readers, then in the case of the latter students, they may ignore important comprehension needs that will tend to limit those children's reading outcomes in the future, even if phonics intervention is effective in addressing the children's decoding difficulties.

With regard to the CCSS, the profile and pattern of reading difficulty can suggest which standards will be most problematic for individual struggling readers. A fourth grader who is a nonstrategic comprehender should be functioning at grade level in relation to foundational standards involving word reading but may require intervention relating to the language standards, with application to standards for reading literature and informational text. Another fourth grader who is a nonautomatic word reader will require intervention involving foundational standards for reading fluency but should have the ability to function at grade level in relation to standards for language and comprehension, although reading grade-appropriate texts may be difficult for him or her. For poor readers who cannot decode grade-appropriate text accurately or fluently, teacher read-alouds can help expose students to increased levels of text complexity by using oral language as a vehicle for developing comprehension, although students also need many opportunities to read at their instructional levels (Haager & Vaughn, 2013).

For all struggling readers, development of prerequisite abilities is essential for future reading progress and bringing students to grade expectations, or at least narrowing the gaps between these students and their peers. Particularly if poor readers are far behind grade expectations, simply providing them with more challenging texts without systematic intervention to develop the abilities necessary for reading and comprehending these texts is a recipe for continued reading failure. Moreover, as noted previously, recent studies (Gamson et al., 2013; Hiebert & Mesmer, 2013) suggest no decline in elementary-level text complexity in recent decades; indeed, at some grade levels such as Grade 3, complexity has actually *increased* (Gamson et al., 2013). Further increases in text complexity in the early grades as part of implementation of the CCSS, especially without accompanying attention to providing strong Tier I instruction in foundational reading abilities, may only serve to create more struggling readers requiring intervention. Many poor readers know all too well what it is like to struggle with highly challenging texts; if doing so could solve their reading problems, we would need many fewer reading interventionists, special educators, and books such as this one.

Implications for Researchers

Theoretical models such as the one described in the last two chapters have the power to inform research as well as practice. Knowledge about common profiles and patterns of reading difficulties has important implications for many areas of reading research, including studies on reading interventions and RTI (e.g., Aaron et al., 2008; Denton et al., 2010; Simmons et al., 2011); ASD (e.g., Huemer & Mann, 2010; Norbury & Nation, 2011); ELLs and students from low-SES backgrounds (e.g., Kieffer, 2010; Lesaux & Kieffer, 2010); written expression (e.g., Berninger et al., 2006); assessment of reading comprehension (e.g., Keenan et al., 2008; Nation & Snowling, 1997; Spear-Swerling, 2004b); and genetic underpinnings of reading problems (e.g., Betjemann, Keenan, Olson,

& DeFries, 2011; Keenan, Betjemann, Wadsworth, DeFries, & Olson, 2006). These implications have sometimes been far-reaching. For instance, Nation and Snowling (1997) showed that struggling readers' reading comprehension performance on tests with different formats (e.g., question answering versus cloze) varied as a function of poor readers' profiles (SWRD versus SRCD), a line of work extended by a number of other researchers (e.g., Cutting & Scarborough, 2006; Keenan et al., 2008). More recently, Betjemann and colleagues (2011) applied findings from this line of research to show that different choices of reading comprehension measures could influence the outcomes of genetic analyses and perhaps account for discrepancies in findings of twin studies of reading comprehension.

For both practitioners and researchers, a model linking reading difficulties and typical reading development is imperative for at least two reasons. First, this type of model is necessary for mapping reading difficulties over time—for understanding common reading problems at different grade levels as well as how individual children's reading difficulties may change across grades. For instance, understanding why some reading difficulties emerge early and others emerge later requires a model that considers typical developmental processes and grade expectations as well as reading impairments. Second, as many investigators have pointed out, an understanding of typical reading development offers numerous insights into common reasons some children experience difficulty learning to read. Without an accurate theory of reading development, misconceptions about the nature of reading difficulties—such as that they involve seeing letters or words backward or that they stem from an inability to use multiple cuing systems to read words—can lead to fundamentally wrongheaded assessment and intervention approaches. The next two chapters review research on reading assessment (Chapter 5) and instruction (Chapter 6), with conclusions about evidence-based practices in both areas for typical readers as well as those with different types of reading problems.

5

Research-Based Practices
for Assessment in Reading

As increasing numbers of school districts in my state have begun to implement RTI, I have heard some recurrent grievances from teachers. One common set of complaints involves procedures for universal screening. The screening assessment in one K–3 school, which I will call Jones Elementary School, provides an illustration of some of these problems. The universal screen at Jones Elementary employs a type of assessment known as an *informal reading inventory* (IRI), in which children read graded passages aloud and answer a series of comprehension questions after each passage. Teachers score children's oral reading accuracy using running records that highlight not only percentages of errors but also the nature of errors (e.g., whether or not children's errors change the meaning of the text or are consistent with its meaning); in addition, educators score students' responses to different types of comprehension questions (e.g., literal versus inferential questions). Testing is stopped when passages become too difficult for the child to read or comprehend. Teachers say that this particular screen was chosen by the district because administrators wanted an assessment that reflected "real reading in authentic contexts," one that would provide information about comprehension, the ultimate goal of reading. Timing is not used because administrators do not want to encourage children to rush reading at the expense of comprehension. Concerns about timing and "inauthentic" assessments led administrators to reject the use of a type of universal screen frequently employed in RTI models: brief timed probes called curriculum-based measures (CBMs).

Teachers at Jones Elementary do view some of the information from the screening instrument as instructionally useful; however, one of their biggest complaints about these screening procedures involves how long they take to administer. Teachers must administer most reading assessments in the early grades individually, and the IRI screen can take a good 20–30 minutes or more per student. For a general educator screening a class of 20–25 students, total screening time therefore consumes anywhere from about 400 to as much as 750 minutes (6.7–12.5 hours). Furthermore, to monitor children's progress throughout the school year, the district requires repetition of the screening in the winter and spring, meaning that upward of 20–36 hours of instructional time is lost every year to this one set of assessment procedures. (Of course, teachers also give many other required assessments, including the state-mandated reading assessment in Grade 3.) Even worse, the screen often misses at-risk readers, especially those with difficulties specific to word decoding or fluency.

The problems in screening at Jones Elementary reflect some legitimate disquiet, as well as some widespread misunderstandings, about assessment in reading. As many investigators have noted (e.g., Johnston & Rogers, 2002; Rand Reading Study Group, 2002; Shepard, 2000; Valencia et al., 2010), assessment tends to shape instruction. Administrators' concerns that the use of timed assessments might lead teachers to overemphasize timed activities in teaching, or speed reading at the expense of reflective reading and comprehension, are not unfounded, and assessment information about children's comprehension is indeed important, especially for children with difficulties in this area. Moreover, the use of a one-stage screen, including ones involving CBMs, may entail other problems, as discussed later in this chapter. In addition, any assessments involved in classifying children, whether in screening for tiered interventions or for special education placement, can exert powerful influences on children's educational futures, and it is certainly wise to be cautious about their use.

Nonetheless, ignoring early signs of reading difficulty or employing time-consuming and cumbersome screening procedures like the ones at Jones Elementary, which do not even accurately identify at-risk readers, clearly are not a good solution for these concerns. Solving these and other assessment-related problems requires consideration of the purpose of assessments, cautious and well-informed choice and interpretation of assessments, distinction of tasks appropriate for use in assessment from those appropriate for instruction, and guidance by a research-based theory of reading development and reading problems. For example, as discussed in the previous chapters, word-recognition difficulties, usually involving phonological decoding skills, are central to most reading difficulties in the primary grades; when reading text, children with weak decoding can sometimes compensate by using context clues. Although the screen in use at Jones Elementary likely detects children with the most severe decoding problems, it is not highly sensitive to those problems. Using a screen that is not sensitive to decoding problems in the primary grades is like trying to scan the night sky for comets with the naked eye; you will find the brightest ones, but without a telescope, you will also miss a lot.

This chapter focuses on research-based practices for assessment in reading. I begin with a broad overview of different types of assessment, basic standards for choosing assessments, and issues in assessing ELLs. Next, I consider some widely used categories of reading assessments, including the utility of these assessments within an RTI framework. The third section of the chapter considers the use of assessment to determine children's profiles and patterns of reading difficulty; the fourth section examines the role of clinical diagnosticians in assessment and evaluation of struggling readers.

OVERVIEW OF READING ASSESSMENT

The term *assessment* encompasses a wide variety of measures, including checklists and observational data as well as formal and informal tests. Other kinds of information are also vital adjuncts to assessment. For example, two particularly relevant pieces of information for early identification of reading problems (see, e.g., Scarborough, 1998, 2005) are whether children have a history of early language delay (even if they no longer receive speech-language services) or whether there is a significant family history of reading difficulties (assuming that family members had adequate educational opportunity to learn to read). Although early language delay or a family history of reading difficulties does not automatically mean that a child will have reading problems, they are clear indicators of risk. This type of information usually is readily available from parents and should be considered routinely in decision making about individual children's need for intervention or eligibility for special education.

Purposes of Assessment and Broad Types of Assessments

Authorities interested in reading assessment (e.g., Kame'enui et al., 2006) have distinguished four main purposes of assessment. *Screening* assessments are used with large groups of children to facilitate early identification of at-risk children needing intervention. Usually educators administer screening assessments early in the school year to all children in a class. *Progress-monitoring* assessments are used in Tier I to ensure that students are continuing to progress well throughout the school year and often involve readministration of an assessment similar to the initial screen in the winter and spring. Progress-monitoring assessments are also required for children receiving tiered interventions, although these entail more frequent administration than Tier I progress-monitoring assessments and will vary for students receiving different types of interventions (e.g., phonics versus comprehension interventions). Because screening and progress-monitoring assessments are given to large groups of students on a relatively frequent basis, they must be not only reasonably accurate in identifying students at risk but also reasonably quick and easy to administer; otherwise, they will consume large amounts of instructional time, as at Jones Elementary. *Diagnostic* assessments pinpoint individual students' specific strengths and weaknesses in reading (e.g., in different component areas such as vocabulary, fluency, decoding, and comprehension) in order to help target instruction and intervention appropriately. Although diagnostic assessments can be relatively time-consuming to administer, teachers do not need to give these assessments to all children, only to those whose difficulties require closer examination. Finally, some assessments involve *evaluation of outcomes* at a particular point in time, often at the end of the school year; most state-mandated achievement tests fall into this category.

Several other distinctions among assessments are commonly made. These distinctions tend to overlap somewhat with the ones described earlier as well as with each other. *Formative* assessments are employed primarily to inform instruction and help promote student learning, whereas *summative* assessments sum up students' cumulative learning over time. *Criterion-referenced* measures assess students' specific skills in a circumscribed domain such as word decoding or math computation, whereas *norm-referenced* tests assess students' performance in relation to a norm group, a large group of students used in standardizing the test. Criterion-referenced tests usually yield scores expressed as percentages correct or in terms of meeting a goal; norm-referenced tests most often yield age or grade equivalents, standard scores, and percentile ranks. Some measures assess students' *specific skills* in particular areas, such as the five components of reading, whereas others are broad *performance-based* measures that try to duplicate the more complex demands of everyday or academic reading. Many state-mandated achievement tests in reading are broad performance-based measures, such as the Partnership for Assessment of Readiness for College and Careers as well as Smarter Balance assessments tied to the CCSS. Evaluating students' learning of complex literacy demands is important, of course. However, in the absence of additional diagnostic assessments, when students have difficulty on broad performance-based measures, the reason for their difficulty, and hence the appropriate remedy, is often unclear. Students might do poorly for myriad reasons on a performance-based test of reading comprehension requiring extensive written responses: slow handwriting, slow reading, poor written expression skills, poor decoding, or vocabulary limitations, to name only a few. Likewise, educators using broad performance-based assessments to evaluate the quality of their educational programs may not be able to draw unambiguous inferences about necessary improvements in curriculum or instruction.

Different types of assessments all have the potential to offer valuable information, depending on the context and purpose of assessment. A teacher who wants information about how to plan phonics instruction for a student with decoding difficulties would probably find a criterion-referenced measure of decoding more useful than most norm-referenced tests. However, a norm-referenced test would be more useful than a criterion-referenced test for obtaining information about how a student is performing in decoding relative to national norms—that is, for deciding how far "behind" a student is. Multiple measures are always important for evaluating students' performance, and the different types of measures described earlier can often complement each other; diagnostic assessment using a well-chosen battery of component reading measures can help clarify why a student is doing poorly on a performance-based, broad reading comprehension measure. Finally, the most important use of assessment data is not to evaluate *children* but rather the effectiveness of *instruction and intervention*. If many students in Grade 4 demonstrate vocabulary weaknesses on assessments, these data suggest the need for greater attention to vocabulary in the Tier I primary grade curriculum; if a student in tiered interventions is not demonstrating progress, the intervention needs to be changed.

Basic Standards for Choosing Assessments and Types of Scores

To be useful for any purpose, assessments must have certain basic technical qualities, including adequate reliability and validity. Reliability refers to whether a test is accurate and yields consistent scores across different testers, test items, and test administrations. Commercially available tests often contain detailed information in the test manual about test reliability by age group. A common standard for reliability is that educational assessments used to make high-stakes decisions for individuals, such as decisions about retention or special education placement, should have reliabilities of at least .90; tests used for screening should have reliabilities of at least .80 (Salvia, Ysseldyke, & Bolt, 2013). Validity involves whether a test measures what it purports to measure or is believed to measure. Sometimes validity can be determined in part through the correlations between a given test and other, well-studied tests with known validity; again, for published tests, at least some validity information would often be available in the test manual. Teachers should also consider whether test items seem appropriate for the children they are testing as well as whether the children would have had opportunities to learn test content, either in or out of school. If children did not have the opportunity to learn test content, then their test scores may mean something quite different from what they imply for children who did have this opportunity. For example, if teachers are trying to determine a student's profile of reading difficulty in English, tests of English language abilities can be useful with ELLs as well as with monolingual English children. However, most of the former children obtain low scores on tests of English language abilities merely because of lack of exposure to English, whereas a monolingual English child with low scores, especially one not from a poverty background, may be more likely to have genuine language disabilities.

A crucial type of validity to consider for screening measures is *predictive validity*: whether a screen accurately predicts children's future reading performance—for instance, on a broad outcome measure such as a state-mandated test of reading achievement. A related construct is *classification accuracy*: accuracy in classifying children into at-risk and not-at-risk groups. Screens with good predictive validity and classification accuracy will also be reliable. The screen described in the opening to this chapter was problematic because it had poor classification accuracy, and it was very time-consuming as well.

Norm-referenced tests must employ an adequate norming (standardization) sample: one reasonably representative of the students being assessed in terms of gender, race, ethnicity, and socioeconomic status. Teachers would not want to use a test normed only on boys to assess a female student or a test normed only on affluent white children to assess children who are socioeconomically and ethnically diverse. Up-to-date norms are also important. Salvia and colleagues (2013) suggest that norms for achievement tests should be from within the past 7 years in order to be reasonably up-to-date.

When using norm-referenced tests, educators must decide which scores to report and interpret. Generally, testing authorities recommend the use of percentile ranks or standard scores in test interpretation (e.g., Salvia et al., 2013), not grade or age equivalents. Many types of standard scores exist, but the most common score used in education has a mean of 100, a standard deviation of 15, and an average range of either 85–115 (percentile ranks of 16–84) or 90–110 (percentile ranks of 25–75). In addition, standard scores and percentile ranks can use age norms (which compare a child to other children of the same age) or grade norms (with comparisons based on grade). The use of grade instead of age norms can result in substantially different scores for children who are not the typical age for their grade; students with a history of retention may score within average range in relation to current grade-mates but be significantly below average in relation to age-mates. Decisions about whether to use grade or age norms are somewhat complex, but in interpreting students' performance, teachers must attend to which types of norms have been reported, and they should employ consistent types of norms for comparison purposes, as when examining a student's performance on the same test over time (Farrall, 2012). It also is important to keep in mind that standard scores and percentile ranks express a child's relative standing in a group. Suppose a child's standard score of 82 on a test of word attack remains the same from one school year to the next. Assuming the use of the same test and types of norms, this pattern implies that the child made progress in word attack skills, because he or she maintained the same standing relative to peers (who are now 1 year older or advanced one grade). However, he or she is likely not *closing the gap* with peers; to narrow that gap, the student's standard score would need to increase significantly. Significantly decreasing standard scores and percentile ranks imply that a student is falling further behind same-age or -grade peers.

Finally, information about reliability and validity is typically lacking for certain assessments, such as informal, teacher-made assessments. Unfortunately, whether or not published statistics are available, it still matters whether the test yields accurate, consistent scores and measures what it purports to measure. In this situation, teachers should consider issues such as whether test directions are clear, scoring is consistent, individual items are reasonable to expect students to know, and individual items appropriately sample the domain being tested. An advantage of many commercially published tests is their inclusion of data on technical adequacy. Further information about technical standards for tests can be obtained from many sources, including professional organizations (e.g., American Educational Research Association, American Psychological Association, & National Council on Measurement in Education, 1999) and comprehensive textbooks on assessment (e.g., Salvia et al., 2013). For examples of well-informed reviews of published tests, see Salvia and colleagues (2013), Farrall (2012), and the Buros Center for Testing (http://buros.org/test-reviews-information), which has online test reviews available for a modest fee. Kame'enui and colleagues (2006) provide a thoughtful, sobering review of the adequacy of available K–3 reading assessments with a useful framework for evaluating assessments.

ASSESSMENT OF ENGLISH LANGUAGE LEARNERS IN READING

ELLs often have difficulty learning to read English simply because of their limited experiences with English language and literacy. These difficulties may not be apparent in everyday conversation because children can have well-developed conversational abilities but still lack the command of academic language needed for success in school, especially at upper grade levels. (Despite many years of studying French and Spanish in school, I myself would do much better conversing in one of these languages with a waiter about menu options than, say, taking an advanced physics course in French or Spanish.) Appropriate assessment to determine and address ELLs' educational needs is essential but also involves many challenging issues, and the use of multiple assessments to guide decision making, including sources such as parent reports and language sampling as well as standardized testing, is particularly important (Goral & Conner, 2013; Rivera et al., 2008).

Where feasible, assessments should employ tests of component language and literacy abilities in a child's native language as well as in English. If a child is in a bilingual educational program, assessment of component abilities in both languages provides information directly relevant to planning instruction; even for children in English-only programs, assessment of native language and literacy abilities may provide important insights about the child's strengths and weaknesses. For instance, a child who has age-appropriate phonemic awareness and decoding abilities in Spanish, but weaknesses in the same areas in English probably has the ability to make good progress in English decoding if provided with explicit instruction and intervention that helps the child catch up to classmates. A dual-language evaluation is quite possible for a few languages such as Spanish, where appropriate norm-referenced tests and bilingual examiners are generally available. However, appropriate tests do not exist for some languages, and informal translations of English tests are problematic in numerous ways. Suppose that a student speaks only Tagalog, a language of the Philippines, for which standardized reading tests are not available. Even if by an amazing stroke of luck a school district had a Tagalog-speaking examiner on staff, having that examiner translate test items for the student from a standardized English test is undesirable because (among other reasons) translated items may not be comparable across the two languages (Salvia et al., 2013). In these situations, providing test instructions in the native language may be helpful, even if the actual items are administered in English (Rivera et al., 2008).

Examiners should interpret formal assessment results in light of information about the student's experiential and cultural background (August & Hakuta, 1998; Salvia et al., 2013). English language assessments should be interpreted with particular caution, because they often reflect children's lack of exposure to English or typical developmental patterns involved in learning a second language (Goral & Conner, 2013; Genesee, Paradis, & Crago, 2004). Furthermore, if children have not had opportunities for ongoing native language development and instruction, examiners should interpret even native language assessments with great care (Rivera et al., 2008), as they too may simply reflect lack of opportunity to learn. In addition, ELLs come overwhelmingly from low-SES populations (August & Hakuta, 1998), and reading difficulties in these children sometimes may reflect the influence of SES more than language-minority status (e.g., Kieffer, 2010). Nevertheless, for ELLs as well as other children, component language and literacy measures are valuable in planning a reading program. For example, whether or not a child's English vocabulary weaknesses reflect lack of exposure or an intrinsic learning difficulty, the child needs increased instruction on English vocabulary in order to learn to read well in English.

Of course, ELLs can have intrinsic learning problems, including disabilities requiring special education. RTI models designed specifically for ELLs can help ensure that all ELLs in a school receive appropriate core instruction. In addition, RTI may assist teachers in differentiating genuine disabilities from reading difficulties associated mainly with lack of exposure to English or lack of opportunity to learn (e.g., Gerber & Durgunoglu, 2004; McCardle, Mele-McCarthy, Cutting, & Leos, 2005; Rivera et al., 2008). Examiners evaluating the reading abilities of ELLs should obtain information from parents or other family members about children's developmental histories (e.g., any history of early language delay in the native language), their native language abilities, and any literacy skills the child has in the native language. Factors such as a history of significant language delay in the native language or serious problems learning to read in the native language despite adequate opportunities to learn should be strongly considered in decisions about referral for comprehensive evaluation or special education placement.

SOME SPECIFIC CATEGORIES OF ASSESSMENTS IN READING

This section reviews several specific categories of assessments in reading: CBMs, measures of reading comprehension, and IRIs. Although many other types of reading assessments also are important, I include further discussion of these three particular categories of assessments because of their wide use in education and certain issues surrounding their interpretation.

Curriculum-Based Measurement in Reading

CBMs are short, timed probes often used in RTI models for universal screening and progress monitoring. CBMs evolved from research intended to test the effectiveness of a special education intervention model called *data-based program modification* (Deno, 1985, 2003; Deno & Fuchs, 1987; Deno & Mirkin, 1977). Early CBMs were developed from local curricula involved in this research. However, in recent years, many generic CBMs have been published that work as well as these original, locally developed CBMs (Brown-Chidsey & Steege, 2005); see the web site of the National Center on Response to Intervention (http://www.rti4success.org/toolschartsLanding) for helpful information on the technical adequacy of commercially available CBMs. It also is important to distinguish CBMs from curriculum-based assessment, a broad category that includes not only CBMs but also many types of informal assessments, such as teacher-made tests of specific content knowledge, which are not CBMs.

Reading CBMs employ a variety of timed tasks, including those that require children to give letter sounds, read sets of nonsense words, read passages orally, or comprehend passages. A reading comprehension CBM might employ a 3-minute maze task in which children read passages with blanks in them, picking from a set of multiple-choice options the word that best fits in each blank. Another commonly used CBM involves oral reading fluency (ORF). In a Tier I ORF CBM, children read a set of grade-appropriate passages aloud for a brief interval, such as 1 minute; for Tier II or III progress monitoring, educators generally use a set of passages at or slightly above the child's instructional level. Passages are all at the same grade level, not graduated in difficulty as in an IRI. The primary score of interest on an ORF CBM involves the number of words the child can read correctly within the specified time interval—that is, words correct per minute across several trials, with the child's median score across trials typically used to interpret the results. Teachers compare this median score to published benchmarks by grade to determine whether the child is at risk of reading difficulties (in Tier I screening), or teachers use scores to chart progress during intervention.

CBMs are particularly useful for screening and progress monitoring because they are relatively quick and efficient to administer, and therefore, they do not consume a great deal of instructional time. In addition, they have multiple equivalent forms, so unlike most standardized tests, they can be readministered frequently to check children's progress in reading, and they are much more sensitive to incremental progress than are standardized tests. However, most CBMs are quick proxy measures of overall reading competence; they are not intended to provide fine-grained diagnostic information about individual children's strengths and weaknesses in reading. A typical Tier I reading comprehension CBM could reveal which at-risk read-ers are failing to meet grade-appropriate benchmarks in comprehension but not the specific nature of individual children's comprehension weaknesses. A typical ORF CBM could tell educators which children are below grade expectations for overall word-reading accuracy and fluency but would not provide detailed information about the specific patterns of words that chil-dren can decode.

An often-used analogy to CBM (e.g., Shinn, 2008) involves measurement of temperature. As with CBM scores below grade benchmarks, an elevated temperature signals the need for attention as well as the urgency of that attention; a temperature of 103 degrees should inspire more urgency than one of 100.5 degrees, just as a CBM score far below grade benchmarks should inspire greater urgency than one slightly below the benchmark. Physicians would not treat a fever only by prescribing medication to reduce temperature; they would try to figure out the source of the fever and then treat the underly-ing problem. Similarly, educational interventions for children with poor ORF or maze comprehension should not focus on practicing ORF or maze compre-hension tasks but should pinpoint and treat the child's underlying reading dif-ficulty using research-based interventions.

In the early- and middle-elementary grades, ORF CBMs are especially useful as an initial screen for reading problems because, at these grade levels, many at-risk children have a decoding component to their reading difficul-ties (i.e., they have a specific word-recognition or mixed reading difficulty profile). However, as mentioned in Chapter 1, one-stage universal screens such as ORF CBM, if used with cutpoints set high enough to identify most at-risk readers, also tend to have high false positive rates. This problem has led a number of researchers (e.g., Fuchs, Fuchs, et al., 2012; Fuchs & Vaughn, 2012; Johnson et al., 2009) to suggest two-stage or multistage screening pro-cedures. In a multistage screen, the first step (e.g., an ORF or a word iden-tification CBM) identifies the children who are doing well, those definitely not in need of intervention. A subsequent step, for the children who score below the cutpoint on the initial screen, might employ an individually admin-istered battery of component language and cognitive subtests (Fuchs, Comp-ton, et al., 2012); use dynamic assessment, which considers the amount of scaffolding children require to learn to read novel pseudowords (Compton et al., 2010); or monitor children's response to Tier I instruction over several weeks (Compton et al., 2010) to find those who are nonresponders to Tier I instruction. This second step of screening increases accurate identification of at-risk readers, reducing the larger pool of children identified by the initial screen to a smaller group more truly in need of intervention. Although mul-tistage screens obviously are more time consuming than a one-stage screen, as Fuchs and colleagues (2012) point out, one-stage screens may result in providing many hours of intervention to children who do not actually need it, an even more time- and resource-consuming endeavor.

ORF CBMs tend to miss children whose difficulties center only on comprehension—that is, those with a specific reading comprehension difficulty profile (Riedel, 2007; Valencia et al., 2010). These inaccuracies become especially worrisome at the upper end of the elementary range (and beyond), in which a larger proportion of struggling readers have the SRCD profile, or with certain populations in which SRCD is relatively more common, such as those involving children from low SES backgrounds or those who are ELLs. Including language measures in screening, such as assessments of vocabulary or listening comprehension (e.g., Riedel, 2007; Scarborough, 2005) as well as reading comprehension CBMs, may help to identify at-risk readers with SRCD. In addition, schools often have students' reading comprehension data readily available because of yearly state-mandated testing requirements; it certainly makes sense to use these data in initial screens for reading problems. Screening for reading difficulties must continue throughout the elementary grades and even beyond because some children's reading problems emerge only after the primary grades.

When CBMs are used to monitor children's progress in tiered interventions or special education, such measures may be relatively conservative indicators of progress; struggling readers tend to have more difficulty meeting a fluency-based reading criterion than an analogous untimed criterion (Denton et al., 2010; Mathes et al., 2005). For example, a struggling reader might show good progress on a decoding measure that assesses only accuracy but might perform more poorly on a similar measure that is timed. Therefore, educators may wish to consider both types of measures, timed and untimed, in evaluating students' progress. Moreover, the use of any single measure for evaluation of progress is likely to be problematic (Barth et al., 2008).

Assessment of Reading Comprehension

Measures of reading comprehension vary widely in format and specific task requirements. Three common formats used to assess comprehension in listening as well as in reading include fill-in-the-blank cloze or maze measures, question-answering measures in which the child reads (or listens to) a passage and answers questions about it, and retellings of what a child has read or heard. Any of these formats may be timed or untimed. Measures of reading comprehension vary in many other potentially important ways, such as in whether they allow reference to the text when the child responds, whether they require lengthy written responses, passage length and genre, and specific administration and scoring procedures (see, e.g., Cutting & Scarborough, 2006; Farrall, 2012; Keenan et al., 2008).

The influence of some features of reading comprehension tests on student performance is relatively obvious. For example, a nonautomatic word reader who can read text accurately at grade level but reads very slowly will likely do worse on a reading comprehension measure with stringent timing

than on an untimed measure. However, the influence of other test characteristics on student performance may be equally important but less apparent. In
particular, although all reading comprehension tests tap both word reading
and language comprehension, a number of studies (e.g., Keenan & Betjemann,
2006; Keenan et al., 2008; Nation & Snowling, 1997; Spear-Swerling, 2004b)
indicate that tests with certain characteristics appear to tap word reading
relatively more heavily than language comprehension. Such measures include
cloze or maze format tests or tests with single sentences, in which comprehension often rests heavily on the decoding of one word in the sentence. Other
types of tests, such as those involving passages and question-answering formats, show the reverse pattern, tapping language comprehension relatively
more heavily than word decoding, perhaps because, on these types of tests,
children can more easily compensate for weaknesses in decoding by using context or background knowledge. Thus, children with a profile of specific word-
recognition difficulty may tend to do worse on cloze, maze, or single-sentence
comprehension measures than on longer-passage, question-answering measures; those with a specific reading comprehension impairment profile, who
often have associated language comprehension weaknesses, may tend to
show the reverse pattern.

To complicate matters further, for some tests, the relative contributions
of language comprehension and word reading vary by developmental level
(Keenan et al., 2008). In addition, question-answering measures sometimes
employ passage-independent questions, that is, questions that do not actually
require the child to read the passage accurately in order to answer the question correctly. Examples of these types of questions include those tapping the
meaning of a vocabulary word or background knowledge, knowledge a child
may already have without reading the passage. Passage-independent questions can inflate a child's score, especially in the case of children with SWRD
(Keenan & Betjemann, 2006), who often have strong background knowledge
and vocabularies. Inclusion of writing requirements on reading comprehension measures, especially *extended* writing requirements, introduces other
sources of variance into reading comprehension assessments (Jenkins, Johnson, & Hileman, 2004). For example, some state-mandated reading assessments include open-ended comprehension questions for which children are
expected to write lengthy answers. Children with weaknesses in writing may
do poorly on these assessments not because they have poor reading comprehension but because of limitations in handwriting, keyboarding, text composition, or other aspects of writing.

Because good reading comprehension is universally regarded as indis-
pensable to reading success, and reading comprehension is widely employed
as an outcome measure, research findings on the potential variability in children's reading comprehension performance by test are critical for educators
to consider. Plainly, if only one reading comprehension test is administered,
then which children are identified as having SRCD will depend on the chosen

test, and that test will likely miss other children who also have comprehension problems (Keenan et al., 2008). High-stakes evaluations of reading comprehension should ideally employ more than one type of comprehension task, and analyses of struggling readers' performance on any comprehension measure should consider individual children's profiles and patterns of reading difficulty as well as the specific task demands of the test. For example, if a child with specific word-recognition difficulties performs within average range on a question-answering comprehension measure, this performance may reflect test format or the use of passage-independent questions; it is not a sign that the child's word-reading difficulties are trivial and require no intervention. If a maze measure is used to monitor progress in a student with a language-related SRCD, that measure may not be highly sensitive to the student's underlying language problems. If decisions about reading intervention are based solely on a comprehension measure that requires writing, then some children whose only difficulties involve writing will likely be inappropriately identified as poor comprehenders. Interpreting struggling readers' reading comprehension performance in this manner requires the use of appropriate component reading (and perhaps component writing) measures.

At upper grade levels, standardized measures of reading comprehension rarely approximate the types of sophisticated reading demands expected of children (Allington & McGill-Franzen, 2008)—for instance, reading two novels and comparing their plot development, characters, and themes, with reference to specific evidence in the text. Especially beyond the primary grades, children may score within average range on tests of reading comprehension but still have difficulties meeting grade expectations for reading comprehension. At all grade levels, assessment of reading comprehension should include consideration of everyday classroom performance as well as children's abilities to complete homework with expected levels of independence and without herculean amounts of adult support.

Finally, research on measurement of reading comprehension has important implications for researchers as well as educators. Without consideration of these findings, the results of studies of reading comprehension may depend heavily on the nature of the specific comprehension measure used rather than permitting broader inferences about reading. Children's performance on measures of oral language comprehension, as well as reading comprehension, likely varies depending on specific test characteristics, which also may affect the results of studies employing these measures, especially if multiple measures are not used.

Informal Reading Inventories

IRIs, like the one described in the opening to this chapter, may be commercially published or developed informally by teachers. Educators often employ these tests to help place children at a particular text level for instruction or independent reading, as well as to obtain detailed information about children's decoding and comprehension strategies when reading text. As described previously, IRIs require children to read a series of successively more difficult graded passages aloud, with scoring of children's word-reading accuracy and comprehension. An initial set of graded word lists is often used to decide where to have individual children start their reading of passages.

One issue that affects all IRIs (as well as other types of tests) involves the challenges of assigning grade levels to particular passages—that is, the accuracy of text leveling. Different readability procedures for assigning grade levels to texts can yield very different estimates of text grade level, with, say, a given text graded as late third, fourth, or even early fifth grade, depending on the formula used for estimating its grade level. (With regard to ORF CBM passages, considerable progress has been made in the past 10 years on the issue of equating passages using methods other than readability formulas; see Fuchs & Vaughn, 2012. As yet, this approach does not seem to be widely applied to the development of IRIs.) This variability greatly limits the utility of most IRIs by themselves as estimates of children's grade level of functioning in reading. Furthermore, many published IRIs either do not report reliability information or have inadequate reliabilities for purposes such as those illustrated in the opening to this chapter (Farrall, 2012; Spector, 2005). Other issues in the use of these measures include the fact that graded word lists usually employ only real words, not nonsense words, which will not be sensitive to some children's decoding problems; passage-independent questions may be used, with their attendant problems described earlier; and the same child may perform differently depending on the length or genre of passages.

So how are these tests useful, if at all? IRIs do help teachers determine the appropriate levels of text to use for individual children's instruction and independent reading, as well as find individual children's frustration levels—that is, text levels that are too difficult for them. If struggling readers are placed repeatedly in books at their frustration level—a common problem—they tend to lose motivation for reading, and they find it hard to build fluency and comprehension. Especially for these readers, an IRI can be useful in helping teachers approximate initial text levels for instruction and independent reading, with further monitoring and adjustment to ensure that children have been appropriately placed. Authorities in reading offer varying cutoffs for independent and instructional levels, but Morris (2014) provides one useful set of guidelines. Morris suggests that *independent level* is the level at which children can read with 98%–100% word accuracy and 90%–100% comprehension; *instructional level* is the level at which children can read with 95%–97% word accuracy and 75%–89% comprehension. Scores a few points below either criterion, word accuracy or comprehension, are a "gray area" requiring further analysis; those substantially below either criterion would be frustration level, even if the child does well on the other criterion. For example, a text on which a child only achieves 50% comprehension is frustration level even if the child's word accuracy is perfect.

Criteria for instructional level may also need to change somewhat across grades, especially in relation to word-reading accuracy. Border-line word accuracy of 92% may be sufficient for good comprehension and engagement in a beginning first grader who is only reading a couple of lines of text on each page. However, the same percentage of word accuracy would yield an average of 16 errors per page for a child reading fifth- or sixth-grade text containing a couple of hundred words per page, an error rate dubious for supporting good comprehension and engagement at these grade levels. Placement of struggling readers in appropriate texts must consider numer-ous additional factors, including automaticity of reading as well as individual children's background knowledge and interests. A child with a strong inter-est in and background knowledge about soccer might be able to read a rel-atively challenging text about soccer, even if most other texts at the same reading level are too difficult for him or her.

IRIs can also be useful in providing information about children's com-prehension and their application of decoding skills to passage reading. Anal-yses of children's text-reading accuracy should consider whether children are applying known decoding skills to reading text, as opposed to guessing at words based on context, as well as whether children appear to monitor comprehension as they read. Overreliance on context to aid word reading is suggested when children frequently substitute words that fit the context of the passage but that differ substantially from the actual word on the page (e.g., the child reads *Mary went to the butterfly garden* as *Mary walked to the butterfly gate*). Lack of comprehension monitoring is suggested by repeated failure to try to correct errors, especially ones that yield a nonsensical read-ing (e.g., the child reads *Mary went to the butterfly garden* as *Mary went to the butter graden* and then just keeps on reading). Analyses of children's oral reading must be based on a sound theory of reading development, one that recognizes the role of accurate, automatic word reading in driving reading progress. Morris (2014) provides a thoughtful approach to the use of oral reading inventories in instructional planning.

DETERMINING PROFILES AND PATTERNS OF READING DIFFICULTY

To determine a child's profile and pattern of reading difficulty, examiners must employ focused assessments of component language and reading abili-ties, such as those described in Tables 2.1 and 2.2. Table 5.1 shows examples of commercial, standardized norm-referenced tests or subtests that assess various components of reading and language, including information such as whether the tests are timed or untimed. Many other tests (not shown in the table) certainly may be used as long as they are technically adequate, measure specific component abilities, and provide up-to-date norms or benchmarks for interpreting performance relative to grade or age. A thorough reading evaluation for children experiencing reading difficulties should include stan-dardized, technically adequate measures of all the following: reading real

Table 5.1. Examples of standardized, norm-referenced tests or subtests for assessing component reading and language abilities

Component reading-related ability	Examples of tests/subtests
Word recognition, real words (timed or untimed)	KTEA-II Letter and Word Recognition (both timed and untimed subtests); TOWRE-2 Sight Word Efficiency (timed); WIAT-III Word Reading (timed); WJ-III Letter-Word Identification (untimed)
Word decoding, pseudowords (timed or untimed)	KTEA-II Nonsense Word Decoding (both timed and untimed subtests); PAT 2 Decoding Section (untimed); TOWRE-2 Phonetic Decoding Efficiency (timed); WIAT-III Pseudoword Decoding (timed); WJ-III Word Attack (untimed)
Text reading accuracy (oral only)	GORT-5 Accuracy; WIAT-III Oral Reading Fluency—Accuracy Score
Text reading fluency/rate (oral or silent)	GORT-5 Rate (oral); GORT-5 Fluency (oral); WIAT-III Oral Reading Fluency—Rate Score (oral); WIAT-III Oral Reading Fluency Composite (oral); WJ-III Reading Fluency (silent)
Reading comprehension (overall format; early items / later items)	GORT-5 Comprehension (passage reading and question answering); KTEA-II Reading Comprehension (match word to picture / passage reading and question answering); WIAT-III Reading Comprehension (passage reading and question answering); WJ-III Passage Comprehension (match phrase to picture/cloze)
Oral language—receptive vocabulary	PPVT-IV; ROWPVT-4; WIAT-III Receptive Vocabulary
Oral language—expressive vocabulary	EOWPVT-4; WIAT-III Expressive Vocabulary; WJ-III Picture Vocabulary
Oral language—broad listening comprehension, sentences or paragraphs (overall format)	CELF-5 Receptive Language Composite (varied formats); CELF-5 Understanding Spoken Paragraphs (listening and answering questions); KTEA-II Listening Comprehension (listening and answering questions); WIAT-III Oral Discourse Comprehension (listening and answering questions); WJ-III Oral Comprehension (cloze)
Oral language—phonological processing (including phonemic awareness)	CTOPP-2 Phonological Awareness, Phonological Memory, and/or Rapid Naming Quotients; KTEA-II Phonological Awareness; PAT 2 Phonological Awareness Section; WJ-III Sound Awareness
Oral language—pragmatics	CELF-5 Pragmatics Profile; SLDT-Elementary; TOPL-2
Spelling	KTEA-II Spelling; TOWL-4 Spelling; WIAT-III Spelling; WJ-III Spelling

Note: CELF-5 = Clinical Evaluation of Language Fundamentals, 5th edition (Semel, Wiig, & Secord, 2013); CTOPP-2 = Comprehensive Test of Phonological Processing, 2nd edition (Wagner, Torgesen, Rashotte, & Pearson, 2013); EOWPVT-4 = Expressive One-Word Picture Vocabulary Test, 4th edition (Brownell, 2010a); GORT-5 = Gray Oral Reading Test, 5th edition (Wiederholt & Bryant, 2012); KTEA-II = Kaufman Test of Educational Achievement, 2nd edition (Kaufman & Kaufman, 2004); PAT 2 = Phonological Awareness Test 2 (Robertson & Salter, 2007); PPVT-IV = Peabody Picture Vocabulary Test, 4th edition (Dunn & Dunn, 2007); ROWPVT-4 = Receptive One-Word Picture Vocabulary Test, 4th edition (Brownell, 2010b); SLDT = Social Language Development Test (Bowers, Huisingh, & LoGuidice, 2008); TOPL-2 = Test of Pragmatic Language, 2nd edition (Phelps-Terasaki & Phelps-Gunn, 2007); TOWL-4 = Test of Written Language, 4th edition (Hammill & Larsen, 2009); TOWRE-2 = Test of Word Reading Efficiency, 2nd edition (Torgesen, Wagner, & Rashotte, 2012); WIAT-III = Wechsler Individual Achievement Test, 3rd edition (Wechsler, 2009); WJ-III = Woodcock-Johnson Tests of Achievement, 3rd edition (Woodcock, McGrew, & Mather, 2007). Newly revised, 2014 editions of both the WJ-III and KTEA-II became available just as this book became available as this book was at press.

words in isolation, reading nonsense words in isolation, text-reading accuracy and fluency, oral vocabulary, broad oral comprehension (i.e., comprehension of sentences and/or longer discourse), and reading comprehension. For children with limitations in decoding, teachers also should assess phonemic awareness; for these children, a measure of letter–sound knowledge (including sounds for common letter patterns such as *sh, ai,* and *er*) is often useful as well. For children with core comprehension weaknesses—reading comprehension problems not attributable to decoding difficulties—more in-depth assessment of comprehension usually is needed, including measures of language as well as reading comprehension.

In addition, examiners should consider multiple aspects of reading fluency in assessment, especially for students with difficulties in this area. For example, measures of ORF often provide information about prosody of reading, typically using a rating scale, as well as about rate (i.e., words correct per minute). Although good prosody and a fast rate tend to go together, this generalization does not always hold true, and a disjunction between prosody and rate may be informative. A child who meets words-correct-per-minute benchmarks for his or her grade but has poor prosody may have reading difficulties driven by comprehension weaknesses rather than decoding. One of the best examples of this type of pattern that I have encountered involved a 9-year-old girl with autism who had excellent word-reading skills but very limited comprehension. On an ORF CBM, this child read words quickly and flawlessly but in a monotone voices, with no pauses for punctuation, and she was obviously not reading for meaning; at the end of every line of text, she stopped reading abruptly, and I had to urge, "Keep going! Keep going!" Still, the ORF CBM was useful in ruling out a decoding-related fluency weakness and in confirming a broad pattern of comprehension-related weaknesses in this student.

Table 4.1 displayed the performance that one would expect on these assessments for children with different profiles and patterns of reading difficulty. Information about a child's past reading history, if it is available, may also be useful in determining whether reading difficulties are early or late emerging; in the latter case, teachers and parents may find it reassuring to learn that a child's difficulties were not simply overlooked but actually emerged after the early grades. Analyses of children's reading histories also must consider that patterns of reading difficulty may shift over time; for instance, a third-grade nonalphabetic or inaccurate word reader may respond well to phonics intervention but may have lingering fluency problems, resulting in a pattern of nonautomatic word reading in later grades.

THE ROLE OF SPECIALISTS AND CLINICAL DIAGNOSTICIANS

Knowledgeable specialists can play a valuable role in reading assessment, whether those specialists have generalized assessment expertise (e.g., school psychologists, special educators) or domain-specific expertise in areas relevant to children's reading performance (e.g., reading specialists, speech-language pathologists, licensed clinical social workers). Most elementary schools have a range of such specialists available—albeit often overworked ones. These specialists can consult or collaborate with general educators about individual students or, in some cases, perform evaluations and help administer classroom assessments. In RTI models, specialists with strong assessment backgrounds can assist in analyzing universal screening data, administering second-stage screens, and interpreting progress-monitoring data.

Independent educational diagnosticians, retained by either parents or school districts, also can play valuable roles in assessment. Knowledgeable independent diagnosticians can be important sources of information about research-based approaches to assessment and intervention. They can help evaluate students' responses to past intervention and special education and, for students who have been unresponsive, suggest changes in programming and intervention that may be helpful. They can translate comprehensive test results into educationally relevant, useful recommendations and, if they are impartial and constructive, may help mediate conflicts between parents and schools. For instance, occasionally schools may adopt ill-advised reading programs for individual students because of parental pressure. The parent may be desperate to find something that will work for the child and may respond to descriptions of programs on the Internet, or elsewhere that promise miraculous gains in achievement but that are not supported by research. The opposite also occurs, of course; sometimes educators are not familiar with evidence-based practices for struggling readers with a particular type of problem, and the parent has the right idea. In either case, educators and parents may accept a recommendation from a neutral third party who is knowledgeable and who offers practical, constructive, research-based guidance for meeting the child's instructional needs in reading.

Although sometimes conceptualized as mutually exclusive alternatives to identification of LDs, clinical diagnosticians and school-based RTI approaches to identification of LDs do not have to be pitted against each other. RTI approaches to identification of LDs do necessitate, however, that everyone involved in assessment and identification seriously consider the influence of instruction and experience in diagnosis of any disability. As required by IDEA 2004 for all disabilities, not only LDs, educators and diagnosticians certainly should not identify a student with a disability if the primary cause of a student's reading problem is inadequate instruction or lack of opportunity to learn. Moreover, because all reading problems occur and develop in an educational context, consideration of this context is vital in addressing any type of reading difficulty, whether or not it involves a disability. To evaluate the quality of instruction, diagnosticians must not only be knowledgeable about research-based interventions but also have more than cursory information about the type of instruction the child has received; they must actually observe instruction and intervention. For example, a child might be receiving a research-based phonics intervention, but if he or she is placed in a text for classroom reading that does not provide opportunities for application of decoding skills, or if the teacher does not provide appropriate cues and feedback to errors, then the entire phonics intervention may be undermined. The next chapter reviews research on the features of effective core curriculum and instruction in reading as well as examples of research-based interventions for students with various types of reading difficulties.

6

Research-Based Practices for Reading Instruction and Intervention

An interesting study by Cunningham, Zibulsky, Stanovich, and Stanovich (2009) investigated the preferred instructional practices in reading of a group of 121 first-grade teachers. The researchers asked educators to plan a 2-hour language arts block in the manner they thought best as well as provide detailed descriptions of specific instructional activities, including the amount of time they would allocate to each activity. The findings showed that many teachers planned little or no time for important components of literacy, such as phonemic awareness and vocabulary, and an average of only about 12 minutes for phonics instruction, despite the centrality of this area to first graders' reading progress. Another study that my colleague Jamie Zibulsky and I did (Spear-Swerling & Zibulsky, in press) replicated these findings and extended them to the K–5 grade range as well as to components of written expression. Taken together, both studies suggest that in schools lacking a research-based, comprehensive core literacy curriculum, many teachers might allocate instructional time in ways inconsistent with consensus recommendations of scientific investigators of literacy (e.g., Graham & Hebert, 2010; NRP, 2000; National Research Council, 1998). Although some teachers would no doubt allocate instructional time wisely, variability across teachers would surely create problems for children's achievement, manufacturing reading difficulties in some children who could have done well with appropriate instruction, exacerbating difficulties in others, and likely creating a steady stream of children requiring intervention.

An effective core (Tier I) literacy curriculum can be achieved in a variety of ways: through the adoption of research-based, comprehensive core reading programs; through the adoption and integration of multiple programs to address multiple components of literacy; and through the development of instructional activities by groups of highly knowledgeable educators within a school or district over time. However a comprehensive literacy curriculum is achieved, data from children's assessments, such as Tier I progress-monitoring assessments, should be used on an ongoing basis to determine whether the curriculum works for most children, with appropriate adjustments in the curriculum as needed. One challenging issue for educators is that most commercial programs claim to be "research based" whether or not they involve practices consistent with basic research findings on reading. In deciding whether a curriculum, program, or intervention is actually research based, educators should keep in mind that most research studies have not directly compared specific commercial programs; for example, research comparing published core reading curricula is scant, although there is some evidence to suggest differences in the efficacy of specific curricula (Crowe, Connor, & Petscher, 2009). Furthermore, a variety of approaches to instruction and intervention may be effective (e.g., Mathes et al., 2005; Torgesen et al., 2001), and effectiveness may well vary for different subgroups of students.

How should educators make these high-stakes decisions about choices of reading curricula and interventions? Although there are no easy answers to this question, such decisions are extremely important because poor choices may completely undermine instruction or intervention efforts and, given the costs involved, are not easily reversed. Therefore, educators and administrators who are knowledgeable about interdisciplinary research on reading and who use research-based resources to inform their selections should make the decisions. For choices of core reading curricula, two examples of valuable research-based resources include the guidelines from the Florida Center for Reading Research (2007) for reviewing reading programs and the consumer's guide for evaluating K–3 reading programs from the University of Oregon (Simmons & Kame'enui, 2003). In making curriculum choices, educators must also consider the nature of the school population that they serve. For example, students who are ELLs benefit from comprehensive, explicit instruction in the five components of reading just as native English speakers do. However, language-minority children also need a particular emphasis on oral language development in English, an emphasis that should be incorporated into the curriculum from the early grades (August & Shanahan, 2006; Rivera et al., 2008).

RESEARCH-BASED TIER I READING CURRICULUM AND INSTRUCTION

Research-based resources on Tier I curriculum and instruction in reading, such as those mentioned at the end of the previous section, emphasize the importance of addressing the key component abilities discussed in Chapter 2, including not only the five components of reading but also specific comprehension abilities and knowledge, such as knowledge about text structure. Children can develop many of these abilities in tandem with each other. However, as suggested by the research on typical reading development reviewed in Chapter 3, certain component abilities do require different emphases depending on grade level. For example, phonemic awareness is critical for typical readers in kindergarten and early Grade 1, and omitting this area in beginning reading instruction will put children at risk. However, typical readers will not require instruction in this area beyond about the first half of

Grade 1 because, by this point, typical readers will already have the threshold level of phonemic awareness necessary for decoding printed words (O'Connor, 2011)—although older poor readers certainly may still benefit from intervention in phonemic awareness. Conversely, emphasis on developing comprehension strategies generally should await Grades 3 and 4 even for typical readers, because prior to that point, most children's word reading and text fluency are not sufficiently developed for them to profit much from comprehension strategy instruction (Willingham, 2006–2007). If a core reading curriculum is not based on knowledge about typical reading development—if Grade 3 or 4 looks a lot like Grade 1, merely with more difficult books—then the curriculum will not work well for many children. In addition, specific components of reading and writing are mutually facilitative, and instruction in a given writing component may help to develop the corresponding reading component (Graham & Hebert, 2010). Spelling activities can help to develop phonemic awareness and decoding skills in beginning readers; language-focused written expression activities can further children's reading comprehension. Therefore, a literacy curriculum should provide skillful integration of reading and writing activities as well as comprehensive writing instruction for its own sake. Other practices very important to effective core instruction include making instruction as motivating and engaging as possible, ensuring that children experience a range of text genres, and providing a language-rich classroom environment (Duke & Pearson, 2002; Guthrie et al., 2004).

Because children's reading abilities vary widely from the earliest grades, differentiation of instruction is essential for not only poor readers but also high achievers: children who may enter school as good decoders or who may respond quickly to initial decoding instruction, progressing rapidly through the beginning phases of reading. A first-grade teacher might provide differentiation of instruction through small flexible groups, with one group for children who need additional work in phonemic awareness or phonics and a different group for those needing additional work in vocabulary or comprehension. While the teacher works with flexible groups, high achievers could do independent reading, writing, or project work, with teacher feedback provided later.

Research reviews (e.g., NRP, 2000; National Research Council, 1998) strongly support the value of explicit, systematic instruction in the important component areas of literacy. *Explicit* means that educators teach important skills and concepts directly; children are not expected to infer them only from exposure. *Systematic* means that instruction is planned and organized, with prerequisite skills taught before more advanced ones. In a systematic reading program, children are not expected to decode complex words like *author* or *illustrator* before they can decode *book* (although they might well learn the meaning of those words orally); they are not expected to comprehend text with many long, complex sentences if they cannot yet understand text with simple sentences.

Explicit, systematic instruction requires not only knowledgeable, highly skilled teachers supported with a comprehensive, research-based curriculum but also adequate resources, especially access to ample numbers of children's books on a wide range of reading levels and topics. Children's access to books that are at an appropriate reading level for them and on topics of interest is vital for fostering wide independent reading, a key vehicle for building reading fluency, background knowledge, spelling, vocabulary, and other literacy-related abilities (Cunningham & Stanovich, 1991; Mol & Bus, 2011; Stanovich, 2000). For economically disadvantaged children, a population often having inadequate access to books (Neuman & Celano, 2001, 2006), providing those children with self-selected trade books during the summer may ameliorate the summer reading loss common in these students (Allington et al., 2010). Moreover, a comprehensive review (Mol & Bus, 2011) concluded that low achievers' reading abilities related even more strongly to their print exposure, via activities such as independent pleasure reading, than did those of high achievers. As this review notes, however, finding appropriate texts for struggling readers can be challenging and may require help and scaffolding from adults.

Research provides some specific recommendations for core instruction in different components of reading. I describe these recommendations next.

Phonemic Awareness and Phonics Instruction

The meta-analysis of the NRP (2000) found significant benefits of phonemic awareness instruction on children's real-word reading, word decoding, spelling, and reading comprehension. The benefits of phonemic awareness instruction were greatest when instruction focused on just one or two specific phonemic awareness skills, especially phoneme blending and segmentation, as opposed to many phonemic awareness skills, as well as when teachers included phonemic awareness instruction with phonics instruction, particularly in activities involving children's manipulation of letters. Furthermore, studies devoting modest amounts of time to phonemic awareness instruction (e.g., 5–18 hours) actually yielded *higher* effect sizes than those devoting greater amounts of time to phonemic awareness instruction (Ehri, 2004). This finding suggests that relatively small amounts of time devoted to research-based phonemic awareness instruction during the appropriate developmental period (pre-K to early Grade 1 for typical students) can yield substantial benefits for children's reading and spelling.

Decades of research (e.g., Adams, 1990; Anderson et al., 1985; Chall, 1967; Liberman & Liberman, 1990) established the value of explicit, systematic phonics in teaching young children to read even before the advent of the NRP (2000) report. However, the NRP and more recent studies (e.g., Christensen & Bowey, 2005) suggest particular benefits for a specific type of phonics instruction, synthetic phonics, as opposed to whole-word, analytic phonics approaches. Whole-word approaches emphasize decoding an unknown word by analogy to a known word or inferring phonics relationships through analysis of known, whole words. In these approaches, a child might learn to decode the unfamiliar word *bright* by comparison to the known word *might* or by learning word families such as *might, sight, right,* and *tight,* during which the child is expected to infer the pronunciation of *-ight* and apply it to *bright.* In contrast, synthetic phonics involves parts-to-whole instruction; children learn sounds for letters and letter patterns as well as how to blend those sounds to form words (e.g., by sounding out /b/, /r/, /i/, /t/ then blending those sounds into *bright*).

The size of the initial unit employed in synthetic phonics approaches also can vary. Onset-rime approaches to beginning reading instruction emphasize intrasyllabic linguistic units called *onsets* and *rimes.* The onset of a syllable is the initial consonant sound or sounds, and the rime involves all sounds from the vowel to the end of the syllable. In *smack, sm-* is the onset and *-ack* is the rime; in *shake, sh-* is the onset and *-ake* the rime; *ice* has only a rime and no onset. In an onset–rime approach to phonics instruction, children begin by learning consonant sounds and common rimes such as *-ack, -it,* and *-ake,* with application to decoding unfamiliar words. Later, children make the transition to decoding individual phonemes. In contrast, in a grapheme–phoneme phonics approach, children learn to decode at the phoneme level right from the start. A word such as *smack* would be decoded by blending only two parts in an onset–rime approach, the sounds represented by *sm* and *ack.* A grapheme–phoneme approach would require blending four parts, the sounds represented by *s, m, a,* and *ck.* (Letter-by-letter decoding will not work for many English words, so even in a grapheme–phoneme approach, children must learn sounds for letter patterns such as *sh* and *ck.*)

Synthetic phonics approaches at the grapheme–phoneme level are relatively demanding of children's phoneme blending skills, but they also appear to yield larger benefits for children's word decoding, spelling, and reading comprehension than larger-unit approaches (Christensen & Bowey, 2005; Ehri, 2004), perhaps because they force early attention to all the letters in a word. Close attention to all the letters in a word is an important habit to develop for children learning an alphabetic orthography. Anyone who has ever taught word families to beginning readers has probably seen that, once some children know what the rime is, they attend only to the initial letter of the word. Obviously, however, focusing only on the initial letter will not enable the child to recognize the word when it appears in a book as opposed to a word family list.

As children advance beyond the earliest phases of reading to second and third grade, phonics instruction for typical readers should begin to emphasize syllabication and structural analysis of multisyllabic words. Furthermore, continued and differentiated phonics instruction in these grades may provide a second chance for success to at-risk or struggling decoders (Connor, Morrison, & Underwood, 2007). Although research on morphological awareness instruction is still emerging (Carlisle, 2010), instruction in this area can help develop children's spelling and vocabularies as well as their word reading, and these areas should be included in instruction. For example, as children learn that the prefix *tele-* means *distant,* they can also learn its spelling and that this spelling will remain stable across words; hence, *telivision* and *telavision* cannot be correct spellings for *television*. Moreover, morphological instruction not only benefits children in the middle- and upper-elementary grades but actually appears to have its greatest effects in the early grades (Goodwin & Ahn, 2013), perhaps because of a synergistic relationship between morphology and phonology (Bowers, Kirby, & Deacon, 2010). Another advantage of early morphological instruction is that in the first few grades, children know the meanings of many base words and affixes that they are learning to decode (e.g., *lamp, lamps; jump, jumped; sing, singer; lock, unlock*), whereas they often know fewer root word and affix meanings for advanced, multisyllabic words of Greek or Latin derivation (e.g., *exportation, thermodynamic*). Therefore, even in kindergarten and Grade 1, decoding instruction should include teaching about grade-appropriate aspects of morphology as well as phonology.

Text Reading and Reading Fluency

Texts for children's reading are key ingredients of any reading curriculum. Yet a fundamental challenge in beginning reading instruction is that nearly all children have language comprehension abilities far exceeding their reading abilities, and finding engaging texts for them to read can be difficult. Holistic approaches to reading instruction, such as whole language, have often resolved this issue by using *predictable* texts—that is, texts employing repetition of words, phrases, and sentences in conjunction with pictures that help children predict the words of a simple text with relatively natural language. An important pitfall of these texts, however, is that children may attend to the pictures more than to the print, and the books may encourage guessing based on context rather than application of decoding skills. (One struggling reader I observed, reciting a predictable text from memory, exclaimed to his teacher, "Look, Mrs. M., I can read with my eyes closed!") Alternatively, phonics or code-emphasis approaches have often employed *decodable* texts, with most words controlled to fit the specific phonics patterns that children have learned. Decodable texts vary greatly in the extent to which they control word choice and phonics elements, but the most highly controlled decodables sound stilted and often do not lend themselves well to developing comprehension (e.g., *Jan can fan the cat. The fan is tan.*). Less stringently controlled decodables sound much more like natural language and can work well for many beginning readers (see, e.g., http://www.flyleafpublishing.com). A leveling system incorporating multiple criteria, including both predictability and decodability, can also benefit beginning readers, including those at a range of ability levels (e.g., Menon & Hiebert, 2005; Mesmer et al., 2012).

Research does not support rigid prescriptions about the types of texts to use in beginning reading instruction, but there is a substantial consensus among researchers that beginning readers should read texts that provide opportunities for them to apply their decoding skills (e.g., Ehri, 2004; Vadasy, Sanders, & Peyton, 2005), opportunities not provided by some popular text-leveling systems (Cunningham et al., 2005). In the early phases of reading, appropriate feedback to children's oral reading by a teacher or other knowledgeable adult—for example, feedback that encourages careful attention to the print as opposed to feedback that encourages guessing at words based on context—is especially important. As typical readers advance beyond the earliest phases of reading into late first and second grade, many children can decode well enough to read a variety of reasonably engaging materials, such as trade books, with some independence. Appropriate texts that meet the needs of a range of readers must be available for independent reading, and texts used in reading instruction should be at individual children's instructional levels. Decisions about which texts to use in a curriculum at particular grade levels, and for specific subgroups of readers within grade levels (e.g., high achievers versus average achievers), should be based on multiple considerations. These considerations include quantitative information (e.g., Lexile level, an indicator of vocabulary complexity); qualitative information (e.g., knowledge demands of the text); and information about the readers and tasks (e.g., children's phases of reading development and the degree to which children must function independently on the reading task). See Hiebert (2012b) for a helpful discussion of how to use these multiple sources of information in choices of texts for children's reading as well as Brown (1999/2000) for thoughtful examples of how different types of texts (e.g., decodables versus children's literature) can be useful for different instructional purposes with beginning readers.

For typical readers later in Grade 1 and in Grade 2, the curriculum should begin to emphasize activities for developing text reading fluency. If phonemic awareness and phonics skills have been taught well in kindergarten and first grade, then most typical readers will have the foundation of word accuracy that they require to begin building text fluency, although even for typical students, phonics instruction should continue, as discussed previously. Many classroom activities can be used to promote fluency, including guided oral reading with appropriate teacher feedback, structured partner reading, repeated oral reading of the same text with feedback, and wide independent reading monitored by the teacher (Kuhn & Stahl, 2003; NRP, 2000). Relatively challenging texts can be used in fluency development if there is appropriate scaffolding from a teacher and children are highly motivated to read the texts (Hasbrouck, Ihnot, & Rogers, 1999; Stahl, 2004). The key is for teachers to provide well-structured, well-motivated opportunities for reading practice, with monitoring and guidance, not merely a block of time for reading.

Vocabulary and Comprehension

Two broad approaches, direct and indirect, exist for building children's vocabulary knowledge. *Direct* approaches involve explicit teaching of specific words, with careful consideration of which words should be taught. Beck and colleagues (2002) suggest that explicit vocabulary instruction should focus on second-tier words, relatively unusual words unlikely to be known by most children but also generalizable across a wide range of texts. For typical second graders, examples of second-tier words might include *astonished, fond,* and *dislodge.* In contrast, first-tier words are common ones (e.g., *mouse, happy, run*), whose meanings most children will already know; third-tier words are unusual but not highly generalizable words (e.g., *owlet, talon, pellet*). In addition to second-tier words, educators should explicitly teach third-tier words that children need to know in order to comprehend specific texts and learn content subjects as well as common morphemes to help expand children's vocabularies. Another consideration in direct vocabulary instruction involves whether to teach a relatively small number of vocabulary words intensively, with many opportunities to practice words, or to provide children with briefer exposure to a larger word set. Biemiller and Boote (2006) argue that brief instruction on a larger word set is more effective and better meets the needs of a classroom of children, who will inevitably vary in their knowledge of specific words.

Indirect approaches to vocabulary instruction teach children to use picture, sentence, or passage context to infer the meanings of unknown words. (This teaching differs from using context to guess at words in decoding, as discussed in Chapter 3.) Use of context to infer word meanings is a potentially powerful strategy for increasing vocabulary knowledge, but without explicit teaching of important words, many children, especially at-risk readers, will not acquire the vocabulary knowledge necessary to comprehend academic texts and function well in school. Therefore, most literacy authorities (e.g., Beck et al., 2002; Nagy & Scott, 2000; NRP, 2000) recommend using a combination of direct and indirect approaches for vocabulary instruction. All reading curricula must address vocabulary, but certain populations, such as ELLs and low SES children, are particularly likely to have vocabulary weaknesses, so it is especially important for schools serving these populations to address vocabulary development explicitly, beginning in the earliest grades (Biemiller, 1999).

Also, educators should directly teach important text comprehension skills and knowledge using techniques such as teacher modeling, clear explanation, unambiguous examples, and think-alouds. A third-grade teacher might model attention to informational text structure by reading an informational text aloud and drawing children's attention to specific features of the text such as headings, subheadings, and emboldened vocabulary words. ("Hmm, I notice the word *amphibian* is in bold, which means that it is an important word to pay attention to. . . . Let's keep reading to see what it means.") In addition, the meta-analysis of the NRP (2000) strongly supported explicit teaching of specific, multiple-comprehension strategies such as the use of graphic organizers, summarization, generating and answering questions, and comprehension monitoring. *Comprehension monitoring* refers to active monitoring of meaning during reading, with application of appropriate remedies (e.g., rereading) when comprehension fails. The inclusion of practices designed to foster students' motivation, such as affording choices to students and using hands-on activities in conjunction with comprehension strategy instruction, appears more effective than comprehension strategy instruction alone (Guthrie et al., 2004).

Comprehension strategy instruction in reading has its roots in models such as reciprocal teaching (Palincsar & Brown, 1984) and transactional strategies instruction (Pressley et al., 1992). Willingham (2006–2007) notes that, although educators should teach research-based comprehension strategies, the point of strategy instruction is not actually the specific strategies themselves but, rather, fostering a strategic approach to reading in general to "push the reader toward a new understanding of reading" (p. 45) in which the focus is on gaining meaning from text. He further notes that the benefits of comprehension strategy instruction can sometimes be achieved in as few as six sessions and that this instruction should be deferred until children have reasonably accurate and fluent decoding, around third to fourth grade for typical readers.

A different approach to comprehension development emphasizes content instruction focused on the discussion of a specific text with the use of open-ended questions, meaningful talk about the text, and ample student–student as well as teacher–student interaction (e.g., Applebee, Langer, Nystrand, & Gamoran, 2003; Beck & McKeown, 2006; Chinn, Anderson, & Waggoner, 2001; McKeown, Beck, & Blake, 2009). There is evidence that well-implemented, content-based approaches can be as effective as or perhaps even more effective than comprehension strategy instruction (McKeown et al., 2009). Content-based approaches may be especially useful in comprehension development as children advance into the upper-elementary grades and beyond.

Finally, oral language is a crucial vehicle for comprehension development, especially when children have not yet mastered accurate or fluent decoding. Many children can learn new vocabulary or comprehension strategies, such as question generation, or develop other comprehension abilities, such as analyzing the author's craft, in the context of teacher read-alouds well before they can read well enough to develop such abilities in the context of their own reading. Such knowledge and abilities, developed orally, can transfer to reading comprehension as children's decoding and reading fluency improve.

Influence of the Common Core State Standards

Implementation of the CCSS, with their attendant increases in text complexity, has escalated expectations for text-reading accuracy, fluency, vocabulary, and comprehension across the K–12 grade range. The standards also emphasize close reading—that is, attentive reading, rereading, and analysis of challenging texts in a manner that engages with their deep meaning. Close reading goes far beyond understanding the basic content of a text to include, for example, analyzing the author's craft, citing textual evidence to support a particular interpretation of a text, and integrating information across texts. In close reading, multiple readings of a text might involve an initial reading to grasp its basic points, followed by a second reading focused on the author's use of language, followed by a third focused on the relationship of the text to other texts the children have read (e.g., Shanahan, 2013). Not all texts, and probably not many of those used in the earliest grades, are suited to this kind of reading although even in the early grades, children could develop some of the abilities and dispositions involved in close reading through listening activities, as discussed previously. Nevertheless, expectations for careful, attentive reading and analysis in the CCSS begin relatively early. By the end of Grade 3, for instance, students are expected to be able to distinguish their own points of view from that of a story narrator or character and to refer explicitly to a text as the basis for their answers to questions.

With good instruction, most children are quite capable of meeting these expectations, and if appropriately implemented, the CCSS could greatly improve the college and career readiness of many ending high school students. Furthermore, international test comparisons, such as the Program for International Student Assessment given to 15-year-olds, suggest that American schools badly need to raise the educational bar if they are to prepare students to succeed in a rapidly changing world (Ripley, 2013). The CCSS appropriately increase expectations for the kinds of critical thinking and higher order literacy skills that students now require to compete successfully in a global economy. However, successful implementation of the standards for text complexity and advanced comprehension depends on the development of solid foundational skills such as word decoding and reading fluency in the early grades—skills that, especially for at-risk children, require a research-based reading curriculum and explicit, systematic instruction. If children do not develop strong foundational skills early in development, they will not be able to focus their mental resources on the complex, higher-level reading comprehension abilities that are the ultimate goal of the standards. Their "close reading" will involve a struggle simply to decode the words on the page or extract the most basic meaning from the text, not to engage with the deep level of meaning envisioned by the standards.

EFFECTIVE INTERVENTIONS FOR DIFFERENT PATTERNS OF DIFFICULTIES

Even with a strong core curriculum in reading and generally effective, differentiated instruction, some children require additional intervention to progress in reading. All schools should provide opportunities for intervention as part of the general education system, whether or not these interventions involve a formal MTSS model. Decisions about choice and delivery of interventions involve some important considerations.

Issues in Selection and Delivery of Interventions

One central decision for educators involves whether to use a standard protocol approach, with one standardized, research-based intervention for all children having a particular type of reading difficulty (e.g., decoding), or a problem-solving approach, with individualized interventions based on analysis of students' needs (Fuchs et al., 2010). Standard protocols exist for many poor readers at the elementary level, especially for those with difficulties involving decoding and as discussed in Chapter 1, standard protocols have several advantages, such as minimizing time required for choosing and planning intervention, as well as for teachers' initial professional development, because teachers require training on a relatively small number of interventions. Standard protocol approaches also provide greater consistency of intervention in relation to consideration of nonresponsive students for special education than do problem-solving approaches. On the other hand, no intervention works for all struggling readers, and standard protocols do not yet exist for all reading difficulties, especially for those involving core comprehension abilities. A hybrid approach, such as the use of available standard protocols in Tier II interventions with more individualized interventions for nonresponsive Tier II students, provides one reasonable solution to these issues.

Teachers must also decide whether to employ single-component or multicomponent interventions. Single-component interventions focus on one area of need, such as fluency or comprehension, whereas multicomponent interventions address multiple components of reading, usually including phonics, fluency, text reading, and comprehension. Multicomponent interventions can be quite effective (e.g., Denton et al., 2010; Gelzheiser, Scanlon, Vellutino, Hallgren-Flynn, & Schatschneider, 2011), and they address the needs of children with a variety of difficulties. Another potential advantage of multicomponent interventions involves good integration across different components of reading, an important quality (Denton, Vaughn, & Fletcher, 2003; Mathes et al., 2005; Torgesen et al., 2001). However, educators can achieve good integration of single-component interventions through thoughtful planning and dovetailing of children's interventions with the rest of their literacy instruction. An example of a poorly integrated decoding intervention is providing poor decoders with classroom spelling instruction that requires spelling many difficult words that the children cannot yet decode—words that the children are not likely to retain, even if they manage to perform well on a weekly spelling test. Educators could improve integration of the children's intervention with an alternative spelling program or through the selection of a subset of words consistent with the children's decoding skills.

In delivery of interventions, group size is another important consideration. Effective interventions do not necessarily have to be delivered one-to-one, but they often require small homogeneous groups—for example, no larger than about one teacher to three or four students (Elbaum, Vaughn, Hughes, & Moody, 1999; Iversen, Tunmer, & Chapman, 2005; NRP, 2000; Torgesen, 2004). Inevitably, some situations will require one-to-one tutoring, such as those in which homogeneous grouping is not feasible or if a child has other (e.g., social or emotional) difficulties that make functioning even in a small group too challenging. Educators also should strongly consider well-structured peer tutoring models of intervention that have a strong research base (e.g., Fuchs & Fuchs, 2005).

The system of interventions must be designed with enough flexibility to "fast-track" certain students to special education when warranted (Fuchs, Fuchs, Compton, et al., 2012). For example, educators might choose to increase intensity of intervention for a third grader with weak responsiveness to initial intervention if the child has no prior history of ongoing reading difficulties, language delay, or family reading problems. However, a nonresponsive student with a history of language delay and a family history of language-based LDs should probably receive a comprehensive evaluation for special education. Also, students who already are functioning far below grade expectations should be fast-tracked to more intensive levels of intervention without having to demonstrate unresponsiveness in less intensive levels first (Vaughn, Denton, & Fletcher, 2010). Educators who deliver interventions must have appropriate knowledge and expertise, with greater levels of expertise required for those who teach children with the most persistent reading difficulties, including special educators.

In general, effective reading interventions involve increases in explicitness and intensity of instruction (Torgesen, 2004) as opposed to instruction that differs qualitatively from effective general education practices. Furthermore, interventions successful with broad groups of poor readers also can work for special populations. For instance, ELLs typically benefit from interventions effective for monolingual English-language children (Rivera et al., 2008), and students with ASD may benefit from some widely used comprehension interventions such as peer-mediated and strategy interventions (Kamps, Barbetta, Leonard, & Delquadri, 1994; Whalon & Hanline, 2008) originally developed for broad groups of poor readers. However, intervention design must also consider children's unique needs. Children with ASD may require a much greater emphasis on pragmatic language and perspective-taking in reading comprehension than do most struggling readers; ELLs and children from low SES backgrounds often require a particular emphasis on learning English vocabulary and academic language.

Effective Interventions for Phonemic Awareness and Phonics

The most effective interventions for poor decoders involve highly explicit, systematic, synthetic phonics, with considerable intensity required for children with the most severe decoding difficulties (Ehri, 2004; Torgesen, 2004).

If assessments indicate that a child lacks phonemic awareness in areas likely to interfere with decoding and spelling, such as phoneme blending and segmentation, then phonemic awareness intervention must be included and well integrated with phonics intervention. Nonalphabetic word readers, including children with MRD who have a pattern of nonalphabetic word reading, are particularly likely to require phonemic awareness as well as phonics intervention. Inaccurate word readers also may require intervention in phonemic awareness.

Effective phonemic awareness interventions have often used concrete tokens with letters on them; concrete manipulatives with letters help children focus on sounds, which are ephemeral and coarticulated in speech (Ehri, 2004; O'Connor, 2011). These interventions might have children move the appropriate tokens in place while segmenting and blending phonemes in simple words provided by the teacher (e.g., *sun, man, flip*), or children may write letters representing phonemes in empty boxes (e.g., Elkonin, 1973) when provided appropriately structured chains of words (e.g., *at, sat, sit, slit, slip*). Phonemic awareness interventions for children in the earliest grades, pre-K and kindergarten (e.g., Boyer & Ehri, 2011), or for older poor decoders with severe problems in phonemic awareness (e.g., Lindamood & Lindamood, 1998; Torgesen et al., 2001) have found teaching of articulatory cues beneficial. For example, children may look at pictures that show how a particular sound is formed with the lips and tongue, or they may learn to classify similarly articulated sounds (e.g., /b/ and /p/ are formed similarly with the lips and tongue, but /b/ is voiced whereas /p/ is not).

Effective phonics interventions include word-building interventions (Beck, 2005; McCandliss, Beck, Sandak, & Perfetti, 2003; Spear-Swerling & Brucker, 2004); well-structured peer tutoring models such as Peer Assisted Learning Strategies (PALS; Fuchs & Fuchs, 2005); highly scripted direct instruction programs (Adams & Carnine, 2003) such as Reading Mastery (Engelmann & Bruner, 1988); and multisensory structured language (MSL) programs such as the Orton-Gillingham approach (Gillingham & Stillman, 1970) or Wilson program (Wilson, 1988). All these programs involve a central foundation of highly explicit, systematic, synthetic phonics, but other aspects of the programs may vary. For instance, in addition to explicit, systematic decoding instruction, MSL programs include teaching of higher-level aspects of language structure, such as sentences and discourse, as well as multisensory activities, such as those involving simultaneous tracing, looking at, and saying of letter sounds and words. A letter pattern such as *sh* might be learned by having children look at the printed letters and repeatedly trace them with a pencil while simultaneously articulating the sound /sh/. Phonics interventions can be successful with or without the multisensory component, but appropriate multisensory activities may be especially helpful in focusing children's attention on print, a vital habit for learning to decode and spell. (See Birsh, 2005, for an extremely useful, detailed explanation of MSL teaching.) In addition, phonics interventions vary in intensity; a classroom-based word-building intervention or peer tutoring model might be especially appropriate choices for initial intervention or for children with relatively mild decoding problems, whereas an intensive MSL program is likely more appropriate for a student with persistent, severe reading difficulties.

Phonics intervention should encompass teaching of two-syllable and multisyllabic words, with systematic teaching of syllabication strategies, structural analysis, and morphology. This type of advanced phonics intervention may be required for nonautomatic word readers as well as other struggling decoders. One example of a research-based intervention that includes these areas is the Phonological and Strategy Training word-reading intervention of Maureen Lovett and her colleagues (Lovett et al., 2000; Lovett, Barron, & Benson, 2003), which combines teaching of grapheme–phoneme blending with strategies such as peeling off prefixes and suffixes in a multisyllabic word. Other examples of valuable approaches to teaching advanced decoding skills and morphology include Gillingham and Stillman (1970) and Henry (2010). Goodwin and Ahn (2013) found that morphological interventions benefited struggling readers, including ELLs and students with LDs, at least as much as typical readers.

Finally, children's application of their phonics skills to reading text is a critical component of any phonics intervention. If children develop decoding skills for isolated words during intervention but do not actually apply those skills to reading text with appropriate teacher guidance, or if they are expected to read grade-level texts that are much too difficult for them, the phonics intervention may not generalize to children's reading in books. Vadasy and colleagues (2005) found that an intervention combining explicit phonics with application to oral reading of appropriate texts was even more effective than explicit phonics alone in developing the oral reading accuracy and rate of struggling first-grade decoders. Spear-Swerling (2011b) provides sample teaching scripts for both a word-building intervention and children's application of decoding skills to oral text reading with a teacher.

Effective Interventions for Reading Fluency

Two types of interventions that benefit children's fluency in the early- to middle-elementary grades are repeated reading and continuous wide reading (O'Connor, White, & Swanson, 2007). Both types of interventions typically involve oral passage reading with feedback from a teacher or partner. In repeated reading, the child reads the same text multiple times, whereas in continuous wide reading, the student reads a range of texts or different sections of a long text. With young children, repeated reading, which researchers have studied more intensively than continuous wide reading, appears to have a moderately beneficial impact on reading rate, though not always on comprehension (Chard, Vaughn, & Tyler, 2002; Meyer & Felton, 1999; NRP, 2000). However, continuous wide reading appears to benefit rate of reading as much as repeated reading does and may provide better benefits in relation to comprehension development (O'Connor et al., 2007; Wexler, Vaughn, Roberts, &

Denton, 2010). Peer tutoring models that pair stronger readers with weaker readers for fluency practice can also be effective—if there are strong readers available to model fluent reading and to provide appropriate feedback (McMaster, Fuchs, & Fuchs, 2006).

Especially if implemented in the early grades, these types of interventions can benefit nonautomatic word readers as well as children with MRD who have a pattern of nonautomatic word reading. Furthermore, some inaccurate word readers require supplemental fluency intervention in addition to phonics intervention. A useful rule of thumb for deciding whether or not struggling readers require supplemental fluency intervention (Carnine, Silbert, Kame'enui, & Tarver, 2004) involves comparing children's fluency levels with their reading levels as opposed to their grade placement. For example, struggling fourth graders who have an instructional reading level of third grade would only require supplemental fluency intervention if they failed to meet *third*-grade (not *fourth*-grade) fluency benchmarks.

Poor fluency can also accompany SRCD. For instance, some ELLs, as well as some children with ASD, may decode accurately and automatically but read with poor prosody because they do not comprehend what they are reading. For this type of student, whose fluency problems are not linked to decoding, vocabulary and comprehension development, which could be implemented in conjunction with a continuous reading intervention, may be more beneficial than repeated reading. For all struggling readers but especially those with comprehension weaknesses, fluency intervention should not inadvertently discourage comprehension monitoring. If interventions involve timed, repeated readings of passages without comprehension checks, children may rush reading in order to improve their times without attending to meaning as they read. Inclusion of comprehension questions as part of the fluency intervention (e.g., Hasbrouck et al., 1999) may help to avoid this unintended consequence.

Unfortunately, research on older children with persistent, severe reading problems has tended to yield disappointing findings in relation to fluency, with fluency difficulties often being resistant to intervention in these students (Torgesen et al., 2001; Wexler et al., 2010). Fluency difficulties in children with long-standing reading problems may sometimes reflect a cumulative lack of practice that is very hard to overcome (Torgesen et al., 2001). These difficulties do not mean that schools should abandon attempts to improve fluency in older students, but they underscore the importance of early intervention efforts. Also, for all poor readers, even those who would rather eat spinach /have a root canal / clean the toilet than read, efforts to encourage independent reading are essential once children have the ability to read independently. Many poor readers do have this ability, especially if provided with some guidance from adults in finding and selecting appropriate books. Independent reading can be a powerful adjunct to struggling readers' school programs because of its potential to help develop many reading-related abilities over time (Cunningham & Stanovich, 1998; Mol & Bus, 2011).

Effective Interventions for Vocabulary and Comprehension

Vocabulary interventions have usually targeted vulnerable populations such as ELLs, economically disadvantaged children, or at-risk readers. Interventions for the youngest children, pre-K through Grade 1 (e.g., Beck & McKeown, 2007; Loftus, Coyne, McCoach, Zipoli, & Pullen, 2010; Pullen, Tuckwiller, Konold, Maynard, & Coyne, 2010), have often used storybook reading coupled with direct teaching of target words in the stories as well as activities to promote further engagement with those words, such as generating sentences using the words. These interventions, typically used within an RTI/MTSS model that also provides strong core instruction in vocabulary, suggest that supplemental vocabulary intervention improves vocabulary knowledge in at-risk children, although short-term interventions may not lead to robust, long-term gains (Pullen et al., 2010). Vocabulary interventions for middle-elementary or older students (e.g., Carlo et al., 2004; Lesaux, Keiffer, Faller, & Kelley, 2010; Nunes et al., 2006) have often emphasized explicit teaching of morphology and strategies for using context to infer word meanings as well as reading of informational text with direct teaching of target academic words. Such interventions can improve vocabulary knowledge with transfer to reading comprehension; furthermore, they appear especially beneficial for ELLs and struggling readers (Bowers et al., 2010; Goodwin & Ahn, 2013).

Interventions for reading comprehension have often emphasized explicit, systematic teaching of comprehension strategies such as comprehension monitoring, questioning, and teaching about text structure. Research indicates that comprehension strategy interventions, which can be implemented within cooperative learning (e.g., Palincsar & Brown, 1984) or peer mediated (e.g., Fuchs & Fuchs, 2005) models, do improve reading comprehension for both ELLs (Rivera et al., 2008) and students with LDs (Gersten, Fuchs, Williams, & Baker, 2001). These interventions are especially important for nonstrategic comprehenders, who lack a strategic approach to comprehension.

In designing interventions for reading comprehension, educators should also address oral language development, particularly in children with any indication of oral language weaknesses. Clarke, Snowling, Truelove, and Hulme (2010) implemented interventions designed to improve reading comprehension in a group of children ages 8 to 9 years old. In a randomized controlled trial, the investigators compared a wait-listed control group with the following: a text comprehension strategies intervention based on the Reciprocal Teaching model of Palincsar and Brown (1984); an oral language intervention that taught oral vocabulary as well as figurative language and spoken activities paralleling Reciprocal Teaching; and a combination of the two preceding interventions. All the interventions lasted 30 hours in total, and all significantly benefited children's reading comprehension on the WIAT-II (Wechsler, 2005) as compared to the control group. However, the oral language intervention group made greater gains in reading comprehension than did other intervention groups during an 11-month follow-up period after the intervention ended. Also, the oral language and combined intervention groups made significantly greater gains in expressive vocabulary than did the control group; furthermore, for the oral language intervention group only, these gains generalized to performance on untaught words as well as on a standardized vocabulary measure, a subtest of the Wechsler Abbreviated Scale of Intelligence (Wechsler, 1999). These findings provide encouraging evidence of the power of oral language and vocabulary intervention to improve children's reading comprehension.

Because so many abilities influence comprehension, appropriate targeting of interventions is essential, both for nonstrategic comprehenders and for suboptimal comprehenders. Students with ASD, for instance, may have particular difficulties with anaphoric reference, such as tracking the antecedents of pronouns used within a text, as well as with perspective-taking and theory of mind (Frith, 2012). Reading intervention research on students with ASD is still in its infancy (Whalon, Al Otaiba, & Delano, 2009), but preliminary indications are that interventions targeting these specific difficulties may be effective in improving these students' language or reading comprehension. For example, the use of anaphoric cuing techniques—such as having students decide on the referent of a pronoun during reading via a multiple-choice task—appears beneficial (O'Connor & Klein, 2004), as does developing perspective-taking through oral narrative interventions that teach children to take the perspective of different story characters (Dodd, Ocampo, & Kennedy, 2011).

If well implemented, the close reading practices called for by the CCSS may particularly benefit suboptimal readers. These readers have a solid foundation of word decoding, fluency, and basic comprehension abilities but lack more advanced comprehension abilities. As Snow (2013) notes, "warm" close readings that employ motivating, interesting texts and that require close reading for a meaningful purpose that makes sense to the students are likely to be more successful than "cold" close reading activities, which lack attention to these motivating factors.

Finally, educators should implement all interventions in the context of a broad, well-integrated, comprehensive program of literacy instruction. For example, an inaccurate word reader with strong oral language comprehension abilities, such as a typical dyslexic student, will not usually require *intervention* in vocabulary or comprehension. However, like any child, this student does require ongoing vocabulary and comprehension *instruction*, which usually can be delivered within the core (Tier I) program if necessary modifications or accommodations (e.g., in text reading demands) are made. For students with MRD, who require a combination of decoding and comprehension interventions, achieving reasonable integration of these interventions may require setting some different priorities at different points during the intervention. For instance, a child who is both an inaccurate word reader and a nonstrategic comprehender may not yet possess sufficiently developed decoding and fluency to benefit from learning reading comprehension strategies; teaching of those strategies in the context of the child's own reading might best await some improvements in the child's word-reading skills. However, development of oral vocabulary and oral comprehension should start right away and might well yield later improvements in reading comprehension, as found by Clarke and colleagues (2010).

A Checklist for Evaluating Reading Interventions

Table 6.1 summarizes important features of interventions for all struggling readers as well as features specific to interventions for poor decoders and for poor comprehenders. The table may be useful as a checklist to help plan or evaluate interventions employed with students who have various types of reading difficulties. In the next three chapters, I consider in detail specific examples of children who have different profiles and patterns of reading difficulties, with recommendations for intervention for each student.

Table 6.1. Checklist for K–6 reading interventions

Type of reading difficulty	Important features of intervention
All types of difficulties	___ Group size is appropriate to the child's needs, with homogeneous groups.
	___ Intervention time is appropriate for the child's needs.
	___ Intervention and instruction are generally clear, unambiguous, and engaging.
	___ The intervention is well integrated with other components of literacy in a comprehensive curriculum of literacy instruction.
	___ If the child is capable of independent reading, he or she is reading reasonably engaging texts at an appropriate level of difficulty (i.e., independent level), with appropriate teacher monitoring and guidance.
Word decoding difficulties (nonalphabetic, inaccurate, and nonautomatic readers)	___ The intervention employs explicit, systematic, synthetic phonics.
	___ The intervention appropriately targets the child's decoding needs (e.g., word patterns studied are not too easy / not too hard).
	___ If the child has difficulties with phonemic awareness, appropriate intervention in this area is included with phonics intervention.
	___ The interventionist provides appropriate examples of words for the child to decode (i.e., words that fit the phonics generalization being studied) as well as appropriate feedback to the child's errors (e.g., pointing to letters or parts of words that a child may have overlooked).
	___ The child has sufficient practice in oral reading of text containing words he or she is capable of decoding, at his or her instructional level, with a teacher.

___ During oral reading, the interventionist provides appropriate scaffolding and feedback to errors (e.g., pointing to words and providing other cues to assist in application of decoding skills).

___ Explicit, systematic spelling instruction is well integrated with the decoding intervention.

___ The intervention addresses automaticity of word reading, including the use of supplemental fluency interventions for children whose rate of reading is low relative to their reading level.

Comprehension-based difficulties (including non-strategic and suboptimal comprehenders)

___ The intervention provides explicit, systematic teaching of important comprehension abilities, including comprehension strategies, if appropriate.

___ The intervention appropriately targets the child's specific comprehension needs (e.g., inferencing versus vocabulary knowledge versus knowledge about text structure).

___ If the child has weaknesses in vocabulary knowledge, vocabulary intervention, including teaching of morphology, is provided and is appropriately integrated with comprehension intervention (e.g., vocabulary intervention addresses word meanings needed for success in the broader comprehension intervention).

___ The interventionist is sensitive to possible sources of poor comprehension (e.g., word meanings a child might not know) and addresses those needs in the intervention.

___ The interventionist asks appropriate comprehension questions before, during, and after reading, including open-ended questions that promote thinking and discussion.

___ The interventionist employs oral language activities at the child's listening level as well as reading activities to develop comprehension.

___ The child reads instructional-level texts (not too easy / not too hard) in intervention that provide ample opportunities to apply the comprehension abilities being taught.

___ The interventionist provides appropriate feedback to vocabulary and comprehension errors (e.g., questions/ cues that will assist comprehension as opposed to merely providing answers or calling on another child).

___ Appropriate writing activities to develop vocabulary and comprehension are integrated with reading.

___ The interventionist addresses prosody of oral reading and reading fluency, if appropriate.

7 Students with Specific Word-Recognition Difficulties

Several years ago I had a graduate student in my classes whom I will call Tim. From the first week of classes, Tim stood out as an extremely capable, insightful student, one who asked unusually perceptive questions and clearly grasped important concepts easily. He also had a dry, quick-witted sense of humor that greatly amused his classmates (and me). However, on in-class exams, Tim's writing evidenced numerous spelling errors, although his vocabulary was excellent and his understanding of content was flawless. Eventually, Tim revealed that he had been diagnosed with dyslexia as a child. In his elementary years, he "hated school with a fiery passion" and did not learn to read until he was 8 years old, when a teacher used an MSL program to help him begin to decode words. Even with no accommodations, Tim did extremely well in his graduate program because he had learned how to compensate effectively for his ongoing weaknesses, which were mainly in spelling (e.g., by carefully editing reports and papers), and because he brought many strengths to his graduate education, including not only a thoughtful intelligence but also a deep empathy for children with disabilities. He ultimately decided to pursue a Ph.D. and gained acceptance, with full funding, to a widely recognized doctoral program in another state.

This chapter provides examples of students with a broad profile of SWRD and one of the three patterns for this profile discussed in Chapter 4: nonalphabetic, inaccurate, or nonautomatic word reading. Children with SWRD are certainly not all dyslexic, but they all do have at least age-appropriate oral vocabulary and listening comprehension coupled with difficulties involving word-level reading skills; thus their reading comprehension difficulties are attributable entirely to problems in word reading and do not involve core comprehension weaknesses (see Table 4.1). Likewise, if children with SWRD have poor reading fluency, these difficulties stem from word-level reading problems, not from broad language comprehension problems. The underpinnings of these word-level problems, typically phonological in nature, result in impaired spelling and decoding. Because of their oral comprehension strengths, children with SWRD can often function well in situations in which information is provided verbally.

For each of the three children in this chapter, I begin with general background information about the child followed by a discussion of recent assessment data with a table of scores; conclusions about the child's pattern of difficulties, including whether he or she appears to have any disabilities; and recommendations for intervention. The assessment data are organized similarly to Table 4.1 but also include sections for written expression and mathematics as well as other potentially relevant data (e.g., whether the child has a history of preschool language delay or has received intervention). Although the focus here is on reading, a consideration of performance in specific components of writing (including spelling) as well as math is often helpful for confirming the child's profile and pattern of reading difficulties; the underlying weaknesses characteristic of different profiles and patterns tend to manifest in predictable ways across other academic areas.

Because the three children range in age and come from different school districts, varied measures were used to assess their component abilities. Most of these assessments have been discussed in Chapter 5 (see, e.g., Table 5.1); if they have not, further explanation is provided in the text. All standard scores use age norms, and I employ 90–110 (not 85–115) as the average range for all academic achievement standard scores, with 8–12 for scaled scores such as those from the Gray Oral Reading Test-5 (GORT-5; Wiederholt & Bryant, 2012); discussions of IQ test data and oral language testing employ 85–115 as average range. The logic of a standard score cutoff of 90 for low achievement in academic areas was explained at the end of Chapter 2; a more stringent cutoff (i.e., below 85) makes it difficult to identify children with relatively mild, but still significant, weaknesses in reading (or writing or mathematics).

Also, where available, I include data from IRIs, with information based on the child's *highest* independent, instructional, and listening levels; for example, if a child scored at the independent level on both second- and third-grade passages, the independent level would be given as third grade. As discussed in Chapter 5, IRIs are problematic in some key ways (e.g., because they often lack or have inadequate reliability data); however, the information they provide may still be useful, especially when considered as part of a comprehensive data set. One important use of IRIs is to help guide initial placement of children in texts for instruction. Teachers should always view these initial placements as very rough estimates because (among other reasons) many factors can influence the readability of a specific text for an individual child, such as the child's background knowledge and motivation for reading it. Experimentation with a variety of texts in instruction may reveal that certain texts are particularly engaging and motivating for specific students, and motivation and engagement play important roles in reading comprehension as well as amount of reading (Duke & Pearson, 2002; Guthrie et al., 1999). Moreover, strong motivation for reading a relatively challenging text can certainly help students' willingness to grapple with reading it—up to a point—and may help them improve their reading more than they otherwise would.

BRETT

Brett is an ending second grader, age 7 years, 10 months, from a suburban school district. He received speech-language services for language delay as a preschooler, but his language problems seemed to have resolved before he entered kindergarten, and services were discontinued. Brett's problems in learning to read were evident by late kindergarten; he had difficulty remembering letter sounds, particularly vowels, and even when he knew the letter sounds, he often had difficulty blending them. Core kindergarten and first-grade instruction in Brett's school included phonemic awareness and phonics, but the instruction was not highly explicit or systematic, an especially bad fit for Brett. However, although there were no formal universal screening procedures, his second-grade teacher did quickly recognize Brett's decoding difficulties and immediately included him in a supplemental phonics group in her class. When his progress in that group lagged well behind that of the other children, his teacher recommended him for reading intervention. Brett has been receiving highly explicit, systematic intervention in phonological skills, decoding, and spelling for the past 6 months in a small group with one other student well matched to him and delivered by a well-trained, capable reading specialist. The reading specialist works with Brett and the other child for 45 minutes a day, 4 days per week. Brett has made some modest gains in his intervention, but Aimsweb passage reading fluency probes (see http://www .aimsweb.com), used to monitor his progress, show that he still is not closing the gap with grade-mates at all; as the school year has progressed, he has increasingly expressed anxiety about his reading difficulties. Brett's parents are very concerned about his reading. Recently, they requested a comprehensive evaluation for special education, a request with which Brett's second-grade teacher, as well as his interventionist, concurred.

Recent Assessment Data

Table 7.1 displays some key data from Brett's recent evaluation. The Wechsler Individual Achievement Test–Third Edition (WIAT-III; Wechsler, 2009) Word Reading and Pseudoword Decoding subtests, as well as other assessments, document that Brett has significantly below-average decoding skills. On the CORE Phonics Survey (CPS; Consortium on Reading Excellence [CORE], 2008), a criterion-referenced measure that provides words in different phonics categories for the child to decode in isolation, Brett could capably decode only one-syllable words with short vowels (e.g., *hog, laz, shut, wheck*); he could not even attempt two-syllable words. As an ending second grader, Brett should be able to decode a much wider range of one-syllable patterns (e.g., *time, sharp, steam*) as well as some longer words (see Table 3.1). Results from the Basic Reading Inventory (BRI; Johns, 2005) indicated that Brett read both isolated word lists and passages at about an ending first-grade instructional level, roughly 1 year behind his grade placement. His consistent attempts to

Table 7.1. Recent assessment data for Brett, an ending second grader, age 7 years, 10 months

Word recognition and phonological skills	Text reading accuracy and fluency	Oral vocabulary and comprehension	Reading comprehension	Written expression and math	Other
WIAT-III Word Reading standard score (SS) = 78; Pseudoword Decoding SS = 77 CTOPP-2 Phonological Awareness SS = 84 CORE Phonics Survey (CPS): mastery of all short-vowel categories; all other one-syllable categories < 60%; did not know sounds for many common vowel patterns; could not attempt two-syllable category Basic Reading Inventory (BRI) word lists: independent = primer; instructional = end of Grade 1	WIAT-III Oral Reading Accuracy SS = 81; Oral Reading Rate SS = 95 BRI passages: no independent level; highest instructional level = end of Grade 1; at this level, child does not attempt to self-correct errors and apply decoding skills, although his oral reading tends to be choppy and monotone; rate consistent with instructional level Aimsweb passage reading fluency probes show inadequate progress in intervention	PPVT SS = 105 WIAT-III Receptive Vocabulary SS = 109 WIAT-III Oral Discourse Comprehension SS = 106 Does well answering questions during teacher read-alouds	WIAT-III Reading Comprehension SS = 95 WJ-III Passage Comprehension SS = 84 Comprehension errors on the BRI related entirely to decoding weaknesses	WIAT-III Spelling SS = 82; Sentence Composition SS = 80, due mainly to errors in mechanics, especially spelling; handwriting is good WIAT-III Math Fluency: Addition SS = 105, Subtraction SS = 99 WIAT-III Numerical Operations SS = 98 WIAT-III Math Problem-Solving SS = 102 Spelling errors indicate that Brett consistently tries to spell all sounds in words but often does not know the correct letter pattern	Stanford-Binet: Verbal IQ = 90, Nonverbal IQ = 82, Full-Scale = 86 CTOPP-2 Phonological Memory = 90; Rapid Symbolic Naming = 98 History of preschool language delay and K–1 problems in phonemic awareness; no history of significant medical, hearing, or behavior problems; no family history of reading problems 20/20 vision with glasses Tier II intervention—6 months

Note: CTOPP-2 = Comprehensive Test of Phonological Processing, 2nd edition (Wagner, Torgesen, Rashotte, & Pearson, 2013); PPVT-IV = Peabody Picture Vocabulary Test, 4th edition (Dunn & Dunn, 2007); WIAT-III = Wechsler Individual Achievement Test, 3rd edition (Wechsler, 2009); WJ-III = Woodcock-Johnson Tests of Achievement, 3rd edition (Woodcock, McGrew, & Mather, 2007).

self-correct decoding errors, though not always successful, are a positive sign because they show that Brett monitors his comprehension and grasps the alphabetic principle. In line with a profile of SWRD, Brett's oral vocabulary and oral comprehension were firmly average.

Brett's text reading accuracy score on the WIAT-III was below average at 81, and he was described as having poor prosody of oral reading, but the overall pattern of his performance—significant decoding weaknesses coupled with age-appropriate oral language abilities—strongly suggests that his fluency difficulties relate to decoding problems. Similarly, Brett's low Woodcock-Johnson III Tests of Achievement (WJ-III; Woodcock-Johnson, McGrew, & Mather, 2007) Passage Comprehension score is likely attributable to his poor decoding, and his performance on comprehension questions on the BRI support this view because his comprehension errors related entirely to poor decoding. For example, in one passage, he could not decode the word *animal* in the phrase *animal tracks*, so he answered a question involving this segment of the text incorrectly, inferring a reference to railroad rather than animal tracks; however, when queried orally later and asked to explain what *animal tracks* are, he easily answered correctly. On the WIAT-III Reading Comprehension subtest, Brett scored in average range, perhaps because this test uses a question-answering format and permits the child to retain access to the passage when answering questions. Other assessments show, however, that Brett's decoding problems do impair his reading comprehension.

Brett's writing and math scores also reflect an SWRD profile. His spelling was below average, consistent with his weak decoding, and he had difficulties with sentence composition that reflected poor spelling and other problems in mechanics (e.g., punctuation), not problems in areas such as vocabulary. Math also was a strength, with both his calculation skills and problem-solving skills well within average range. (Some children with Brett's profile have difficulties with automatic recall of math facts, which may in turn impair calculation skills, but this was not the case for Brett.) Brett's phonological awareness composite on the Comprehensive Test of Phonological Processing, Second Edition (CTOPP-2; Wagner et al., 2013) was below average; his history of blending problems also suggests past difficulties with phonological awareness. Two other CTOPP-2 phonological composites, Phonological Memory and Rapid Symbolic Naming, were within average range. In addition, Brett's school psychologist administered an IQ test, the Stanford-Binet-5 (Roid, 2003). This test has an average range of 85–115; Brett scored within average range for verbal abilities and somewhat below average for nonverbal abilities. His full-scale IQ, taking both sets of abilities into account, was 86, a score that, though considered within average range, upset his parents and surprised his teachers.

Conclusions

Brett has an overall profile of SWRD, with a pattern of inaccurate word reading. He does have some decoding skills, and he has definitely grasped the alphabetic principle, so he does not exemplify a nonalphabetic pattern. However, he has not yet mastered decoding skills even for most one-syllable words (except for those with short vowels), so he is not a nonautomatic reader. Some inaccurate word readers have fluency weaknesses beyond what their poor decoding accounts for; a student with these types of problems might read text very slowly or laboriously, even when placed at an instructional level. However, Brett does not seem to have these dual problems; his WIAT-III Oral Reading Rate score is within average range, and his rate of passage reading is consistent with his instructional reading level (end of first grade). This pattern suggests that, although Brett certainly needs attention to fluency development in his overall reading program, he probably does not require intensive fluency intervention. Brett does require substantial intervention in phonemic awareness, decoding, and spelling, and these areas should continue to be integrated together via the systematic decoding and spelling activities provided in his current intervention program.

Other information about Brett suggests that he has dyslexia. His long-standing reading difficulties clearly relate to central difficulties in phonological skills and decoding, and he has additional difficulties characteristic of dyslexia as well, such as poor spelling. His history of preschool language delay, although not universal among individuals with dyslexia, also suggests an intrinsic vulnerability to language and reading problems. His reading difficulties are not primarily attributable to another disability, ELL status, or economic disadvantage. Brett's early reading instruction definitely left much to be desired; for example, he might have benefited greatly from more explicit attention to phonemic awareness instruction in kindergarten, which might have prevented at least some of his decoding problems. Nevertheless, he has had appropriate intervention for 6 months, preceded by his supplemental phonics group with his classroom teacher, yet he is still not beginning to narrow the gap with grade-mates.

With regard to specific identification criteria for LDs, not only does Brett have low achievement in reading, but based on the data provided, he also appears to meet exclusionary criteria and shows inadequate response to intervention. Thus, in most RTI approaches to identification of LDs, he would likely be eligible for services in the LD category. (Some RTI approaches might require a Tier III intervention first—more on this in the next section, "Recommendations for Intervention.") Brett would also likely be eligible for services in some states that have a separate dyslexia category (Youman & Mather, 2013) as well as with the use of a listening comprehension–reading comprehension discrepancy because he has a nearly 30-point gap on the WIAT-III (standard score = 106 for Oral Discourse Comprehension versus 77 and 78 for word reading).

However, in many states requiring an IQ–achievement discrepancy for identification of LDs, Brett would likely *not* be eligible because his IQ of 86 yields no more than a 9-point discrepancy with any of his component reading scores. In this situation, a Section 504 plan could provide Brett with general education accommodations and modifications. Section 504 is part of civil rights legislation that includes the Americans with Disabilities Act (ADA) of 1990 (PL 101-336), which protects people with disabilities from discrimination; moreover, 2008 amendments to the ADA broadened its considerations to include reading (Cortiella, 2011). However, Section 504 does not provide the same detailed procedural safeguards and rights accorded to students eligible for special education under IDEA 2004, and it is meant to ensure equal educational opportunity for students with disabilities, not the kind of specialized, intensive instruction provided under IDEA (Martin, 2013). Brett clearly requires this kind of intensive instruction, but using an IQ–achievement discrepancy, he likely would be ineligible for special education services—at least until he fell even further behind in reading. Furthermore, his modest IQ may lead educators, and even his parents, to lower their expectations for his reading progress.

Recommendations for Intervention

Brett should be "fast-tracked" to special education rather than undergoing Tier III interventions because an appropriate Tier II intervention has not been successful in accelerating his progress, and his decoding skills are far below expectations. Recent research (Fuchs, Compton, et al., 2012; Vaughn et al., 2010) supports this kind of fast-tracking. Also, Brett's patterns of difficulties and history are consistent with dyslexia. His explicit, systematic, synthetic-phonics intervention should continue, with an initial focus on the one-syllable patterns that he cannot decode (e.g., silent *e* words and words with common vowel patterns), then progress to strategies for syllabicating longer words with known syllable patterns (e.g., dividing between two consonants in a word with a closed plus silent *e* syllable like *invite*). To begin to close the gap with grade-mates, Brett will need to make a great deal of decoding progress; achieving this kind of progress will require a substantial increase in intensity of his phonics intervention (e.g., 1 hour a day, 5 days per week, one to two or one to one). Brett's phonics intervention also should include substantial application of his phonics skills in oral reading of text with his special education teacher, who should provide appropriate scaffolding and cuing that helps Brett apply his decoding skills (not guess at words based on context) and that continues to encourage his good comprehension monitoring. Oral reading of text should help Brett generalize his phonics skills and build his text reading fluency. Given his current decoding limitations, he may need to read somewhat controlled, decodable texts initially, but he can later make the transition to a wider range of texts at his instructional level. In addition, Brett's teachers and parents should certainly continue to read to him and to encourage his own reading for enjoyment at home, a pursuit that may become more appealing as his decoding skills improve. Spelling intervention should continue to be well integrated with his decoding intervention.

Brett's teacher should assess his progress via regular probes of his decoding, spelling, and ORF gains, including both timed measures (e.g., Aimsweb passage reading fluency passages) and untimed measures (e.g., records of his decoding and spelling accuracy on unfamiliar words used during his intervention sessions). If progress monitoring over several months does not indicate some acceleration in Brett's decoding gains, then his program should be reconsidered and attempts to improve it should be made.

ALICIA

Alicia is a beginning first grader, age 6 years, 2 months, attending a K–8 interdistrict magnet school. This school serves a substantial language-minority population, including many children from low-income backgrounds; Alicia is a monolingual English child from this type of background. She spent her kindergarten year in an urban, high-poverty school district that did not provide her current school with any kindergarten assessment data. However, Alicia's first-grade teacher was concerned about her from the first few days of school because she could tell from Alicia's classroom performance that her basic decoding and spelling skills were very limited, even relative to those of other beginning first graders. On writing tasks, Alicia had legible, well-formed handwriting, although she sometimes reversed letters. She also clearly understood most basic print concepts such as left-to-right progression and separating printed words with spaces. However, she demonstrated little use of letter–sound correspondence, except occasionally for the first letters of words; for example, she spelled *sun* as *smht* and *girl* as *knx*. She had no ability to read text, even very simple decodable text with closed single-consonant words; if given a predictable text from a teacher read-aloud, she could use pictures and verbatim memory to "reread" the story, but she could not identify individual words from that text presented in isolation except for *the*. She tended to guess wildly at unknown words based on picture clues or, sometimes, the first letter of a word. If shown a word such as *man* in isolation, rather than looking carefully at the word and attempting to decode it, Alicia might guess *me, moon,* and *mice* in rapid succession, watching the teacher's face intently for evidence of a correct answer.

As a new student to a class in which most other children already knew each other, Alicia was initially quiet and shy. However, after the first week or two of school, she began to make friends, and she opened up in class, revealing an outgoing, articulate child. She clearly enjoyed daily teacher read-alouds of children's books and did very well retelling stories and answering questions orally. The magnet school has a strong Tier I reading program, including a strong vocabulary component, and Alicia has been very successful in these oral vocabulary activities. Her math skills are also grade appropriate.

Recent Assessment Data

Table 7.2 displays recent assessment data for Alicia. Because of concerns about Alicia's foundational literacy skills, the reading specialist at Alicia's

Table 7.2. Recent assessment data for Alicia, a beginning first grader, age 6 years, 2 months

Word recognition and phonological skills	Text reading accuracy and fluency	Oral vocabulary and comprehension	Reading comprehension	Written expression and math	Other
Dynamic Indicators of Basic Early Literacy Skills (DIBELS) Next Phoneme Segmentation Fluency = well below benchmark; Nonsense Word Fluency (correct letter sounds [CLS]) = well below benchmark PAT 2 Phonological Awareness Section SS = 78; Grapheme Test SS = 80 BRI Word Lists, read two words on pre-primer list	Reads predictable texts emergently (e.g., using verbatim memory and picture clues), with knowledge of basic print concepts Guesses wildly at unknown words, often based on picture clues, rather than attempting to decode Cannot yet read even preprimer text in the conventional sense	PPVT-IV SS = 99 Grade-appropriate performance on a curriculum-based listening comprehension assessment Does well answering questions during teacher read-alouds	Not yet testable because child cannot read connected text	Classroom writing samples show child misspells almost all words but often spells first letters of words correctly; confuses *b* and *d* Writing shows evidence of knowledge of basic print concepts: writes left-to-right, top-to-bottom on a page; uses spaces correctly between words; handwriting is legible and well formed Math assessments are grade appropriate	No history of preschool language delay No history of significant medical, hearing, or behavior problems; no apparent family history of reading difficulties No interventions yet

Note: BRI = Basic Reading Inventory (Johns, 2005); PAT 2 = Phonological Awareness Test 2 (Robertson & Salter, 2007); PPVT-IV = Peabody Picture Vocabulary Test, 4th edition (Dunn & Dunn, 2007).

school administered the Phonological Awareness Test 2 (PAT 2; Robert-son & Salter, 2007) in early September. This test yields standard scores for phonological awareness, grapheme–phoneme knowledge, and decoding. Alicia could not attempt the decoding test, and she scored below the aver-age range on both the phonological awareness and grapheme–phoneme sections. Although she could give sounds for most single consonant letters (except for *h, x, w, b,* and *d*) as well as for short *a*, she did not know any other vowel sounds nor could she apply her knowledge of letter sounds in attempting to decode words. On the BRI (Johns, 2005), she attempted the preprimer word list, but she read only two words correctly, so test-ing on the graded word lists was discontinued. The BRI graded passages could not be attempted due to Alicia's weak word-reading skills. However, on a curriculum-based listening comprehension assessment, in which the teacher read first-grade passages aloud to Alicia, she performed very well, answering nearly all comprehension questions correctly. The reading spe-cialist also administered a measure of receptive vocabulary (the Peabody Picture Vocabulary Test-IV [PPVT-IV]; Dunn & Dunn, 2007), on which Alicia scored well within average range.

In mid-September, the magnet school did universal screening using Dynamic Indicators of Basic Early Literacy Skills (DIBELS) Next (Good & Kaminski, 2011) CBMs. Two DIBELS Next subtests were administered to beginning first graders: Phoneme Segmentation Fluency (PSF), a timed phonemic awareness measure that requires students to segment orally pre-sented words such as *stuff* by phoneme (/s/, /t/, /u/, /f/), and Nonsense Word Fluency (NWF), a timed decoding measure that involves out-of-context non-sense words (e.g., *mip*). Examiners score NWF for both correct letter sounds (CLS) and whole words read (WWR) correctly without sounding out. On all these indicators, Alicia's performance was below benchmark, with both PSF and NWF-CLS well below benchmark. (Although Alicia had a score of 0 on NWF-WWR, below benchmark is the lowest possible category for a begin-ning first grader on this indicator.) On PSF, she could sometimes segment the first phoneme correctly but not other phonemes. She approached NWF as if giving sounds for single letters, without attempting to blend those sounds into words. Her low score on NWF-CLS stemmed from her lack of knowledge of most vowel sounds, confusions of *b* and *d*, and frequent skipping of letters; on this subtest as well as on all other reading tasks, Alicia tended to glance quickly at words rather than looking carefully at the print.

At a parent–teacher conference to review the screening results, Alicia's mother indicated that Alicia's early language development and other mile-stones were typical and that Alicia was a healthy child with no chronic medi-cal, hearing, or vision problems. School screenings in these areas also were typical. Although Alicia's parents and extended family members do not have high levels of formal education, no unusual family history of reading difficul-ties appears to exist.

Conclusions

Alicia's assessment data as well as her everyday classroom performance suggest a profile of SWRD with a pattern of nonalphabetic word reading. Although Alicia does have some basic literacy skills, such as an understanding of basic print concepts and knowledge of many letter sounds, her tendency to guess wildly at words, her utter lack of attempts to decode words, and her inability to spell most sounds in words all suggest that Alicia does not fully grasp the alphabetic principle. She also clearly has accompanying difficulties in phonemic awareness. Although she has not yet had the kind of extensive testing that Brett had as part of his comprehensive evaluation, her grade-appropriate math skills, social skills, vocabulary knowledge, and language comprehension all suggest an intellectually typical child with specific problems in decoding. Alicia's letter reversals and confusions of *b* and *d* are very common for a child at her emergent reading level; they do not imply that she has an LD.

Because Alicia has not yet had any intervention, and because there is currently no evidence of a disability (e.g., speech-language impairment, other health impairment) affecting her educational performance, a referral to special education is not appropriate at this time. However, Alicia's ongoing literacy difficulties, which persisted into October despite her teacher's attempts to differentiate instruction for her, as well as her universal screening data support the need for Tier II intervention. This intervention should occur in a small, homogeneous group of no more than three to four children, including Alicia. Alicia's performance in intervention can be used to help guide decision making about any subsequent steps that may be required.

Recommendations for Intervention

Alicia's Tier II intervention should emphasize explicit, systematic teaching of phonemic awareness, letter sounds (including sounds for vowels), decoding, and spelling skills. Instruction must focus Alicia's attention on letter sequences in words and help her grasp the alphabetic principle—for example, through the use of word-building activities with letter tiles or of phoneme–grapheme maps, with single-phoneme changes in chains of words (e.g., *map, man, fan, ran, rag*). These activities also would require Alicia to blend and segment phonemes in words, developing her phonemic awareness. Instruction should begin with continuous-sound phonemes (e.g., *m, f, r, s*) that are easiest to blend rather than stop consonants (e.g., *b, c, d, g*). Although Alicia needs to learn short vowel sounds, the interventionist should avoid introducing multiple short vowel sounds, which are highly confusable together; Alicia and the other children in her group should learn one new short-vowel sound at a time. Initially, Alicia can read simple decodable texts, with the teacher providing appropriate cues that focus Alicia's attention on the print and discourage guessing based on pictures or context. Later, instruction can employ less controlled types of texts at Alicia's instructional level. Alicia should also have structured opportunities to apply her phonics skills in spelling and writing activities.

Alicia's progress in intervention should be monitored regularly (e.g., once every couple of weeks) through timed and untimed measures of her developing phonemic awareness, decoding, and spelling skills. For instance, equivalent forms of DIBELS PSF and NWF could be used to monitor progress under timed conditions, with DIBELS ORF added later, as Alicia's ability to read passages develops. Untimed measures could include records of her decoding and spelling of *unfamiliar* words in the phonics categories taught during intervention as well as administration of a criterion-referenced measure such as the CPS (CORE, 2008) every few months. If these measures do not show progress adequate for Alicia to catch up to grade-mates, then teachers should consider a change in intervention or additional evaluation, including a referral to special education, if warranted.

In fact, Alicia made very good progress in her Tier II intervention, which lasted through April of Grade 1 and brought her to grade expectations in all areas of reading, including fluency. When followed up early in Grade 3, Alicia was continuing to do well.

HENRY

Henry is a middle sixth grader, age 11 years, 8 months, from a small rural school district. In kindergarten through Grade 3, report cards described Henry as functioning on grade level in reading but hinted at possible problems in phonological skills and at reliance on compensatory strategies. For example, his first-grade report card noted that he "sometimes has trouble blending sounds in words" and "needs to pay closer attention to sounds in words when spelling" but also stated that "use of context clues is a strength." Firm conclusions about Henry's early reading progress are impossible, however, because his school did not administer the kinds of assessments that would have best revealed phonological weaknesses, such as measures of phonemic awareness and out-of-context word-recognition measures including nonsense words. Legibility of handwriting was always a concern. Although Henry's teachers consistently found him to be a likable, sociable boy, they often mentioned his work habits as problematic in literacy areas (e.g., in Grade 3, "Henry needs to try harder to proofread for errors in his written work"). They rarely noted such concerns for math, a subject in which Henry excelled.

In third grade, Henry's teachers did note problems in his ability to decode and spell multisyllabic words as well as in his reading fluency, and he began to receive Tier II intervention for these areas. Intervention involved a small group of children (one teacher to three students) receiving explicit, systematic instruction in phonics, structural analysis, and spelling, first targeting two-syllable, then multisyllabic, words. The interventionist was a special education teacher well trained in several different MSL approaches. To build fluency, the interventionist used timed flashcard practice on common words and repeated readings of texts. Henry received tiered intervention supports for 3 years until very recently, when intervention was discontinued because his teachers stated that he was achieving on grade level in reading. As evidence of grade-level performance, they cited the fact that Henry was obtaining good grades (no term grade below C, with mostly As and Bs) in all his literacy-related classes without any accommodations and that he functioned well in an accelerated math group, in which he did Grade 7 work with A grades. They placed particular weight on the fact that, in the most recent round of testing, he scored at the goal level on the state-mandated reading comprehension assessment. The state test classifies students' scores at five levels: below basic, basic, proficient, goal, and advanced. Students scoring at the goal or advanced level are considered to be doing well.

Henry's father, a widower who has raised Henry on his own, is unhappy with the discontinuation of his intervention and is very concerned about his reading. Henry's father says that extensive help at home has been necessary to enable Henry to achieve good grades in school. The father's immediate concerns involve Henry's accuracy and speed of reading as well as spelling and writing; homework takes much longer than it should because Henry reads slowly, and if he tries to read faster, his comprehension is affected. Henry's father points out wide disparities in his performance on different school assignments; on virtually all oral projects and assignments, Henry achieves A grades, whereas on many written assignments, especially in-class tests, he has obtained grades of C, D, or F—low grades that his father attributes to difficulties in reading test questions and to Henry's problems with handwriting. In the long term, Henry's father is extremely worried about his ability to cope with high school or college literacy demands. In addition, although Henry did not experience early language delay, a maternal uncle has been diagnosed with dyslexia, and Henry's father believes that Henry might also have dyslexia. Recently, he took Henry for a private evaluation by an independent reading evaluator.

Recent Assessment Data

Table 7.3 provides some important assessment data for Henry, including data from his recent independent evaluation. These data show that Henry's phonological awareness (WJ-III Sound Awareness), ability to read real words (WJ-III Word Identification), and text reading accuracy (GORT-5 Accuracy) were all in average range, as were Henry's composite scores on the CTOPP-2 (Wagner et al., 2013). Likewise, IRI data from the Qualitative Reading Inventory (QRI; Leslie & Caldwell, 2006) showed that Henry's instructional level was at grade expectations, sixth grade, in terms of both isolated words and passages. However, other data suggest the presence of mild decoding difficulties as well as significant difficulties in reading fluency. For example, Henry's scores on the WJ-III Word Attack and Reading Fluency subtests, as well as his GORT-5 scaled scores for rate and fluency, were all below average, though not

Table 7.3. Recent assessment data for Henry, a middle sixth grader, age 11 years, 8 months

Word recognition and phonological skills	Text reading accuracy and fluency	Oral vocabulary and comprehension	Reading comprehension	Written expression and math	Other
WJ-III Word Identification SS = 101 WJ-III Word Attack SS = 88 WJ-III Sound Awareness SS = 94 GE Test of Coding Skills: mastered all decoding categories except multisyllabic words, in which his accuracy was 50%; marked difficulties with nonsense words Qualitative Reading Inventory (QRI) word lists, independent level = Grade 4; instructional level = Grade 6	GORT-5 Accuracy SS = 9; Rate = 7; Fluency = 7 WJ-III Reading Fluency = 86 QRI passages: independent level = Grade 3; instructional level = Grade 6; reading at instructional level involved multiple self-corrections, with inconsistent prosody, but child tried hard to decode words and correct errors Word accuracy in Grade 6 texts averaged > 95%; rate was 82 words correct per minute (cpm)	WJ-III Picture Vocabulary SS =110 WJ-III Oral Comprehension SS = 125 QRI listening level = Grade 8	WJ-III Passage Comprehension SS = 96 GORT-5 Comprehension SS = 11 Comprehension errors on the GORT-5 and QRI all appeared heavily influenced by inaccurate or effortful decoding Scored at goal on the state-mandated reading comprehension assessment	WJ-III Spelling SS = 87 WJ-III Writing Samples SS = 116 WJ-III Editing SS = 82 WJ-III Math Fluency SS = 88 WJ-III Math Calculation SS = 109 WJ-III Applied Problems SS = 132 Handwriting is poor Functions well in an accelerated math class doing Grade 7 work	CTOPP-2 composites in average range Some family history of dyslexia; no history of preschool language delay or significant medical, hearing, vision, or behavior problems Possible history of phonemic awareness problems in early grades, but reading progress was considered average in K-2 Received Tier II intervention from Grade 3 through mid-Grade 6; recently discontinued

Note: CTOPP-2 = Comprehensive Test of Phonological Processing, 2nd edition (Wagner, Torgesen, Rashotte, & Pearson, 2013); GE Test = Gallistel-Ellis Test of Coding Skills (Gallistel & Ellis, 1974); GORT-5 = Gray Oral Reading Test, 5th edition (Wiederholt & Bryant, 2012); WJ-III = Woodcock-Johnson Tests of Achievement, 3rd edition (Woodcock, McGrew, & Mather, 2007).

extremely low. Henry was also given a criterion-referenced measure of decoding called the Gallistel-Ellis (GE) Test of Coding Skills (Gallistel & Ellis, 1974); this test is similar to the CPS mentioned earlier but has more differentiation of categories at the two-syllable and multisyllabic stages. On the GE, Henry has not yet mastered multisyllabic words, words that, as a sixth grader, he should definitely be capable of decoding; furthermore, on advanced categories of words, he had marked difficulties reading nonsense words as opposed to real words. The QRI data, showing Henry read Grade 6 passages with multiple self-corrections and inconsistent prosody, strongly indicate limitations in reading fluency, even though Henry attained a sixth-grade instructional level. In addition, the evaluator asked Henry to read unfamiliar passages from his classroom English, science, and social studies texts. Although he consistently read these texts with better than 95% word accuracy, his average rate was only 82 words correct per minute, far below benchmark for a sixth grader (Hasbrouck & Tindal, 2006) and supportive of his father's claims about his homework and in-class testing difficulties.

Consistent with a profile of SWRD, Henry's oral vocabulary and comprehension were strong; in fact, his WJ-III Oral Comprehension score was well above average at 125, and his listening level on the QRI also was above grade expectations. Henry's reading comprehension test scores were well within average range, in line with his ability to score at goal on the state-mandated reading assessment. Despite his handwriting difficulties, Henry also evidenced good language and composition abilities in writing, as suggested by his score on the WJ-III Writing Samples subtest; however, like Brett, he has weaknesses in spelling and conventions of writing (i.e., WJ-III Editing). Although his automatic recall of facts such as multiplication tables (i.e., WJ-III Math Fluency) was slightly below average, Henry's overall calculation skills were at the upper end of the average range, and his math problem solving was well above average.

Conclusions

Henry's pattern of SWRD involves nonautomatic word reading. Henry has mastered decoding skills for most words, but he still needs some work on decoding of multisyllabic words, and his text reading fluency is poor. The lack of appropriate assessment data in the early grades makes it difficult to know for certain when Henry's word-reading problems first emerged. He might have had mild phonological language weaknesses in the early grades that did not significantly affect his word reading until the middle-elementary grades, when he was expected to decode longer, more complex words (Lipka et al., 2006). Conversely, he might have had significant decoding problems early on that his school simply overlooked, especially given Henry's ability to compensate well. Even now, he functions within average range in reading comprehension, probably because his strong language abilities and his ability to remember words by sight help him compensate when reading text. Nevertheless, Henry clearly requires continued intervention because his decoding, reading fluency, and spelling difficulties are affecting his educational performance, and without continued intervention, these effects are likely to grow much worse as Henry advances into junior high and high school.

Henry's school district uses an RTI model to identify LDs and does not administer IQ tests, but if they did, Henry would likely meet IQ–achievement discrepancy criteria with ease. His strong vocabulary, language, and mathematical abilities suggest that he would probably obtain an IQ at least at the upper end of the average range, if not higher, yielding a discrepancy of 20 points or more with his word attack, reading fluency, and spelling skills. Nevertheless, IQ testing is not necessary for Henry to be eligible for LD services; he can and should be eligible with the use of RTI criteria. Henry does have low achievement in decoding and reading fluency as well as in spelling and basic writing skills, but his difficulties are not attributable to another disability or lack of opportunity to learn, and he has had appropriate intervention—still he is having difficulties. Performance on the state-mandated reading comprehension assessment should not be the primary standard for deciding whether Henry requires intervention (let alone special education), because the state assessment is a broad performance assessment that is not sensitive to specific component weaknesses. Furthermore, as a criterion-referenced measure of reading comprehension, it does not yield information about Henry's performance relative to national norms. In addition, other data—including individually administered standardized tests as well as classroom tests and informal measures—show that Henry has a clear pattern of reading difficulties involving multisyllabic word reading and fluency that does affect his educational performance.

Henry should not have another round of tiered interventions because he has already had appropriate interventions for *3 years*; given his continuing need for intervention, he almost certainly should have had a comprehensive evaluation well before sixth grade. Like Brett, Henry's profile of ongoing decoding, spelling, and fluency difficulties, despite intervention, as well as his family history, is suggestive of dyslexia. Henry's word-reading and spelling difficulties are relatively less severe than Brett's, and his compensatory abilities are unusually strong, but special education is still warranted for him.

Recommendations for Intervention

Henry requires decoding intervention focused on structural analysis and decoding of multisyllabic words and integrated with vocabulary and spelling instruction. For example, as Henry learns how to read roots such as *geo* and *psych*, he also can learn the meaning of the roots and that their spelling will remain stable across words, enabling him to spell and perhaps better comprehend words containing these roots. Henry can also benefit from learning common spelling generalizations, particularly those that apply to two-syllable or multisyllabic words (e.g., Eide, 2012). A systematic decoding and spelling program should be employed, but one important source for roots and other word parts to be taught includes words from Henry's content classes, such as social studies and science.

As a nonautomatic reader, Henry requires a focused, systematic fluency-building intervention, such as timed, repeated readings of passages with graphing of scores, feedback to the student, and gradual increase in text difficulty level as the student progresses (e.g., Hasbrouck et al., 1999). Although not typical for his grade, some oral reading of text with his special education teacher emphasizing accurate reading with appropriate prosody might also benefit Henry's fluency; given his sixth-grade instructional level, these oral reading activities could employ texts from his classes. An important adjunct to Henry's intervention program involves encouragement of wide independent reading—for example, as assigned homework or with teacher guidance and monitoring. Given guidance from a supportive adult, Henry certainly reads well enough to find some books that can appeal to him. Another advantage of wide reading is that it can benefit Henry in multiple ways, such as increasing his background knowledge, vocabulary, or spelling, as well as potentially promote his reading fluency.

Handwriting is a key foundational skill that, if weak, can tax children's motivation and ability to compose in written expression (Berninger et al., 2006; Graham, Harris, & Fink, 2000). However, given Henry's age and grade, a focus on word processing technology probably is more appropriate for him than devoting substantial time to handwriting intervention. Educators should ensure that Henry has the keyboarding skills to use word processing efficiently as well as make technology available to him, including during in-class exams. Also, as previously discussed for Brett, Henry's progress should be monitored using both timed and untimed measures of decoding, reading fluency, and spelling, with adjustments to his instruction if these measures do not suggest reasonable progress.

TIER I READING INSTRUCTION AND PROGRESS MONITORING

Students receiving literacy intervention should have those interventions delivered as part of a broader, comprehensive program of literacy instruction, with good integration of interventions, as discussed in Chapter 6. Children with a profile of SWRD, including all three children discussed in this chapter, can generally receive their vocabulary and comprehension development primarily through participation in the Tier I literacy program, with appropriate modifications and differentiation of classroom instruction that takes their decoding and spelling limitations into account. For example, all the children discussed in this chapter can do well in oral activities such as teacher read-alouds, answering questions verbally, and class discussion of content. However, students with SWRD will usually have difficulty reading grade-appropriate texts, and they will often require the use of lower-level texts that match their reading abilities, as is true for both Brett and Alicia.

(Henry can manage reading grade-appropriate texts instructionally but not independently.) Tier I spelling and writing activities will also require some adjustment; for instance, as discussed in Chapter 6, students might require a modified spelling program with words appropriate to their spelling levels. Assistive technology, although potentially helpful for all students with reading difficulties, can be particularly powerful for students with SWRD because of these students' relatively circumscribed difficulties and language strengths. Students with SWRD may benefit from technology that enables them to listen to grade-appropriate texts or access a wide range of texts digitally for school or pleasure reading (see, e.g., *Bookshare*, http://www.bookshare.org) as well as from writing software that helps them compensate for spelling and other mechanical errors (e.g., spell-checkers, grammar-checkers, and word-prediction software). As discussed for Henry, writing software and word processing also are useful for students with significant handwriting problems. For helpful detail about the use of technology to improve literacy in children with reading and writing difficulties, see MacArthur (2013).

Assistive technology is especially critical for older children like Henry, who are faced with a sharply increasing volume of reading and writing. Because the ultimate goal of intervention is to bring students to grade expectations, educators must periodically review the need for accommodations. However, some students may always continue to require specific types of accommodations, such as extended time on exams, and access to appropriate accommodations is important. Without access to accommodations, students may function so poorly at advanced levels of education—high school or college—that they do not take the advanced coursework or obtain the degrees of which they are capable.

Continued participation in Tier I progress monitoring is essential to detect the possible emergence of additional reading problems in the future. For example, some children with a profile of SWRD may have subtle linguistic or cognitive weaknesses that only begin to affect reading as grade expectations in literacy increase. A strong Tier I program, such as Alicia's, may help prevent these kinds of difficulties, but continued Tier I progress monitoring remains vital.

SUMMING UP

Some students with SWRD may differ from Brett, Alicia, or Henry in important ways; for instance, not all students with dyslexia have a family history of dyslexia or a developmental history of language delay. What all these students have in common, however, is a profile of at least average vocabulary knowledge and language comprehension coupled with problems involving nonalphabetic, inaccurate, or nonautomatic word reading. Regardless of the underlying cause of the reading difficulty, the profile and pattern have clear implications for intervention, progress monitoring, and Tier I programming, as this chapter illustrates.

Certainly, for the children in this chapter and in the next two, further detail, especially about each child's specific academic skills and interests, would be valuable to teachers. Information from certain processing measures also might sometimes be helpful. For example, along with the IQ battery that she administered to Brett, his school psychologist administered measures of working memory on which Brett obtained below-average scores. Limitations in working memory could be affecting Brett's decoding, but they do not appear to be directly affecting his comprehension at this point. They could be a factor in the future, however, as Brett advances in reading and must read more syntactically complex text. In addition, some evidence (e.g., Catts et al., 2012) suggests that nonverbal IQ may predict late-emerging reading comprehension weaknesses, perhaps because nonverbal IQ taps executive function types of processes; Brett's nonverbal IQ was somewhat below average. Taken together, these data suggest that Brett's teachers should be especially alert to the possible emergence of comprehension-based reading problems in later grades. However, the information about working memory and nonverbal IQ should not alter teachers' goals for Brett—eventually bringing him to grade expectations in literacy—nor does it change my recommendations for Brett's current intervention in reading. Eligibility recommendations for special education also should not hinge on this kind of information; Henry scored within average range on measures of phonological processing, yet he still can and should be eligible for special education services.

Likewise, IQ test data are not essential to plan interventions or determine eligibility for special education for students with SWRD. Given these students' average or better vocabularies and language comprehension, IQ tests are certainly not needed to rule out IDs in this population. Teachers also did not need an IQ test to tell them that Henry had many cognitive strengths; they already recognized those strengths based on Henry's quick grasp of classroom content, articulate oral language abilities, and superior math performance. Unfortunately, although Brett's good vocabulary and language comprehension are much more relevant to his reading than are his IQ scores, his relatively modest IQ might lead some adults to lower their expectations for him, further jeopardizing his future academic progress.

We can recognize the strengths of students such as Henry without putting at risk students such as Brett. The information essential for planning reading instruction and intervention does not involve measures of processing or IQ but, rather, measures of specific component reading and language abilities, the kind of information given in the "Word recognition and phonological skills," "Text reading accuracy and fluency," "Oral vocabulary and comprehension," and "Reading Comprehension" sections of Tables 7.1, 7.2, and 7.3. The next chapter considers examples of these types of data for students with a different profile of reading problems: SRCD.

8

Students with Specific Reading Comprehension Difficulties

Years ago, I used to bring my teacher education students to do field work in a local K–5 elementary school that served a largely low-income, minority population. This school, which I will call Berson Elementary School, used a highly explicit, systematic phonics program in teaching reading, most definitely not the norm in an era that was the zenith of whole language. In fact, teachers taught phonological skills and decoding so well that it was sometimes difficult for me to find children who required tutoring in decoding, the main focus of the fieldwork course, which involved preparing teacher candidates to teach phonics. For a variety of reasons that had nothing to do with Berson Elementary's quality as a field placement, I eventually had to use a different school for my students' field experience, and I lost contact with the teachers at the school. However, a number of years later, when I revisited the school, I was stunned to discover that the educators there had abandoned their strong decoding program in favor of a more holistic approach to teaching reading—one that emphasized comprehension nearly to the exclusion of phonics, even in the earliest grades. When I asked the principal why teachers were no longer using the decoding program, she said that the children at the school had not performed well on the state-mandated reading comprehension tests given in third grade and beyond. With the phonics program, most children had learned to decode well, but they had other difficulties that affected their reading comprehension. That is, at the time the phonics program was in use, the school tended to generate a large number of struggling readers with SRCD, probably in part because there was insufficient attention in Tier I instruction to vocabulary and other language comprehension abilities. Predictably, the decision to abandon systematic phonics teaching at Berson Elementary was disastrous: Test scores at the school actually went *down* after the program change. Now many students had poor reading comprehension, and they had trouble decoding, too.

This chapter focuses on students with a profile of SRCD: children who have poor reading comprehension despite age-appropriate phonological and word-reading skills and no history of difficulties in learning to decode. These children have a profile opposite to that of SWRD, with reading comprehension problems *not* attributable to poor decoding. Often the reading comprehension problems of students with SRCD stem from weaknesses in oral vocabulary or other aspects of oral language, such as sentence and discourse comprehension. These relatively mild oral language difficulties may not be obvious in everyday conversation and may not result in eligibility for speech-language services; however, especially as children advance in school and reading demands become increasingly sophisticated, problems with reading comprehension begin to emerge or worsen. SRCD can also involve other underpinnings, such as limitations in background knowledge, poor knowledge of text structure, or problems in executive function or working memory.

When students with SRCD have poor reading fluency, their fluency problems typically involve rate of oral text reading as opposed to automatic reading of individual words (Eason et al., 2013). These fluency problems may be based in nonphonological language factors, including those affecting prosody of reading; they do not involve the phonological and decoding weaknesses characteristic of SWRD. For example, students with SRCD can generally read a grade-appropriate passage with high word accuracy—and even read individual words automatically—but still might not meet grade norms for oral passage reading fluency or might demonstrate poor prosody because they do not fully understand the language of the passage they are reading.

Unlike students with SWRD, those with SRCD may have problems comprehending information even when that information is presented verbally, as in classroom discussions of content or teacher read-alouds, because of underlying language limitations affecting both listening and reading. Indeed, some students with SRCD may perform better when reading than listening because of attentional factors and the ability to reread print. As the opening to this chapter suggests, the difficulties of students with SRCD do not necessarily reflect intrinsic limitations or disabilities but sometimes may simply be associated with lack of exposure or lack of opportunity to learn. As the educators at Berson Elementary eventually discovered, the solution to these problems is not to eliminate good decoding instruction in the early grades—that approach only makes things worse by undermining the foundation of accurate, automatic decoding that all students require for good reading comprehension. Instead, educators at Berson Elementary should have continued their research-based decoding instruction but also increased explicit, systematic teaching of vocabulary, language, and other comprehension skills, starting in kindergarten.

This chapter presents three examples of children with SRCD, including both patterns of SRCD discussed in Chapter 4: nonstrategic comprehenders and suboptimal comprehenders. By definition, suboptimal comprehension does not emerge before middle school, when higher order comprehension abilities typically begin to develop. Although this book focuses on the elementary grades, I include an example of an eighth-grade suboptimal comprehender in this chapter to help illustrate the differences between the two patterns of SRCD. The basic format of the chapter follows that of Chapter 7, with background information, assessment data and tables of scores, conclusions, and recommendations for intervention provided for each child. As in Chapter 7, all standard scores employ age norms, and I use an average range of 90–110 for academic achievement tests. I also include scores for components of mathematics and written expression as well as reading. For students with SRCD, an examination of performance across these academic domains often reveals a pattern of difficulties with broad language or vocabulary, coupled with age-appropriate phonological skills and decoding.

MATEO

An ending third grader, age 8 years, 10 months, Mateo came to the United States at age 3 with his parents and two younger twin siblings. Spanish is the primary language spoken at home. Through an interpreter, an aunt, Mateo's parents have indicated that his early language development in Spanish was typical and that he has no unusual health problems; hearing and vision screenings also have been typical. Mateo and his siblings attend an urban school district with a large Hispanic population, one that does have a very good bilingual educational program for Spanish-speaking children. However, Mateo's parents did not consent to his placement in the program because they worried that it might impede his learning of English. They did consent to English as a second language (ESL) services, which Mateo has been receiving since kindergarten. Unfortunately, the ESL teacher is greatly overburdened, and Mateo's ESL time has always been minimal. This year, due to relatively good performance on the English language assessment on which he scored just slightly below the cutoff for discontinuation of ESL services, he has been receiving only about 20 minutes per *week* of ESL time. In fact, Mateo has made excellent progress learning conversational English, and he communicates with ease on everyday topics. An athletic and energetic boy, he has made many friends, both English speaking and Spanish speaking. However, academics, and particularly reading, have been a struggle, especially during the past school year.

In kindergarten and first grade, Mateo's reading and spelling progress were generally grade appropriate. In these grades, he did evidence some phonological confusions related to his Spanish-language background, such as substituting /t/ for /th/ and confusing /sh/ and /ch/ (Barone & Xu, 2007). Nevertheless, these occasional confusions did not significantly limit his overall progress in his school's curriculum for teaching phonics and spelling, which provided highly explicit, systematic instruction in basic reading skills. In contrast, Mateo's English vocabulary, knowledge of academic language, and reading comprehension have always been weaker than his decoding. His limitations in these areas have begun to create particularly serious problems for him during third grade, as the curriculum has begun to focus on content reading as well as extended writing. Furthermore, although

Mateo's early mathematics skills were on grade level, the third-grade math curriculum places more emphasis on language aspects of math as opposed to calculation—for example, on solving word problems, explaining the solution to a problem, and justifying answers. Mateo finds these language-based areas of math substantially more challenging than calculation skills. As a third grader, Mateo recently took his state's high-stakes assessment of reading, writing, and mathematics for the first time, and he scored at the lowest level, below basic, for both reading and writing.

Recent Assessment Data

Because of concerns about Mateo's reading comprehension, the school's reading specialist administered some informal assessments to Mateo, and the special education teacher administered both the PAT 2 (Robertson & Salter, 2007) and the PPVT-IV (Dunn & Dunn, 2007). Table 8.1 displays Mateo's scores on these assessments. As shown in the "Word recognition and phonological skills" section of this table, Mateo's phonological awareness and decoding skills on the PAT 2 were solidly average; likewise, his abilities to read isolated lists of words on the reading specialist's IRI (Burns & Roe, 2007) were grade appropriate. In addition, when Mateo made word-reading errors, these errors tended to relate to lack of vocabulary knowledge, not to poor phonological decoding. For example, he incorrectly read *bargain* as *bar-GAIN*, with the accent on the second syllable and a long *a* in that syllable, because he was not familiar with the spoken word *bargain* or what it meant; he made a similar type of error reading the word *koala* as *cola*.

On the IRI graded passages, Mateo's highest independent reading level was in first-grade passages, and his highest instructional level was in second grade, at least a year below his grade placement; his low performance in passages was almost entirely due to difficulties answering comprehension questions. Most of Mateo's comprehension errors related to limitations in vocabulary and academic background knowledge, difficulties evident in his everyday classroom performance as well. For example, Mateo's class has been reading informational text about the solar system, and many children bring some specific background knowledge with them to this kind of reading— knowing the names of many of the planets or knowing that the planets revolve around the sun—even before they read these facts in the text. Mateo lacks this kind of knowledge, so the comprehension demands of the text are relatively greater for him. Moreover, although Mateo made few word-reading errors on the IRI passages, when he did make an error, he generally failed to try to correct it—that is, he did not appear to monitor his comprehension consistently. When the reading specialist had Mateo read timed, grade-appropriate passages, he scored slightly below benchmark for the rate of oral reading in text.

With regard to oral vocabulary and oral comprehension, although Mateo's listening comprehension was roughly grade appropriate on the IRI, his vocabulary knowledge as assessed by the PPVT-IV was well below

Table 8.1. Recent assessment data for Mateo, an ending third grader, age 8 years, 10 months

Word recognition and phonological skills	Text reading accuracy and fluency	Oral vocabulary and comprehension	Reading comprehension	Written expression and math	Other
PAT 2: Phonological Awareness Section SS = 104; Grapheme Section SS = 99; Decoding Section SS = 98 Burns and Roe's informal reading inventory (IRI), 7th ed., 2007; graded word lists: independent = Grade 2; instructional = Grade 4 Word-reading errors often reflect limitations in vocabulary knowledge as opposed to phonology	IRI passages: independent level = Grade 1; instructional level = Grade 2, due to problems with comprehension Child did not always try to correct word-reading errors Poor prosody of oral reading, mainly reflecting comprehension limitations; rate is slightly below grade expectations	PPVT-IV SS = 75 IRI passages: Listening level = Grade 3 Difficulty with summarization and prediction tasks even when information is presented orally Difficulty with vocabulary questions on the IRI and in classroom tasks Everyday conversational competence in English is good	Comprehension errors on the IRI and in classroom work reflect limitations in academic vocabulary and background knowledge, not limitations in decoding accuracy or automaticity of word reading Scored at lowest level, below basic, on the state-mandated reading comprehension assessment	Represents all phonemes in words when spelling; spells many common words correctly; spelling is generally grade appropriate Poor written expression, due mainly to weaknesses in vocabulary and syntax; scored at lowest level on state writing assessment Math calculation is grade appropriate, but problem solving is somewhat below grade expectations	Native Spanish speaker, arrived in the United States with immigrant parents at age 3; Spanish primary language spoken at home English as a second language (ESL) services since Grade 1, currently 20 minutes per week; no other interventions yet No history of preschool language delay; no significant medical, hearing, vision, or behavior problems; no known family history of reading difficulties

Note: PAT 2 = Phonological Awareness Test 2 (Robertson & Salter, 2007); PPVT-IV = Peabody Picture Vocabulary Test, 4th edition (Dunn & Dunn, 2007).

average. Mateo's classroom teacher has been teaching her class summarization and prediction strategies using teacher read-alouds, and Mateo often has considerable difficulty with these tasks, which do not require him to read. Mateo's vocabulary, language, and background knowledge limitations affect his math performance and his written expression as well as his reading comprehension. Often, he is not sure what key words in a math problem mean (e.g., *expand, distribute*), which interferes with his ability to choose the correct operation to solve the problem. In writing, he has difficulties with elaborating details, correct word choice, subject–verb agreement, and syntax. Many of his grammatical and syntactic errors reflect his Spanish-language background. For example, he is prone to using double negatives (e.g., *He didn't see nothing* instead of *He didn't see anything*) or dropping auxiliary verbs (e.g., *Where she went?* instead of *Where did she go?*), structures that are grammatical in Spanish but not in English. In contrast, Mateo's spelling skills are currently on grade level; he represents all phonemes in words even when spelling unfamiliar words, which is consistent with his good phonological reading skills, and he spells many common words correctly.

Conclusions

Mateo's assessment data and everyday classroom performance suggest that he has a profile of SRCD with a pattern of nonstrategic comprehension. As is typical of children with this profile, his phonological skills are good, as shown in both his reading and his spelling, and his early word-reading development was grade appropriate, though mildly influenced by his language differences as a native Spanish speaker. However, Mateo has obvious reading comprehension difficulties that are accompanied by many corresponding oral comprehension weaknesses, particularly involving vocabulary. His lack of consistent comprehension monitoring as well as his difficulties with summarization and prediction suggest that he does not read strategically. Mateo's profile of abilities indicates that broad language knowledge, not decoding, is the likely culprit in his strategic weaknesses; for example, he may fail to try to correct errors when reading because the linguistic demands of the text overwhelm him with too much that he does not understand. This is a dynamic similar to that of a child with SWRD but with a different underlying cause—language comprehension, not phonology. The types of language difficulties that Mateo is having as well as his apparently typical early development in his native language suggest a child whose problems relate to his ELL status as opposed to a disability, but this conclusion must remain provisional until his response to appropriate intervention is seen.

Mateo desperately needs intervention focused on academic vocabulary and language, including both oral language development and applications to literacy (as well as math). This intervention requires much more time than the current 20 minutes per week he is receiving of ESL services—for example, at least 30 minutes per day—but the intervention could be delivered in a small homogeneous group of children with literacy needs similar to his or perhaps even in an appropriately structured classwide peer-tutoring model (Gersten et al., 2007; Rivera et al., 2008). Given that Mateo's language difficulties seem to reflect his ELL background rather than a disability and that he has not yet had any meaningful literacy intervention, a referral to special education is not warranted. However, Mateo's performance in intervention should guide future decision making, including the possible need for additional standardized language testing and comprehensive evaluation, if appropriate.

Recommendations for Intervention

A helpful approach for Mateo and other ELLs involves direct teaching of target academic words from classroom texts coupled with explicit teaching of morphology, such as the meaning of important roots, prefixes, and suffixes (August et al., 2005). Because Mateo is well below age expectations for English vocabulary, intervention also will need to include below-grade-level vocabulary words, likely including some common words and expressions already very familiar to native English speakers. Vocabulary intervention should build on Mateo's knowledge of Spanish words that have cognates in English (e.g., Spanish *literatura* and English *literature* have similar meanings) but should also address false cognates. For instance, in Spanish, *criatura* is often used to mean *baby* as opposed to *creature*, but in English, referring to an infant as a *creature* might raise a few eyebrows. Visual aids and graphic organizers, such as semantic maps of related words, may be especially useful in Mateo's vocabulary intervention, which should present words in varied contexts and promote active engagement in word learning (Beck et al., 2002) rather than rote memorization of definitions. In addition to direct teaching of important academic words, intervention should also encourage Mateo to use context, when possible, to infer meanings of unknown words. Mateo also requires intervention to develop broader academic background knowledge and language skills, such as knowledge about English syntax and grammar (e.g., avoiding double negatives), text structure (e.g., headings and subheadings in an informational text carry important information), and understanding important cohesive words in text such as *however* and *therefore*. All this intervention should include oral language—for example, teacher read-alouds and oral discussion—as well as applications to appropriate texts, both in reading and in writing.

It is important for teachers to place Mateo for instruction in texts that are at an appropriate level of challenge, a level at which he can learn but at which the comprehension demands of the text do not overwhelm him; overly challenging texts may impede his learning of new language skills. Mateo's assessment data suggest that it might be best to start his intervention with second-grade, not third-grade, text, with increases in text difficulty level depending on his performance in intervention. Because Mateo does not consistently monitor his comprehension when he reads, it would be helpful to include some oral reading of text as a check on whether he is able to monitor comprehension in easier texts and so that the teacher can encourage him to do so. For instance, if Mateo's oral reading prosody suggests that he does not understand a particular segment of text (e.g., reading with flat or halting prosody), the teacher could question him to probe the nature of the problem. She could then emphasize an appropriate strategy for Mateo to apply in the future, such as asking for the meaning of a word, as well as model appropriate prosody. Oral reading of text should include ample discussion and questioning before, during, and after reading and should incorporate direct teaching of comprehension strategies such as summarization and prediction. Also, as Mateo's ability to read independently develops, it will be important to encourage and guide his independent reading in appropriate texts, because (among other reasons) such reading can help promote Mateo's further development of vocabulary and academic language.

Mateo's progress in intervention could be monitored via maze CBMs such as Aimsweb (see http://www.aimsweb.com) and DIBELS Next (Good & Kaminski, 2011) and through informal assessments such as measures of Mateo's knowledge of vocabulary words that have been taught and checks of his comprehension (i.e., responses to literal, inferential, and vocabulary questions) embedded in his intervention. If these kinds of measures do not suggest significant progress in Mateo's vocabulary and comprehension development during fourth grade, then further standardized testing of Mateo's language skills in both Spanish and English should be done. If these language tests suggest the possibility of a language-based disability, or if adjustments to Mateo's intervention do not result in improved progress and some narrowing of the gap in Mateo's reading achievement, then he should have a more comprehensive evaluation with consideration for special education.

Finally, although language-minority parents sometimes believe that native language instruction will impede their children's learning of English, as did Mateo's parents, research suggests that well-designed bilingual instruction can lead to better long-term reading outcomes in English for ELLs than English-only instruction (August & Shanahan, 2006). Even for ELLs with disabilities, evidence does not support an insistence on English-only instruction (Genesee et al., 2004; Goral & Conner, 2013). As is true for all instructional programs, the quality of the bilingual program is critical; furthermore, sometimes it is simply not feasible for schools to provide good bilingual education options for language-minority students—for example, because instructional materials or appropriate teachers are not available in the native language. However, this option did exist in Mateo's case, and it is one from which he might have benefited.

LAUREN

Lauren is a middle fifth grader, age 10 years, 6 months, from a well-to-do suburban school district. Lauren has received special education services since her diagnosis with an ASD at age 2½. Although Lauren's ASD is relatively mild, it was diagnosed early in part because of a family history of ASD: Lauren has an older brother with autism, who is nonverbal, has significant cognitive impairments, and attends a special day school for students with disabilities. Despite a history of social-emotional and language weaknesses, however, Lauren's problems are much milder than are her brother's. She attends her neighborhood school and is heavily included in the core general education program, with some assistance from an instructional aide.

Lauren's early reading progress was good; despite a rather holistic Tier I reading program, she developed strong phonological and word decoding skills. Her kindergarten through Grade 3 report cards, as well as standardized tests from special education, showed reading achievement that was soundly average or better, even in reading comprehension. Likewise, her primary-grade spelling and math skills were well within average range. However, Lauren began to experience literacy difficulties last year, in fourth grade, when the curriculum began to emphasize lengthy independent reading and writing activities as well as relatively advanced types of comprehension and composition skills. Extended reading and writing activities tend to overwhelm Lauren, requiring continual guidance from her aide to keep Lauren on track, and occasionally leading to "meltdowns" as Lauren becomes increasingly frustrated. In reading, she has particular difficulties with higher-level inferential questions. When she reads narratives, questions about characters' motivations and emotions or about figurative language tend to be especially problematic for her; when she reads informational text, the most difficult questions are those about key points or main ideas. In writing, her biggest difficulties involve organization of her thoughts and clarity of writing (e.g., writing for an audience). Lauren's literacy problems have noticeably worsened in fifth grade. Furthermore, in the past school year, she also has begun to struggle with word problems in math, although her computational skills remain strong.

Recently, Lauren had a triennial evaluation that showed significantly lower scores in reading comprehension, as well as in written expression, than she had obtained 3 years earlier, when she was a second grader. These test results greatly upset Lauren's parents, who have always viewed academic performance as a strength for their daughter. They believe that she is rapidly losing ground, particularly in reading. Lauren's teachers understand her parents' concerns, but they pointed out that, although Lauren's standardized reading comprehension scores were below average, those scores were not extremely low. Furthermore, on an IRI, the QRI (Leslie & Caldwell, 2006), administered by Lauren's classroom teacher, Lauren's highest instructional level was at grade expectations, fifth grade. In addition, they noted that Lauren scored at the proficient level on the state-mandated reading comprehension assessment for fourth grade. (Scores for the fifth-grade test were not yet available.) For the state-mandated assessment, a criterion-referenced rather than norm-referenced measure, Lauren did have accommodations involving extended time, frequent breaks, and separate administration in a quiet room.

Recent Assessment Data

Table 8.2 displays data from Lauren's latest triennial evaluation as well as from core general education progress monitoring and informal assessments. As shown in the table, Lauren's standardized reading comprehension scores were all below average, with her Passage Comprehension score on the WJ-III (Woodcock et al., 2007) highest, and her score on the Kaufman Test of Educational Achievement-II (KTEA-II) Reading Comprehension subtest (Kaufman & Kaufman, 2004) lowest. Nevertheless, all Lauren's scores for out-of-context word recognition, displayed in the "Word recognition and phonological skills" section of Table 8.2, were well above average or above grade expectations, even on a standardized measure involving timed pseudowords, the KTEA-II Timed Nonsense Word Decoding subtest. The test data further suggest that Lauren's language weaknesses do not involve single-word vocabulary—her scores on both the Expressive and Receptive One-Word Picture Vocabulary tests (Brownell, 2010a, 2010b) were well within average range—but, rather, sentence and discourse aspects of language comprehension. For example, her total Receptive Language Composite on the Clinical Evaluation of Language Fundamentals-5 (CELF-5; Semel et al., 2013) was slightly below average, and her score on the CELF-5 subtest Understanding Spoken Paragraphs was at the lower end of the average range (using 85–115 for average range as is typical for tests of oral language and intelligence). Both of these language scores were well below Lauren's oral vocabulary performance. Notably, Lauren's pragmatic language skills were particularly weak, as shown by her well-below-average scores on the CELF-5 Pragmatics Profile and on the Test of Pragmatic Language-2 (TOPL-2; Phelps-Terasaki & Phelps-Gunn, 2007). This pattern of language performance was consistent with Lauren's earlier evaluations in which she has always scored within average range for vocabulary but often has had mild weaknesses on other oral language testing, with her lowest performance usually in pragmatic aspects of language. Overall, these data demonstrate that Lauren has excellent phonological skills coupled with broader language weaknesses affecting reading comprehension, a common though not universal profile for students with HFA (Huemer & Mann, 2010; Nation, Clarke, Wright, & Williams, 2006).

Lauren's QRI scores, as well as her scores on tests of written expression and mathematics, also suggest that broad language weaknesses affect her academic performance. On the QRI passages, her highest independent reading level was in Grade 3, 2 years below her current grade placement, and her highest instructional level was in Grade 5, roughly at grade level. However, on a listening comprehension version of the QRI, in which the examiner read text and questions aloud to Lauren, she actually performed less well than when she read passages, because she appeared to have difficulties focusing

Table 8.2. Recent assessment data for Lauren, a middle fifth grader, age 10 years, 6 months

Word recognition and phonological skills	Text reading accuracy and fluency	Oral vocabulary and comprehension	Reading comprehension	Written expression and math	Other
KTEA-II Timed Word Recognition SS = 116	GORT-5 Oral Reading Quotient SS = 103; Accuracy = 10; Rate = 9	ROWPVT-4 SS = 102	WJ-III Passage Comprehension SS = 87	KTEA-II Spelling SS = 107	WISC-IV Verbal Comprehension = 82; Perceptual Reasoning = 112; Working Memory = 88; Processing Speed = 99
KTEA-II Timed Nonsense Word Decoding SS = 122	Met winter benchmark for Aimsweb passage reading fluency; Aimsweb maze was below benchmark (Grade 5 passages)	EOWPVT-4 SS = 106	GORT-5 Comprehension = 7	KTEA-II Written Expression SS = 84; did well with editing tasks; problems with language content and organization	Mild language and social difficulties in preschool years; identified with autism spectrum disorder (ASD) at age 2½; family history is positive for ASD; receiving special education since preschool
QRI word lists: independent = Grade 6; instructional = Grade 7	QRI passages: independent = Grade 3; instructional = Grade 5; higher levels too difficult due to problems with comprehension	CELF-5 Understanding Spoken Paragraphs SS = 86; Receptive Language Composite SS = 84	KTEA-II Reading Comprehension = 74	KTEA-II Math Computation SS = 108	No history of significant medical, hearing, or vision problems; no history of decoding or phonological problems
		CELF-5 Pragmatics Profile = 5	Marked difficulties with inferential questions across all assessments	KTEA-II Math Concepts and Applications SS = 81; difficulty with language-based aspects of math (e.g., word problems)	
		TOPL-2 SS = 68	Comprehension errors on the QRI related heavily to language comprehension	Automatic recall of facts is excellent	
		QRI listening comprehension level = Grade 4; does better when reading than listening	Scored at proficient level on fourth-grade state reading comprehension assessment, with accommodations		

Note: CELF-5 = Clinical Evaluation of Language Fundamentals, 5th edition (Semel, Wiig, & Secord, 2013); EOWPVT-4 = Expressive One-Word Picture Vocabulary Test, 4th edition (Brownell, 2010a); GORT-5 = Gray Oral Reading Test, 5th edition (Wiederholt & Bryant, 2012); KTEA-II = Kaufman Test of Educational Achievement, 2nd edition (Kaufman & Kaufman, 2004); QRI = Qualitative Reading Inventory (Leslie & Caldwell, 2006); ROWPVT-4 = Receptive One-Word Picture Vocabulary Test, 4th edition (Brownell, 2010b); TOPL-2 = Test of Pragmatic Language, 2nd edition (Phelps-Terasaki & Phelps-Gunn, 2007); WISC-IV = Wechsler Intelligence Scale for Children, 4th edition (Wechsler, 2003); WJ-III = Woodcock-Johnson Tests of Achievement, 3rd edition (Woodcock, McGrew, & Mather, 2007).

when she had to listen as opposed to when she read the text herself. On all the QRI passages, Lauren's primary difficulties were with inferential comprehension; she generally did well with questions about the literal content of the text or about vocabulary, and her oral reading of passages in terms of word accuracy was essentially flawless. In written expression, Lauren's difficulties centered on content and organization of writing, and in mathematics, on problem solving; mechanics of writing, spelling, and calculation aspects of math all were well within average range.

A few other test results in Table 8.2 should be mentioned. Lauren's oral reading fluency was age appropriate, as shown by her scaled score for rate on the GORT-5 (Wiederholt & Bryant, 2012), though not nearly as strong as her accuracy and automaticity for reading single words. This rate score was consistent with Lauren's performance on a classroom Aimsweb passage reading fluency assessment on which she met winter benchmarks for fifth grade (although she did not meet the benchmark for maze comprehension). Also, as part of Lauren's triennial, an IQ test was given, the Wechsler Intelligence Scale for Children-IV (WISC-IV; Wechsler, 2003). On this test, Lauren's most significant weakness was on the Verbal Comprehension index, on which her total score was slightly below average; her strongest area involved the Perceptual Reasoning index, on which she had a score at the upper end of the average range. Lauren's score for Processing Speed was solidly average, and her Working Memory index was at the lower end of the average range.

Conclusions

Lauren has a profile of late-emerging SRCD, with strong phonological skills and no history of word decoding problems but weaknesses in reading comprehension first emerging in fourth and fifth grade. Like Mateo, Lauren appears to be a nonstrategic reader, although she functions at a higher reading level than he does. Her tendency to become overwhelmed by extended reading activities and to require constant guidance from her aide, as well as her difficulties inferring main ideas in texts, suggests that she cannot yet consistently apply comprehension strategies such as summarization in reading. Lauren's difficulties are linked not to limited language exposure, as is probably the case for Mateo, but rather to specific cognitive and linguistic weaknesses associated with ASD. For example, her difficulties with answering questions about characters' feelings and motivations in narratives and her difficulties with questions about main idea in informational text likely reflect the difficulties with theory of mind and central coherence characteristic of ASD (Frith, 2012).

Although Lauren's teachers are correct that her current standardized reading comprehension scores are not extremely low, these scores nevertheless are disturbing for at least two reasons. First, Lauren has a consistent pattern of below-average performance on the reading comprehension measures that should be given the most weight: the individually administered standardized measures (i.e., the KTEA-II, WJ-III, and GORT-5 comprehension subtests). Her score on Aimsweb maze comprehension also was below bench-mark. As discussed in Chapter 5, although IRIs can be useful for making initial decisions about placing children for instruction in texts, they typically lack the technical adequacy of standardized measures. In a situation such as Lauren's in which there is conflicting information, standardized measures with good technical adequacy should be weighted much more heavily in evaluating children's performance than IRI data. Likewise, although Lauren scored at the proficient level on the state-mandated reading comprehension assessment, this measure is not norm-referenced, as was also true for Henry's state-mandated test in Chapter 7, so it does not indicate how Lauren performs relative to a norm group of children her age. Moreover, Lauren obtained her score on the state-mandated measure with accommodations. These accommodations were appropriate, but they imply a need for ongoing support in the area of reading.

Second, Lauren's recent reading comprehension performance is worrisome because her performance seems to have declined relative to that of other children her age, based on the information from the standardized, norm-referenced measures. Lauren's reading comprehension scores were within average range in previous evaluations, but her language scores were always somewhat weaker than average, with pragmatic language especially low. Thus, although Lauren's *reading* difficulties are late emerging, they reflect underlying *language* weaknesses that were present from the early grades. These broad language weaknesses at the sentence and discourse level probably did not affect reading comprehension significantly until Lauren progressed beyond the primary grades and expectations for reading comprehension increased. Without appropriate intervention, Lauren's language weaknesses will likely have a mounting impact on her reading comprehension (as well as other academic areas) as she advances in school. Moreover, Lauren's test data and the descriptions of her skills (e.g., low-average working memory and unusual difficulties with planning processes in writing) suggest problems with executive function. This difficulty is common in children with SRCD (Cutting et al., 2009, 2013) and, in the absence of appropriate intervention, may exert an additional negative influence on Lauren's academic achievement as she moves into the upper grades. Overall, although Lauren's difficulties are relatively common among students with HFA, these difficulties should be addressed as soon as possible in order to maximize Lauren's chances for future success in school.

Recommendations for Intervention

Lauren needs intervention focused on inferencing, perspective-taking, understanding figurative language, and other related comprehension abilities in which she is weak. Because Lauren already receives special education services, educators can include this intervention in her special education program, although some increases in special education time may be required.

(However, Lauren's participation in the general education program is very important for her social development as well as her content learning; therefore, decisions about pull-out time for special education must balance competing needs for both general education participation and intervention time.) Intervention should involve both oral language and applications to literacy, so the involvement of the speech-language pathologist, who already provides services to Lauren weekly, is essential. Although reading intervention research involving children with ASD is very limited (Chiang & Lin, 2007; Whalon et al., 2009), a number of activities that have benefited other struggling comprehenders, including children with ASD in some studies, could benefit Lauren. These activities include the use of graphic and semantic organizers, the use of prereading questions to help focus Lauren's attention on important points in the text, and explicit teaching of the meaning of figurative language. Given Lauren's problems with perspective-taking, an especially useful comprehension intervention for her might be perspective-taking through narratives, which includes having children make inferences about and take the perspective of different characters in a story (e.g., Dodd et al., 2011).

Lauren also must be placed at an appropriate level for reading instruction, during both intervention and Tier I participation. Although Lauren's highest instructional level on the QRI was at grade level, her frequent "meltdowns" in extended classroom reading activities suggest that the texts she is reading may be too difficult for her. One option for her teachers to consider is to seek out specific fifth-grade texts that might be easier for Lauren to comprehend. For example, she loves horses and has an excellent knowledge base about horses as well as other types of animals; she might find it easier to learn skills such as inferencing, summarization, and understanding figurative language in the context of these kinds of books. Alternatively, her teachers might try dropping down a grade level in text difficulty (i.e., fourth-grade instead of fifth-grade texts) to see whether she functions better in these easier texts. What matters most is finding texts at a "not too easy, not too hard" level of difficulty in which Lauren can develop the comprehension abilities that she needs to learn.

Because of Lauren's strong basic skills and her tendency to perform better when reading than listening, writing activities may be especially useful to her literacy development. For instance, activities such as writing summaries of texts she has read could benefit Lauren's reading comprehension as well as her written expression (Graham & Hebert, 2010). To benefit Lauren and avoid unduly frustrating her, these activities must be appropriately structured. In writing summaries, Lauren could be taught to identify the main points of a text and to delete less important or repetitive information, with initial coaching from the teacher and then gradually faded coaching over time so that Lauren becomes more independent in her ability to write a summary. Teaching planning processes in writing also is important (e.g., brainstorm ideas, decide on a topic, determine main points, develop a simple outline) and may again benefit Lauren's reading comprehension as well as her written expression.

In addition, teaching Lauren strategies to improve executive function would likely profit her across many academic areas, not only literacy. These strategies should relate strongly to the academic curriculum and should be directly taught. Potentially useful strategies for Lauren include strategies for prioritizing information (e.g., using a highlighter to highlight important ideas in a text), visual aids for organizing academic tasks such as a calendar, and self-monitoring strategies such a personalized checklist to help Lauren monitor completion of her work and become aware of (and correct) her most common mistakes (Meltzer, 2010).

Lauren's progress monitoring should consider her performance on both Aimsweb passage reading fluency and maze comprehension CBMs as well as employ comprehension checks of her everyday performance in curriculum materials. Comprehension checks should include ample numbers of questions that target Lauren's weaknesses (e.g., inferential and main idea questions, questions about figurative language), both in her intervention materials and during general education participation; for purposes of monitoring progress, Lauren must answer questions without coaching from the teacher. In general, to be performing at an appropriate instructional level in curriculum materials, Lauren should answer questions with about 75% accuracy or better (Morris, 2014); lower performance, especially on a frequent basis, indicates that texts are too difficult or that intervention is ineffective. Evaluations of progress should consider not only Lauren's accuracy on comprehension questions but also her text difficulty levels; for example, if she maintains approximately 80% accuracy in increasingly difficult texts, this pattern suggests progress, even though her percentage of accuracy has remained stable. Independent writing samples, such as those involving summaries of texts she has read, may also be useful in evaluating Lauren's comprehension progress. Finally, in determining the success of changes to Lauren's program, educators should consider her performance on readministration of norm-referenced language and reading measures that she has already taken, such as the KTEA-II and CELF-5. These kinds of measures cannot be readministered frequently, and they lack the ability to detect relatively small changes in performance; therefore, they cannot be the sole or primary choice for monitoring progress. Nevertheless, if changes to Lauren's intervention program are effective in bringing her closer to age and grade expectations, educators should see some gains on her norm-referenced test scores over time, in addition to progress on CBMs and informal measures.

MELODY

Melody, who is 13½ years old, attends an interdistrict magnet school similar to the one attended by Alicia in Chapter 7. Like Alicia, Melody is a monolingual English child from a low-income family. She has attended the magnet school since kindergarten, and until recently, teachers have viewed her reading performance as good. She entered school with no history of language delay, and she has no significant health, hearing, or vision problems other than mild asthma that is well controlled with medication. Melody's mother is a single parent who does not have much formal education and who works at multiple jobs to earn a living for herself and her three children; however, there are no apparent reading disabilities in the family. In the primary grades, Melody developed phonemic awareness and word decoding skills as expected, and she routinely met grade benchmarks on ORF CBMs. Her reading comprehension performance also was grade appropriate through most of elementary school, as were her spelling and writing skills. The state-mandated assessment used in Melody's state employs four levels for reporting students' scores: below basic, basic, proficient, and advanced. Melody consistently scored at the proficient level or better on this state-mandated assessment in reading, writing, and mathematics through Grade 6. She is now in the middle of eighth grade and will enter high school next year. However, despite her strong performance in earlier grades, eighth-grade teachers have begun to have some concerns about whether Melody has the literacy skills to do well in high school. Educators' worries escalated when Melody's scores on the seventh-grade state-mandated assessment came back and showed her to be functioning at the basic level in both reading and writing. (The eighth-grade test has not yet been administered.) If Melody's drop in achievement on the state-mandated assessment seemed to be an isolated incident, her teachers might have dismissed it; however, they have also observed some declines in Melody's everyday classroom performance. Educators at the magnet school see many children with much more serious academic difficulties than Melody's, but Melody has always been an exceptionally motivated and engaged student, one that teachers view as quite capable. They want her to continue to do well as she advances in school and eventually have the opportunity to attend college, a cherished goal for Melody and her mother.

Melody has no difficulty reading curriculum materials in her classroom; she reads grade-appropriate texts with a high degree of accuracy, usually 98%–100%. She also performs well on many basic literacy tasks, such as answering literal and inferential questions about texts she has read, predicting what is likely to happen next in a text, and summarizing basic points. Furthermore, Melody clearly monitors comprehension when she reads—for example, she asks questions when something does not make sense or rereads to try to figure out the meaning. However, she struggles with many of the instructional activities included in the eighth-grade literacy curriculum in connection with the CCSS. In reading, her greatest difficulties involve questions about the author's craft (e.g., those involving knowledge of connotations of words or allusions to other texts) as well as integration of knowledge and ideas. Critical analyses of texts—for example, deciding when the evidence presented in an informational text is relevant and sufficient for supporting the claims in a text—are difficult for her. In writing, Melody has many comparable problems with standards involving precise word choice or involving selection, organization, and analysis of content relevant to writing an informational text, for instance. Many other eighth graders also find these advanced comprehension and writing standards challenging, but teachers are particularly concerned about Melody because she always did well in the past and her performance seems to be dropping.

Although educators do not currently view Melody as a candidate for referral to special education, they encouraged her participation in a recent experimental study at the magnet school. The researchers sought participants for a study on seventh and eighth graders' literacy skills and habits. As part of that study, participants would take individually administered, standardized tests of academic abilities as well as some experimental literacy measures. Melody agreed to participate, and her mother provided consent.

Recent Assessment Data

Table 8.3 displays Melody's scores on the standardized study measures. These scores were within average range for all basic skill areas: reading both real words and nonsense words in isolation, reading fluency, spelling, editing of writing, fluency of math facts, and calculation skills. Melody also scored within average range on the WJ-III subtests for Oral Comprehension, Passage Comprehension, and Applied Problems in math. Her weakest areas involved receptive vocabulary (PPVT-IV SS = 85) and content aspects of writing (WJ-III Writing Samples SS = 86), although her scores in these areas were not extremely low.

In addition to these standardized measures, the investigators administered several measures of children's literacy habits such as pleasure reading and exposure to books. One measure was an author recognition checklist, involving names of authors of popular children's books interspersed with fake names or foils; children merely had to circle all the names that they were certain were real authors. (They lost credit for guessing.) Title or author checklist recognition measures are proxy measures of children's exposure to print (e.g., Cipielewski & Stanovich, 1992; Cunningham & Stanovich, 1991, 1997); children who have greater exposure to books—whether through their own reading or through immersion in a literate environment—will tend to recognize more author names and titles than will those with limited exposure to books. Melody was one of only a handful of participants who obtained a score of 0 on this measure; unlike most other students, she did not recognize the names of any authors at all.

Conclusions

Like the other children discussed in this chapter, Melody has a profile of SRCD; she has average phonological and decoding skills, with no history of early word-recognition problems, but nevertheless is experiencing difficulties with reading comprehension. Melody's reading comprehension problems

Table 8.3. Recent assessment data for Melody, a middle eighth grader, age 13 years, 6 months

Word recognition and phonological skills	Text reading accuracy and fluency	Oral vocabulary and comprehension	Reading comprehension	Written expression and math	Other
WJ-III Word Identification SS = 98 WJ-III Word Attack SS = 99	WJ-III Reading Fluency SS = 101 Reads most grade-appropriate text (various curriculum materials) with 98%–100% word accuracy	PPVT-IV SS = 85 WJ-III Picture Vocabulary SS = 88; Oral Comprehension = 93 On classroom tasks, sometimes has difficulty with more nuanced understanding of vocabulary (e.g., connotation versus denotation of words, appropriate word choice)	WJ-III Passage Comprehension SS = 90 Performed at basic level on state-mandated reading comprehension test Uses comprehension strategies such as summarization and questioning; monitors comprehension Having substantial difficulty on classroom tasks involving CCSS for reading comprehension (e.g., author's craft, critical analysis)	WJ-III Spelling SS = 95 WJ-III Editing SS = 92; Writing Samples = 90 WJ-III Math Fluency SS = 99 WJ-III Math Calculation SS = 98 WJ-III Applied Problems SS = 94 Having substantial difficulty on classroom tasks involving CCSS for written expression (e.g., selection, organization, and analysis of relevant content)	No history of preschool language delay; no history of significant medical, hearing, vision, or behavior problems; no apparent family history of reading difficulties; no problems in early reading development, including decoding or phonological skills Score of 0 on an experimental author recognition checklist No interventions yet

Note: CCSS = Common Core State Standards; PPVT-IV = Peabody Picture Vocabulary Test, 4th edition (Dunn & Dunn, 2007); WJ-III = Woodcock-Johnson Tests of Achievement, 3rd edition (Woodcock, McGrew, & Mather, 2007).

are late emerging, similar to Lauren's (although they emerged even later than Lauren's). However, unlike Mateo and Lauren, Melody is a suboptimal comprehender who struggles mainly with higher order comprehension abilities as well as with comparable types of abilities in written expression. Melody's consistent comprehension monitoring, use of strategies when comprehension fails (e.g., rereading, asking for the meaning of a word), and ability to employ basic comprehension strategies such as summarization suggest that she does read strategically. Her primary difficulties are with the more advanced types of comprehension and writing abilities introduced in the later elementary grades and beyond.

Melody's standardized test scores suggest that vocabulary is likely an important factor in her reading comprehension difficulties. Her standard scores on the PPVT-IV and on the WJ-III Picture Vocabulary subtest, in the mid to high 80s, put her in the bottom quarter of the distribution (i.e., below the 25th percentile) for students her age in terms of vocabulary knowledge. Melody may well have had mild vocabulary weaknesses in the early grades, but any weaknesses would have become more problematic as Melody was expected to perform increasingly challenging comprehension tasks in subsequent grades. For example, understanding different connotations of words, such as *stubborn* versus *strong-willed* versus *pig-headed*, and precise choices of words in writing depend on depth and breadth of word knowledge; Melody's vocabulary limitations could certainly affect her ability to meet standards involving these kinds of skills. Also, the experimental author recognition measure suggests that Melody has limited exposure to books compared to her classmates who took the same measure. Exposure to books would affect Melody's vocabulary learning and her ability to recognize literary allusions as well as more broadly affect her academic background knowledge; her experience with models of well-organized, effective writing; and a host of other advanced comprehension and written expression skills (Cunningham & Stanovich, 1998). Although the information presented about Melody does not suggest a disability, it is certainly important for her comprehension and writing difficulties to be addressed. Failure to develop the higher order comprehension and writing abilities required for advanced levels of literacy will seriously jeopardize Melody's dream of attending college as well as her employment opportunities in adult life.

Recommendations for Intervention

Some of the types of intervention warranted for Mateo—in particular, explicit teaching of vocabulary, morphology, and academic background knowledge—also could benefit Melody. This instruction needs to be calibrated to Melody's skill level, which is substantially more advanced than Mateo's and not influenced by Spanish language differences, as is true for Mateo. Melody also needs instruction focused on the advanced comprehension standards in which she is weak, such as critical analysis of texts along with related writing activities such as persuasive writing that makes and defends an argument. Close reading activities involving multiple rereadings of the same text—for example, a first reading to grasp the basic content of the text, followed by a second reading focused on the author's language and craft, followed by a third that analyzes the central theme of the text—should be helpful to Melody if appropriate texts and questions are used (see, e.g., Shanahan, 2013). Melody should not have difficulty reading the words in typical eighth-grade texts, but like the other students described in this chapter, she needs to read books that are at an appropriate level of challenge in terms of vocabulary and comprehension demands. The use of motivating, engaging texts with a clear purpose for close reading that makes sense to Melody also is highly desirable (Snow, 2013). Because many of Melody's classmates are having similar difficulties with meeting advanced comprehension and writing standards, these activities initially could be implemented as part of differentiated general education instruction, with progress monitored through embedded comprehension checks, writing samples, and other types of work products. However, if Melody continues to struggle relative to other students, she should have more intensive, small-group intervention targeting her reading and writing weaknesses.

TIER I READING INSTRUCTION AND PROGRESS MONITORING

Like students with SWRD, those with SRCD should have their interventions delivered as part of a broad, comprehensive program of literacy instruction, with good integration of interventions. Children with SRCD have age-appropriate phonological skills and decoding, and often good spelling as well, so they do not generally require intervention in these areas, but they still need the basic skills instruction appropriate to their grade as well as participation in Tier I progress monitoring. For example, Mateo does not currently require phonics or spelling *intervention*, but he certainly needs the morphological development and spelling instruction that all children need well beyond third grade—instruction that can be delivered through his Tier I participation. Like children with SWRD, those with SRCD may require certain modifications or differentiation of classroom instruction in order to participate effectively in the Tier I literacy curriculum. For example, in order to understand grade-appropriate texts and classroom discussions, students with SRCD may need preteaching of vocabulary and relevant background knowledge, greater scaffolding of instruction during listening or reading activities, and in some cases, placement in somewhat lower-level texts due to comprehension limitations. Although assistive technology can be very valuable for students with SRCD, these students usually benefit from different kinds of technology supports as compared to those with SWRD (Erickson, 2013). Students with SRCD may find supports related to vocabulary, concepts, broad language, and background knowledge particularly helpful, such as illustrative resources (e.g., pictorial examples of a concept), enrichment resources (e.g., supplemental background information related to a text), or translational resources (e.g., synonyms or definitions for difficult words).

SUMMING UP

Intervention and progress monitoring for students with SRCD involve important challenges—hence some of the more cautiously worded recommendations in this chapter as compared to the previous one. Whereas a number of technically adequate progress-monitoring measures, such as CBMs, have been developed for decoding and oral reading fluency, fewer of these are available for comprehension, and the complex issues surrounding measurement of comprehension, discussed in Chapter 5, limit the utility of existing measures. Likewise, progress-monitoring assessments that can measure relatively short-term growth in vocabulary (e.g., over the course of a typical intervention period) are virtually nonexistent. Moreover, for decoding and ORF, there are norms to suggest reasonable expectations by grade (e.g., Hasbrouck & Tindal, 2006) that educators can use to try to determine whether a student is making adequate progress in intervention; determining adequacy of progress is more difficult in the realms of vocabulary and comprehension. Even with relatively effective interventions, significant progress in comprehension or vocabulary simply may take longer than in decoding, and overcoming a large cumulative gap in performance may be especially difficult.

None of the children in this chapter had problems strongly suggestive of an LD in reading comprehension (although Lauren had a different disability that also affected her comprehension: ASD). However, it should be noted that, with the use of RTI criteria (and no IQ–achievement discrepancy), children with SRCD can potentially qualify for services in the area of LDs if their difficulties do not respond to intervention and if exclusionary criteria are met. For example, if Mateo did not respond to intervention, and if his persistent problems did not appear to be primarily due to his language-minority background, then he could potentially be identified as a student with LD, receiving special education services in that category. Indeed, some ELLs do have LDs, and not all those disabilities involve dyslexia; accurate identification of these students, though challenging, is important. However, it would likely be very difficult for a student like Mateo to qualify for LD services with the use of an IQ–achievement discrepancy criterion, because Mateo's language difficulties, and particularly his vocabulary limitations, would likely lower his score on a verbal IQ measure, hence his full-scale IQ as well.

The challenges of surmounting accumulated gaps in vocabulary and academic language further highlight the importance of effective Tier I instruction in these areas, beginning from the earliest grades, especially—though not only—in schools serving vulnerable populations such as ELLs or students from poverty backgrounds (August et al., 2005; Biemiller & Boote, 2006). Insufficient early attention to these areas was likely the initial problem at Berson Elementary, the school discussed in the opening to this chapter. Despite a strong phonics program in the primary grades, Berson Elementary produced a large number of struggling readers, mostly those with SRCD. Unfortunately, however, Berson Elementary's response to this problem—eliminating explicit, systematic teaching of decoding—merely tended to create a stream of children with yet another poor reader profile: MRD. The next chapter considers examples of these struggling readers.

9

Students with Mixed Reading Difficulties

At the end of the classic movie *Casablanca*, the actor Claude Rains, who plays a corrupt police captain, has a famous line: "Round up the usual suspects." Similarly, when children have poor reading comprehension, there are certain "usual suspects." A key suspect, of course—and the easiest to rule in or rule out—is faulty word recognition. Other usual suspects include weaknesses in vocabulary, broad language comprehension, fluency, background knowledge, executive function, and working memory. Just as the usual suspects are not always responsible for a particular crime, the components that I have outlined will not account for every single instance of poor reading comprehension. However, they are certainly a good place to start in trying to understand individual children's comprehension difficulties, because they are associated with many reading problems, and because finding the underpinnings of individual children's reading comprehension difficulties is vital for providing appropriate intervention. In the case of students with MRD, these underpinnings are relatively complex in that they always involve at least two types of difficulties—word recognition and something else affecting comprehension—and sometimes many more than two.

Because of difficulties with core comprehension abilities such as vocabulary, children with MRD may have poor comprehension even when they read text that they can decode well or even in listening, when they are not reading at all. As in the case of students with SRCD, children with MRD frequently have relatively mild language weaknesses not evident in everyday conversation that exert an increasing influence on reading comprehension as children advance into the upper grades. However, unlike students with SRCD, those with MRD need intervention related to not only core comprehension abilities but also word recognition, similar to children with SWRD, with the specific type of intervention dependent on whether they are nonalphabetic, inaccurate, or nonautomatic word readers. In addition, students with MRD often have difficulties with reading fluency, and these difficulties may center on word-level abilities (e.g., poor phonological decoding or slow reading of individual words), broad language abilities (e.g., limited vocabulary knowledge), or both factors.

As the example about Berson Elementary in Chapter 8 illustrates, and like children with other profiles of poor reading, those with MRD do not necessarily have intrinsic learning disorders. Their reading problems can stem from extrinsic factors, such as an inadequate reading curriculum, ill-conceived instruction, or a lack of experience with language or reading. MRD can vary in severity, just as can SWRD and SRCD, and children with MRD certainly can have good outcomes. However, the intervention needs of children with MRD always involve more than one type of difficulty, and sometimes many difficulties. Multicomponent interventions may be particularly useful for these students because of their needs in multiple areas of reading.

This chapter presents three examples of children with MRD. Again, the basic format of the chapter follows that of the two preceding ones, with the same conventions employed as in those chapters (e.g., use of age norms and 90–110 as the average range for academic achievement tests) and with the inclusion of achievement data for math and written expression. As is true for other profiles of reading difficulties, the underlying problems of students with MRD often are evident in academic domains beyond reading. For example, in written expression, students with MRD often have difficulties with both spelling and text-generation aspects of writing, reflecting both phonological and nonphonological language weaknesses. In math, they may evidence difficulties with automatic recall of facts as well as with more language-dependent aspects of mathematics such as solving word problems.

In the previous two chapters, I discussed types of interventions that will be relevant to the three children in this chapter. Therefore, in this chapter, I allude to the interventions but do not discuss most of them at length; readers may wish to refer to the other chapters for fuller descriptions.

DANIEL

Daniel, who just turned 10 years old, is at the end of fourth grade in a small rural school district. As a preschooler, Daniel had some developmental difficulties that primarily involved social development and social communication (e.g., lack of eye contact, lack of imitative play, problems interacting with other children). He was identified with an ASD at age 3. Like Lauren in Chapter 8, he has received special education support since his preschool years, and his ASD is relatively mild; he participates heavily in the general education program with the assistance of an instructional aide. Daniel has responded very well to therapy targeting his behavioral and social difficulties, and these areas have shown considerable improvement over the past few years. Except for occasional challenging situations, such as transitions to a new setting, his need for an aide has been minimal in Grade 4.

Throughout the primary grades, school reports and evaluations in Daniel's file emphasized his behavioral and social needs, not academic needs. Indeed, in these early grades, his reading and other academic skills were well within average range, and no significant concerns about his academic progress were noted. Daniel's school has an excellent Tier I reading curriculum and instruction with universal screening, and early assessments of Daniel's phonological awareness and decoding skills, including his ability to decode nonsense words, were soundly average as well. During fourth grade, however, some concerns about his reading have developed. These concerns have mainly involved two areas: slow reading of text and difficulties with specific aspects of reading comprehension. Daniel's oral reading in fourth-grade curriculum materials is consistently at instructional or independent level in terms of word accuracy (93%–100%), and when he does make an occasional word-recognition error, he usually self-corrects it easily. However, when timed recently by his special education teacher, his rate of reading in grade-appropriate texts was 75 words correct per minute on average, well below expectations for fourth grade (Hasbrouck & Tindal, 2006). Furthermore, educators have been implementing the CCSS into the English/language arts program, and Daniel is having particular problems with fourth-grade standards involving point of view and theme (for narratives) and summarization (for informational text). Sometimes, he also has difficulty keeping track of anaphoric references in a text, especially when the referent and the pronoun are separated by multiple sentences. Daniel is a sweet, hardworking boy; when his comprehension fails, he tends to plow on doggedly through the text without stopping or asking questions, as if oblivious to the fact that things are not really making sense.

Last year, as a third grader, Daniel took for the first time the high-stakes achievement test mandated in his state, with accommodations involving extended time and a quiet room. He scored at proficient level in reading as well as in writing and math. However, Daniel's scores for the fourth-grade test recently came back, and his performance had dropped to basic level for reading and writing (math was still at proficient level). These scores sufficiently concerned his parents that they took him for an independent educational evaluation. They now believe that Daniel has a significant reading problem that educators in his school district completely overlooked in the early grades.

Recent Assessment Data

Table 9.1 displays some test scores from Daniel's recent independent evaluation as well as other relevant assessment data. The scores in the "Word recognition and phonological skills" section do suggest that Daniel has mild difficulties with word-level reading skills, mainly in relation to speed of single-word reading; his standard scores on the Test of Word Reading Efficiency-2 (TOWRE-2; Torgesen et al., 2012) were both in the mid-80s. In addition, on the criterion-referenced GE Test of Coding Skills (Gallistel & Ellis, 1974), he had some difficulty reading words with common suffixes and multisyllabic words, although he did well on other word categories, including all one-syllable categories as well as many two-syllable words and words with endings (e.g., *magnet, candle, brushing*). Consistent with his performance in

Table 9.1. Recent assessment data for Daniel, an ending fourth grader, age 10 years

Word recognition and phonological skills	Text reading accuracy and fluency	Oral vocabulary and comprehension	Reading comprehension	Written expression and math	Other
WIAT-III Word Reading SS = 96; Pseudoword Decoding SS = 93 TOWRE-2 Sight Word Efficiency SS = 86; Phonemic Decoding Efficiency SS = 84 GE Test of Coding Skills: mastered all categories except words with common suffixes and multisyllabic words	WIAT-III Oral Reading Accuracy SS = 94; Oral Reading Rate SS = 72 Does usually attempt to correct word reading errors Oral reading in grade-appropriate curriculum materials is generally accurate (93%–100%) but slow, about 75 words cpm when timed by his classroom teacher	PPVT-4 SS = 109 WIAT-III Receptive Vocabulary SS = 110 WIAT-III Oral Discourse Comprehension SS = 92 CELF-5 Understanding Spoken Paragraphs SS = 94; Receptive Language Composite SS = 98 CELF-5 Pragmatics Profile = 7 TOPL-2 SS = 84	WIAT-III Reading Comprehension SS = 86 Some difficulties on classroom reading comprehension tasks, mainly related to slow reading and strategic aspects of reading (e.g., summarization and use of fix-up strategies for comprehension) Scored at basic level on fourth-grade state-mandated reading comprehension assessment (with accommodations)	WIAT-III Spelling SS = 81; represents all phonemes when spelling; limited knowledge of conventions WIAT-III Essay Composition SS = 71; problems with productivity, elaboration, and text organization Both handwriting and fact fluency in math are very slow; other aspects of math at grade level Scored at basic level on fourth-grade state-mandated writing assessment; proficient in math	WISC-IV Verbal Comprehension = 101; Perceptual Reasoning = 120; Working Memory = 99; Processing Speed = 90 Mild social difficulties in preschool years; identified with ASD at age 3½; special education support since preschool No history of significant medical, hearing, or vision problems; no history of decoding or phonological problems prior to Grade 4

Note: CELF-5 = Clinical Evaluation of Language Fundamentals, 5th edition (Semel, Wiig, & Secord, 2013); GE Test = Gallistel-Ellis Test of Coding Skills (Gallistel & Ellis, 1974); PPVT-IV = Peabody Picture Vocabulary Test, 4th edition (Dunn & Dunn, 2007); TOPL-2 = Test of Pragmatic Language, 2nd edition (Phelps-Terasaki & Phelps-Gunn, 2007); TOWRE-2 = Test of Word Reading Efficiency, 2nd edition (Torgesen, Wagner, & Rashotte, 2012); WIAT-III = Wechsler Individual Achievement Test, 3rd edition (Wechsler, 2009); WISC-IV = Wechsler Intelligence Scale for Children, 4th edition (Wechsler, 2003).

everyday curriculum materials, Daniel's scores on the Oral Reading Fluency subtest of the WIAT-III (Wechsler, 2009) showed that he read text with average accuracy as compared to other children his age; however, his rate of text reading was well below average.

Daniel's oral vocabulary scores were at the upper end of the average range, and his broad language comprehension was also average, except for pragmatic aspects of language tapped by the Pragmatics Profile of the CELF-5 (Semel et al., 2013) and the TOPL-2 (Phelps-Terasaki & Phelps-Gunn, 2007). Daniel's scores in these areas were both below average, although not very low. Likewise, Daniel's standard score on the Reading Comprehension subtest of the WIAT-III was 86, within the bottom quartile as compared to other children his age, but not extremely low.

Daniel's difficulties with speed are noticeable in written expression and mathematics as well as in reading. His fact fluency is weak, and his handwriting, though legible under untimed conditions, deteriorates rapidly when he is pressed for speed. He does well in most aspects of math other than fact recall, but he has myriad difficulties with written expression that extend well beyond handwriting. For instance, his spelling skills are below average, as shown by his WIAT-III score. He does represent all phonemes in words when spelling; his difficulties involve other types of knowledge, such as word-specific spelling knowledge. Examples of typical errors in his daily spelling include *sleaping* for *sleeping*, *pownd* for *pound*, or *graff* for *graph*, in which the intended word is obvious because it is spelled phonetically, but Daniel has not remembered the correct orthographic pattern associated with the word. In addition, he has numerous difficulties with organizational aspects of writing, such as use of appropriate text structure. His weakest area involved the Essay Composition subtest of the WIAT-III, in which he achieved a standard score of 71, a score that stemmed from low productivity, partly related to his handwriting weaknesses, as well as from poor elaboration of details and problems with organization of the text.

Daniel's independent evaluator also administered an IQ measure, the WISC-IV (Wechsler, 2003). Daniel's score on the four composite indices for this test were all within average range, except for Perceptual Reasoning, which was above average (standard score = 120). His lowest index involved Processing Speed, but at 90, this score was still in average range.

Conclusions

Daniel's profile of oral language abilities is reminiscent of Lauren in Chapter 8, with stronger single-word vocabulary than broad language comprehension, and with his weakest area involving pragmatic aspects of language, a frequent area of language difficulty for children with ASD. Overall, Daniel's oral language abilities are stronger than Lauren's are, but unlike Lauren, he has difficulties involving word-level reading skills. These word-level weaknesses primarily center on speed of single-word reading; Daniel is a nonautomatic word reader. (He does also have some difficulties with accuracy of decoding multisyllabic words.) Furthermore, although he does appear to monitor his comprehension in relation to word recognition, his difficulties with summarization and his failure to use strategies when his comprehension is faulty suggest that he is a nonstrategic comprehender. Daniel's nonstrategic approach to comprehension probably relates, at least in part, to the cognitive-linguistic weaknesses associated with his autism. Moreover, these two factors—Daniel's fluency problems and his strategic comprehension weaknesses—likely also interact with each other. For example, slow, dysfluent reading may tend to drain his mental resources for comprehending lengthy fourth-grade texts, making him less likely to generate or employ comprehension strategies when his comprehension fails.

Daniel's reading comprehension problems were clearly late emerging, and they are still relatively mild, although they are likely to worsen over time, especially if not targeted in intervention. The information in Daniel's file suggests that his word-reading problems also were late emerging and did not manifest in the first few grades of school. He might have had subtle phonological weaknesses (Lipka et al., 2006) that were not detected on the types of phonological awareness measures used in his school and that did not affect his word reading until he was expected to decode more complex words in the middle-elementary grades. Alternatively, his word-reading problems might relate to his difficulties developing speed and automaticity, which again might have a bigger impact on his word reading in the middle-elementary grades than in the earliest grades. In any case, it appears that Daniel's teachers did not overlook his word-reading problems in the primary grades; rather, like his reading comprehension weaknesses, his word-reading difficulties actually did not emerge until Grade 4.

Two additional points are important. First, although Daniel has difficulties with speed and automaticity of basic skills across multiple academic domains—handwriting and math facts as well as word reading—he has many cognitive strengths, especially in nonverbal areas, and his broad language comprehension is average; he is not conceptually or intellectually "slow." Second, Daniel provides an example of a student with ASD who has word-level reading difficulties as well as comprehension difficulties. Although some students at the high-functioning end of the autism spectrum are like Lauren—learning to decode with ease even in a holistic instructional program—a significant subgroup of these children do have weaknesses in word-level reading skills (Nation et al., 2006; Norbury & Nation, 2011). Therefore, their instructional programs in reading must provide explicit phonics instruction until the children have learned to decode rather than focus exclusively on comprehension or emphasizing sight word methods. Daniel's school has a strong core reading curriculum with an effective phonics component, so fortunately, he did receive this kind of instruction in the primary grades, which likely did facilitate his learning to decode most words accurately, if not with a high degree of speed.

Recommendations for Intervention

Daniel requires intervention in decoding of multisyllabic words, reading fluency, and developing a strategic approach to comprehension, including explicit instruction for his specific comprehension weaknesses (e.g., point of view and anaphora), all of which can be delivered as part of his special education program. Examples of instructional activities that could benefit him include explicit teaching of morphology integrated with spelling intervention and general-education vocabulary instruction; timed, repeated readings of text and continuous reading; and explicit teaching of comprehension strategies such as summarization and the use of graphic organizers. For his difficulties with anaphora, a technique that helps him track specific referents of pronouns in a text such as highlighting a given pronoun and referent with the same color might be helpful. In addition, like Lauren, he might benefit from an intervention like perspective-taking through narratives (Dodd et al., 2011). As previously discussed in relation to other children, inclusion of oral comprehension activities as well as reading comprehension activities in Daniel's intervention is vital; furthermore, given his fluency difficulties and relatively strong broad oral language comprehension, Daniel might find it easier to learn some comprehension skills, such as summarization, initially in the context of listening rather than reading. An important consideration for Daniel involves ensuring that he has the threshold level of reading fluency necessary for applying comprehension strategies to his reading (Willingham, 2006–2007). For instance, he might be more successful applying summarization strategies in reading if he initially practiced these strategies in texts that he can read fluently (i.e., independent-level rather than instructional-level texts).

Teachers also should include multiple aspects of writing, beyond spelling, into Daniel's reading intervention. Explicit teaching about text structure could benefit Daniel's reading comprehension as well as his written expression; teaching him to write clearly, with unambiguous referents for pronouns such as *he, she,* and *it,* could likewise profit both his reading and writing. Daniel also needs comprehensive writing instruction for its own sake, including ways to address his limited speed of handwriting, such as through assistive technology. Daniel's progress monitoring should employ multiple measures, including those targeting decoding of multisyllabic words (e.g., out-of-context measures of unfamiliar real words or pseudowords), reading fluency (e.g., ORF CBMs), and comprehension (e.g., embedded comprehension checks that emphasize questions tapping Daniel's weaknesses).

In fact, Daniel had an excellent special education program that incorporated intervention in all the mentioned areas of reading; he made good progress in all these areas except for reading fluency. His rate of reading text continues to be relatively slow, and he does require ongoing special education support as well as some general-education accommodations. Now in junior high, he no longer needs an instructional aide, and he generally functions well in mainstream classes. With accommodations involving extended time, he scored at proficient level on the most recent state-mandated reading comprehension assessment.

VALENTINA

Valentina is age 6 years, 11 months, at the end of first grade in a suburban school district. She is a native Spanish speaker, and very few other children in her district speak Spanish, although a handful of other language-minority children speak languages such as Vietnamese and Chinese. Because of the small number of ELLs who speak the same language, the district does not provide bilingual education, although there are ESL services. Valentina did receive ESL services in kindergarten, but she performed well enough on the state's language assessment for these services to be discontinued after her first year of school. She has no history of preschool language delay and no history of significant medical, hearing, vision, or behavior problems. It is unknown whether there is any family history of reading difficulties.

Born in the United States in a large city distant from her current school district, Valentina entered kindergarten with some knowledge of English. However, Spanish is the primary language spoken at home, and Valentina did not attend preschool, so Spanish was her dominant language at the time she started formal schooling. Her conversational English has developed quickly in the past 2 years, and she has had no difficulties making friends or adjusting to most demands of school. She enjoys math and has progressed typically in that subject. However, she has struggled mightily in reading, especially in meeting the burgeoning decoding demands of first grade. Valentina's school has a haphazard, incidental approach to teaching phonemic awareness and phonics, and she did not pick up decoding skills as easily from this approach as did some other children, who tended to have much greater preschool exposure to literacy than she did. She continued to flounder into the middle of first grade, when her classroom teacher sought the advice of the school's special educator. (There was no universal screening program.) The special educator administered several CBMs as well as a criterion-referenced measure of decoding to Valentina, assessments that amply documented her need for intervention. Since late January, the special educator has been providing her with explicit, supplemental phonemic awareness and phonics instruction in a small group with two other classmates; Valentina has shown rapid progress, the best in her small group, although she is not yet meeting grade expectations for decoding. Now that it is June, Valentina's interventionist readministered the previous assessments, along with an IRI, to assess her progress and plan for the next school year.

Recent Assessment Data

Table 9.2 displays Valentina's most recent assessment results, from the end of Grade 1. The "Word recognition and phonological skills" section of the table

Table 9.2. Recent assessment data for Valentina, an ending first grader, age 6 years, 11 months

Word recognition and phonological skills	Text reading accuracy and fluency	Oral vocabulary and comprehension	Reading comprehension	Written expression and math	Other
DIBELS Next Nonsense Word Fluency (Grade 1 curriculum-based measures [CBMs]): CLS = below benchmark; Whole Words Read = below benchmark Tries to decode but does not know some letter sounds, especially those involving vowel patterns such as oo or aw; no difficulty with phoneme blending or segmenting CPS: could decode short and long vowel words; other categories < 40%	DIBELS Next Oral Reading Fluency (Grade 1 passages) = well below benchmark (both accuracy and words cpm) Does not always attempt to self-correct errors Prosody is poor Comprehensive Reading Inventory (CRI) passages (English): no independent level; instructional level = preprimer	CRI listening comprehension level = primer (English narrative passages); CRI listening comprehension level = Grade 2 (Spanish narrative passages) Sometimes has difficulty with oral comprehension questions during teacher read-alouds, mainly due to limitations in English vocabulary knowledge	Difficulties on the CRI passages involved comprehension as well as decoding DIBELS Next Retell (after oral reading fluency [ORF] passages) = below benchmark Sometimes has difficulty answering comprehension questions even when reading books that are at her instructional level	Spells most short-vowel words correctly; difficulty spelling other word types; spelling of common irregular words is poor Written expression is poor due to problems with grammar as well as spelling Math is grade appropriate Handwriting is excellent	Native Spanish speaker, born in United States; mainly Spanish spoken at home No history of preschool language delay; no history of significant medical, hearing, vision, or behavior problems; family history unknown Has been receiving phonemic awareness and phonics intervention since middle of Grade 1; making good progress as shown by CBM but not yet at benchmark

Note: CPS = CORE Phonics Survey (Consortium on Reading Excellence, 2008); DIBELS = Dynamic Indicators of Basic Early Literacy Skills (Good & Kaminski, 2011).

shows that she was still below benchmark for out-of-context word reading on first-grade DIBELS Next CBMs (Good & Kaminski, 2011), although her scores have improved since midyear, when they were well below benchmark. Moreover, at midyear, before intervention, Valentina had not mastered the decoding of *any* word categories on the CPS (CORE, 2008), and she had particular difficulties reading nonsense words. Now, however, she can consistently decode a variety of short-vowel words, including those with consonant digraphs or blends such as *splint, block,* or *smash,* and she can read long-vowel words as well (e.g., *bride, snake, toe*). Furthermore, she read nonsense words in these categories as well as real words, suggesting that she was not relying only on memorization of specific words but has developed the ability to decode unfamiliar words. Phoneme blending, once difficult for her, is no longer a problem. In her most recent round of assessments, she looked carefully at words and attempted to decode them rather than guessing based only on the first letter or two, as she did early in the school year.

Nevertheless, Valentina still does not know sounds for many common letter patterns, especially vowel combination or vowel-*r* patterns such as *oo, ar,* or *ow,* so she cannot decode unfamiliar words with these patterns, as expected by the end of Grade 1 (see, e.g., the Reading: Foundational Skills standards for Grade 1 at http://www.corestandards.org/ELA-Literacy/RF/1). Her text fluency in grade-appropriate text was still well below benchmark as measured by DIBELS Next ORF passages, both in terms of accuracy and rate; furthermore, her performance on retell tasks associated with the ORF passages was below benchmark as well. In grade-appropriate texts, Valentina's oral reading is halting with many decoding errors and poor prosody of reading, mainly because the words simply are too difficult for her to decode. (Her rate is consistent with her instructional reading level.) In grade-appropriate texts, she also does not consistently attempt to correct errors. She reads much more accurately and with better prosody and comprehension monitoring in the simple decodable texts that her interventionist uses. Still, even in these texts, Valentina sometimes has difficulties with comprehension, often due to vocabulary limitations. For example, in one session in which the children in her intervention group were reading a decodable text titled *The Sunset Pond* (Appleton-Smith, 1997), Valentina read with a high degree of accuracy but could not answer questions about the meanings of words such as *dusk.* She also did not know an alternate meaning of the word *bed* (i.e., a bed of flowers as opposed to a bed that one sleeps in). Lack of vocabulary knowledge affected her understanding of parts of the text and her ability to answer some reading comprehension questions. Valentina's classroom teacher has noticed similar vocabulary difficulties in classroom activities involving teacher read-alouds of age-appropriate children's books, difficulties that often involve words well known to most other first graders.

In addition, Valentina's reading interventionist administered the Comprehensive Reading Inventory (CRI; Cooter, Flynt, & Cooter, 2007), an IRI with forms in both English and Spanish. On the English graded word lists, Valentina scored at an independent level on the preprimer (early Grade 1) list and at an instructional level on the primer list (middle of Grade 1). On the English passages, however, she could read only the preprimer passage; that passage was at instructional level for her. She willingly attempted the primer passage but scored at a frustration level due to difficulties with both the decoding demands of the text and limited vocabulary knowledge even of some words she could decode accurately. Reading measures were not administered in Spanish because all Valentina's reading instruction has been in English. Nevertheless, another teacher at the school does speak Spanish, and this educator administered a listening comprehension test using both English and Spanish narrative passages. Valentina's listening comprehension was significantly better on the Spanish passages, a listening level of Grade 2 as opposed to a primer listening level in English.

Finally, although Valentina's math skills are solidly grade appropriate, she has problems with written expression, particularly with spelling of common irregular words (e.g., *have, should*) and with grammar. Many of her grammatical mistakes mirror those of Mateo in Chapter 8, such as use of double negatives. Valentina's handwriting is excellent, and she does spell most short-vowel words correctly, including those with consonant blends and digraphs (e.g., *blast, spend, brush*).

Conclusions

Valentina clearly has grasped the alphabetic principle, but her decoding skills still are not accurate, even for many one-syllable words; she is an inaccurate word reader. However, her reading comprehension difficulties are not entirely attributable to faulty decoding, but also involve English language comprehension and, in particular, limited vocabulary knowledge in English. These difficulties are evident even when she reads material at her instructional level that she decodes well. Therefore, she has a mixed reading difficulty rather than a specific word-recognition difficulty. Valentina's apparently typical early language development in Spanish, the inadequacies in her core reading instruction (e.g., a haphazard approach to teaching phonemic awareness and phonics), and her strong response to phonics intervention all suggest a child who is a curriculum casualty, not one with a disability. Although Valentina's performance on the IRI should be viewed very cautiously because of potential reliability issues (Farrall, 2012; Spector, 2005), her good comprehension when listening to narrative passages in Spanish, as opposed to English, also tends to suggest a child whose difficulties involve limited English exposure rather than an intrinsic language disability. Furthermore, nothing in her performance suggests a possible ID, emotional disability, sensory impairment, attentional disorder, autism, health impairment, or any other disability. Thus, a referral to special education would not currently be appropriate.

Although her decoding problems are similar to those of many children with LDs, Valentina is unlikely to be eligible for services in that category, as most authorities would not view her as a student with LDs, despite her low achievement, for several reasons. First, although she is not yet meeting grade expectations, she has shown a strong response to phonemic awareness and phonics intervention, and she is on a trajectory to catch up in decoding. Second, she does not appear to meet exclusionary criteria, because her reading problems seem mainly due to her limited exposure to English and to inadequate core instruction. And third, her English vocabulary weaknesses would probably make it difficult for her to meet criteria involving either an IQ–achievement discrepancy or a listening comprehension–reading comprehension discrepancy (in districts using these criteria for LDs) because she would have to be very far behind in reading to attain the requisite discrepancy.

Valentina's phonics intervention should continue until she reaches grade expectations in reading but with a crucial addition: Explicit instruction in English vocabulary and academic language must also be included in her intervention. Valentina's vocabulary and language weaknesses already affect her reading comprehension, and without intervention, these effects will certainly worsen. To this point, the impact of vocabulary limitations on her math and written expression performance has been minimal, perhaps because of relatively low vocabulary demands in these areas for Grade 1. However, without intervention, teachers will likely see an increasing influence of vocabulary and academic language limitations on Valentina's math, writing, and reading performance in future grades.

Recommendations for Intervention

Valentina's phonics intervention should continue, with an emphasis on the word categories she cannot yet decode (e.g., one-syllable words with vowel combinations and vowel-*r*). She no longer evidences difficulties with phoneme blending and segmentation, and her decoding and spelling skills also suggest that she has adequate phonemic awareness; for instance, she can consistently read and spell unfamiliar words such as *splint* and *spend* that have five or six phonemes. Thus she no longer appears to require phonemic awareness intervention as part of her phonics program. As her decoding skills develop, Valentina should be able to read a much wider range of texts beyond the decodable books in which she is now placed for intervention; these texts should continue to be at her instructional level and provide practice decoding word categories that she has learned. Continued oral reading of text, with feedback and scaffolding from her interventionist, is very important to help her learn to apply her phonics skills to reading text and to develop reading fluency. Other fluency activities, such as repeated readings of familiar text, may also sometimes be helpful, although Valentina does not appear to require substantial fluency *intervention* because her rate of reading is commensurate with her instructional reading level. (She does require the usual opportunities for practice reading text and fluency-building that most children her age require.)

To develop her academic vocabulary and language, explicit teaching of words that Valentina encounters in texts (e.g., *dusk*) or in the general education curriculum, as well as teacher read-alouds such as vocabulary interventions involving storybook reading (e.g., Beck & McKeown, 2007; Loftus et al., 2010; Pullen et al., 2010), would be useful. Other potentially valuable approaches include explicit teaching about Spanish–English cognates, as discussed in relation to Mateo in Chapter 8, as well as direct teaching of morphology—for example, common roots, prefixes, and suffixes in English. Teaching about morphology can be helpful in multiple ways, benefiting Valentina's decoding and spelling as well as her vocabulary knowledge. Unfortunately, Valentina's core reading instruction does not provide much explicit vocabulary or morphological instruction, especially in the primary grades, and a greater emphasis in these areas could benefit many students, not only Valentina. Nevertheless, given the extent of her vocabulary weaknesses as compared with her classmates, it is likely that, even with stronger core instruction, she would still require supplemental vocabulary intervention.

As Valentina becomes more capable of reading independently, both her classroom teacher and her interventionist should encourage and support her independent reading in appropriate texts. Wide independent reading may help her build not only reading fluency but also vocabulary, academic language, and background knowledge. In addition, writing activities targeting multiple areas, especially spelling, grammar, and vocabulary, could further develop her reading abilities. Some of these activities could be implemented via differentiated core instruction in general education; for example, the classroom teacher could provide feedback and modeling for Valentina of correct English grammar during a classroom writing block in which various students' writing needs are addressed. Valentina's progress in intervention should be monitored through multiple measures targeting decoding accuracy and reading fluency as well as vocabulary and comprehension, with changes to her intervention or further evaluation if these measures do not indicate adequate progress.

KEVIN

Kevin, who attends a large suburban school district, is nearing the end of third grade. He is 8 years and 10 months old. Kevin first received special education services as a preschooler, when he was identified with mild speech-language problems as well as with some behavioral difficulties involving hyperactivity and impulsivity. By the end of kindergarten, standardized tests showed his speech-language abilities to be age appropriate, and his speech-language services were discontinued. However, Kevin had ongoing problems with attention and behavior, and by Grade 2, his pediatrician had identified him with ADHD. He has been receiving special education services in the Other

Health Impaired (OHI) category since the middle of Grade 2. He has no other medical, hearing, or vision problems, and there is no family history of serious reading difficulties.

Kevin participates heavily in the general education program, and most of his special education services involve a "push-in" model that facilitates his inclusion in core general education subjects. He has had difficulties developing automatic recall of addition and subtraction facts as well as passing his weekly Grade 3 spelling tests, and the special education teacher does some supplemental practice with him in those areas. For the most part, however, the focus has been on Kevin's behavioral and attentional needs rather than on academic intervention. For example, he tends to lose interest in or become overwhelmed with lengthy writing tasks, and the special educator helps him plan his writing and stay on task. Similarly, during independent reading blocks, Kevin's attention often wanders, and he gets into trouble in minor ways that annoy both his classmates and teachers, such as repeatedly bumping a classmate because of frequent shifting in his seat. Occasionally, he completely balks at having to do an assignment and, rarely, even has a tantrum.

The approach to universal screening in reading at Kevin's school involves assessments of letter-name knowledge and rhyming in kindergarten, as well as an IRI in the primary grades. Kevin met grade expectations on these assessments in kindergarten through Grade 2 on isolated word lists as well as on passages. Furthermore, on his comprehensive evaluation for special education in Grade 2, he scored within average range on two subtests measuring his reading comprehension and his ability to read real words. However, this year, in Grade 3, Kevin's instructional level in passages was below expectations, and he often did not attempt to correct word-reading errors, reading quickly through the text as if eager to get it over with. Still, Kevin's teachers view his problems as involving effort and attention, not poor reading. His general education teacher, a warm woman who is very fond of Kevin—let us call her Ms. Niceteacher—points out that Kevin does well on classroom reading tasks when he is highly engaged. I observed Kevin in one of these tasks, a reading lesson focused on a children's novel set during a hurricane, which Kevin greatly enjoyed, in part, because he has a strong interest in storms and weather. The children had read a chapter from the book for homework, and the lesson I observed focused on discussion of the story and relating it to another text that the teacher had previously read to the class. Kevin participated eagerly in this lesson and seemed to understand the story well, even adding some insightful observations about one of the characters in the story.

Unlike his teachers, Kevin's parents think he has a significant reading problem, one about which they have become increasingly disturbed over the past year. They say that they often have to read classroom texts assigned as homework to Kevin because he cannot read them himself. Getting him to complete homework can be a nightmare of tears, torn worksheets, and angry outbursts. Although, at the recommendation of their pediatrician, they have him on medication for his ADHD, there have been problems with side effects—mainly Kevin's lack of appetite—and they are considering discontinuing the medication. Now they are not even sure whether he has ADHD at all; they think he might have an LD in reading. They pressed administrators at Kevin's school for an independent evaluation of his reading abilities, and eventually administrators agreed to this request.

Recent Assessment Data

Table 9.3 displays assessment data for Kevin, including scores from his most recent independent evaluation, which involved tests of written expression and mathematics as well as reading. The reading data show that Kevin has difficulties in multiple components of reading, including word recognition and decoding, fluency, and reading comprehension. Although Kevin met grade expectations on the graded word lists of the QRI (Leslie & Caldwell, 2006), standardized subtests from the KTEA-II (Kaufman & Kaufman, 2004) indicated difficulties in his ability to read real words as well as nonsense words but especially the latter. On the CTOPP-2 (Wagner et al., 2013), Kevin's phonological awareness composite was below average, suggesting a phonologically based reading problem.

On the QRI passages, Kevin's highest instructional level was only in Grade 2, a full year below his current grade placement, and on the GORT-V (Wiederholt & Bryant, 2012), both Kevin's word accuracy and his rate were below average. (As was true for Valentina, assessments indicated that Kevin's rate was consistent with his instructional reading level.) Kevin's oral reading sometimes lacked prosody, another sign of fluency weaknesses. In addition, although his scaled score for comprehension on the GORT-V was at the lower end of the average range, Kevin's scores on two other reading comprehension measures, the Reading Comprehension subtest of the KTEA-II and the Passage Comprehension subtest of the WJ-III (Woodcock et al., 2007), were both well below average. On all these reading comprehension measures, although inaccurate decoding accounted for many of Kevin's difficulties, he sometimes made errors even when he had decoded correctly. For instance, if he did not immediately know the answer to a comprehension question, he was inclined to shrug his shoulders and respond, "Don't know." The examiner often could not persuade him to make an attempt at the question, even when the answer involved a relatively easy "common sense" type of response for which he probably could have received some credit. On other occasions, when he had decoded correctly and did try to answer a comprehension question, he simply seemed to miss the point of a sentence or passage.

As displayed in the "Oral vocabulary and comprehension" section of Table 9.3, Kevin scored within average range on all standardized assessments of his oral vocabulary and oral language comprehension and also scored at grade expectations for listening comprehension on the QRI. Nevertheless, he has academic difficulties in math and written expression as well as reading.

Table 9.3. Recent assessment data for Kevin, an ending third grader, age 8 years, 10 months

Word recognition and phonological skills	Text reading accuracy and fluency	Oral vocabulary and comprehension	Reading comprehension	Written expression and math	Other
KTEA-II Word Recognition SS = 87 (untimed) KTEA-II Nonsense Word Decoding SS = 80 (untimed) CTOPP-2 PA Composite SS = 84; other composites in average range QRI word lists: independent = Grade 2; instructional = Grade 3	GORT-5 Oral Reading Quotient SS = 85; Accuracy = 7; Rate = 7 QRI passages: independent level = Grade 1; instructional = Grade 2 Does not consistently attempt to self-correct errors; prosody is also inconsistent	ROWPVT-4 SS = 95 EOWPVT-4 SS = 99 KTEA-II Listening Comprehension SS = 90 WJ-III Oral Comprehension SS = 94 QRI listening comprehension level = Grade 3	KTEA-II Reading Comprehension = 70 WJ-III Passage Comprehension = 78 GORT-5 Comprehension = 8 Comprehension errors did not always reflect problems in decoding Tends to become frustrated in classroom reading tasks; gives up or is unwilling to attempt task	KTEA-II Spelling SS = 80 KTEA-II Written Expression SS = 78 KTEA-II Math Computation SS = 90; Math Concepts and Applications SS = 82 Difficulty on classroom spelling tests Difficulties with mechanics as well as text generation and planning aspects of writing Automatic recall of facts is poor Handwriting is often illegible	Stanford-Binet: Verbal IQ = 90; Nonverbal IQ = 88; Full-Scale = 89; some problems with working memory and executive function History of early problems with speech/language as well as impulsivity and hyperactivity; identified with attention-deficit/hyperactivity disorder (ADHD) in Grade 2; receiving special education in Other Health Impaired (OHI) category No other significant medical, hearing, or vision problems; no family history of reading difficulties

Note: CTOPP-2 = Comprehensive Test of Phonological Processing, 2nd edition (Wagner, Torgesen, Rashotte, & Pearson, 2013); EOWPVT-4 = Expressive One-Word Picture Vocabulary Test, 4th edition (Brownell, 2010a); GORT-5 = Gray Oral Reading Test, 5th edition (Wiederholt & Bryant, 2012); KTEA-II = Kaufman Test of Educational Achievement, 2nd edition (Kaufman & Kaufman, 2004); QRI = Qualitative Reading Inventory (Leslie & Caldwell, 2006); ROWPVT-4 = Receptive One-Word Picture Vocabulary Test, 4th edition (Brownell, 2010b); WJ-III = Woodcock-Johnson Tests of Achievement, 3rd edition (Woodcock, McGrew, & Mather, 2007).

In mathematics, his performance on a measure of math concept knowledge and applications from the KTEA-II was below average, as was his performance on the KTEA-II written expression subtest. In writing, he had multiple areas of difficulty, including problems with not only spelling but also other mechanics of writing such as punctuation, text generation aspects of writing (e.g., elaboration of detail), and organization and planning. Kevin's handwriting also often has poor legibility.

Finally, although an IQ measure was not part of Kevin's recent academic evaluation, an IQ measure was given when he was in Grade 2 as part of his evaluation for special education. The scores from this administration are in the "Other" section of Table 9.3 and indicate that on the Stanford-Binet (Roid, 2003), Kevin had a full-scale IQ of 89, a verbal IQ of 90, and a nonverbal IQ of 88, all at the lower end of the average range (using 85–115 as average range). Additional tests administered by this evaluator suggested difficulties in working memory and executive function, consistent with Kevin's diagnosis of ADHD.

Conclusions

As Kevin's parents have maintained, he does have significant reading problems. His reading difficulties partly involve inaccurate word reading based in phonological weaknesses, with inaccurate reading affecting his reading fluency; although he sometimes reads quickly, he cannot truly be fluent if he is not accurate as well as fast and effortless in reading words. Kevin's inconsistent prosody in oral reading is further evidence of his lack of fluency. In addition, Kevin has reading comprehension difficulties as shown by his performance on standardized measures in these areas. (As discussed for Lauren in Chapter 8, in deciding whether Kevin functions below expectations, educators should weigh his performance on standardized measures of reading comprehension much more heavily than his performance on an IRI.) Moreover, inaccurate decoding does not account for all Kevin's reading comprehension difficulties, because he sometimes has difficulty in comprehending material he has decoded correctly; he has a mixed reading difficulty, not a specific word-recognition difficulty. Kevin's lack of consistent comprehension monitoring and his tendency to become overwhelmed by reading tasks, as shown by his unwillingness to even attempt some comprehension questions and his outbursts both at home and in school, suggest that he is a nonstrategic comprehender.

What about Kevin's strong performance in the classroom reading lesson with Ms. Niceteacher? This kind of performance persuaded many of his teachers that his difficulties were more about behavior and effort than about reading (and not all viewed him quite as warmly as Ms. Niceteacher did). Indeed, Kevin was able to perform well in instructional contexts that provided a great deal of oral discussion, support, and engagement, and his participation in such instructional activities should certainly continue, because he can benefit from them. However, activities like the one involving the book set during a hurricane involve *oral language* more than actual *reading*; when required to read—at home or at school—Kevin often did not do well. Moreover, requirements for independent reading on a wide array of topics, not all of which Kevin will find as fascinating as he does hurricanes, will escalate as he advances in school, likely leading to more reading comprehension difficulties unless his underlying reading needs are remediated.

Kevin's lack of strategic reading has somewhat different underpinnings than Daniel's. First, Kevin obviously has decoding difficulties that have not yet been addressed in intervention and that likely cause considerable frustration for him. It is difficult to know exactly how early these problems emerged, because, as in the case of Henry in Chapter 7, Kevin's school was not using screening measures sensitive to phonological decoding difficulties; such measures were not even employed in his Grade 2 comprehensive evaluation for special education. He might well have had mild decoding weaknesses in kindergarten or Grade 1 for which he was able to compensate by using sight word knowledge and context, functioning at grade expectations on graded word lists and passages. These word-level difficulties clearly have begun affecting his reading in third grade, if not before then, taxing his mental resources for focusing on the meaning of the text, and making his development of strategic comprehension—just beginning in third grade for typical readers—much more difficult. Kevin's unrecognized reading problems very likely contributed to his behavioral and attentional difficulties, because children often cannot sustain attention to work that is not at an appropriate level of difficulty for them, and some children will act out behaviorally when frustrated.

Second, Kevin appears to have difficulties with executive function and working memory, problems implicated in attentional disorders (Barkley, 1997) and that can make an independent contribution to reading comprehension (Eason et al., 2012; Sesma et al., 2009). Executive function and working memory also influence children's writing development (Altemeier, Jones, Abbott, & Berninger, 2006; McCutchen, 2000), and Kevin has numerous difficulties with written expression that could partly reflect underlying problems in working memory and executive function—for example, difficulties with planning and organization of writing. Kevin's problems with hyperactivity and impulsivity manifested even before he started kindergarten and before difficulties in learning to read would have affected his behavior, tending to support the view that Kevin has ADHD. Also, Kevin's history of early speech-language problems implies an intrinsic vulnerability to reading difficulties; his overall pattern of poor phonological awareness, decoding and spelling weaknesses, and poor automatic recall of facts suggests the *possibility* of dyslexia, although, despite nearly a year and a half of special education services, he has not yet had appropriate intervention for his reading problems! Unfortunately, in Kevin's case, a vulnerability to phonologically based reading difficulties was likely compounded by lack of prompt intervention, attentional and behavioral issues, and an ineffective approach to assessment. Although many of Kevin's teachers, such as Ms. Niceteacher, were well intended and truly wanted to help him, inappropriate screening assessments and failure to assess phonological skills in his comprehensive evaluation contributed to their overlooking his reading difficulties.

Recommendations for Intervention

Kevin clearly requires phonics intervention integrated with spelling intervention at his current level of functioning, which will very likely involve the use of different words and word patterns than the spelling program used in his third-grade classroom. Although Kevin's intervention could be delivered through a variety of models, including both "push-in" and "pull-out" services, it will require much more than simply supporting him in doing classwork; Kevin needs phonics and spelling intervention that targets his specific weaknesses. To design this intervention, more focused assessment of Kevin's decoding (and spelling) skills is necessary, through a test that provides information about his ability to decode specific word patterns (e.g., a test such as the CPS [CORE, 2008] or the decoding section of the PAT 2 [Robertson & Salter, 2007]). Kevin's interventionist also should further assess his phonological awareness, specifically his phoneme blending and phoneme segmentation skills; if he demonstrates problems in these areas that interfere with his decoding and spelling of unfamiliar words, then phonemic awareness instruction should be included with his phonics and spelling interventions.

In addition to the types of intervention mentioned already, Kevin needs to practice applying his decoding skills in oral reading of text at his instructional level with his interventionist, which can help him build fluency and will also provide opportunities for his interventionist to guide his development of other important reading abilities, such as comprehension monitoring. With regard to comprehension, Kevin might benefit from the types of "executive function" strategies discussed in relation to Lauren in Chapter 8, especially as he advances into fourth grade. These strategies must be tailored to his specific needs in reading comprehension as well as written expression and should be explicitly taught (Meltzer, 2010). As with many of the other children discussed here, writing activities can reinforce and further develop his reading skills, but a comprehensive writing program, beyond its benefits for reading, is also very important. Kevin's writing needs are extensive, involving not only spelling, planning, and organization but also punctuation, capitalization, and handwriting.

Given Kevin's considerable academic needs and the fact that he already receives special education, it would make sense for his literacy interventions to be delivered through his special education program by his special educator. Kevin's primary disability is unclear, and he could be eligible for special education in different categories, including his current category of OHI (if his primary disability is decided to be ADHD) or LDs (if his primary disability is determined to involve reading). Eligibility in the area of LDs would require him to meet additional criteria besides the low reading achievement documented in Table 9.3, including insufficient response to intervention (if that criterion is used by his district) or an IQ–achievement discrepancy (if used by his district). However, Kevin probably would not meet IQ–achievement discrepancy criteria in relation to basic reading, as opposed to reading comprehension, because of the relatively small gap between his full-scale IQ of 89 and his word-reading scores; basic reading is one of his most important instructional needs, without which intervention in other areas such as reading comprehension will likely fail. In any case, the most important issue educationally is not Kevin's designated eligibility category but for him to receive appropriate help.

Although research-based literacy intervention may certainly improve Kevin's problems with behavior and attention, he may well require further support in these latter areas. Kevin's parents should certainly discuss their concerns about medication side effects further with their pediatrician. Although with good medical management, medications do appear helpful to many children with attentional disorders, authorities on ADHD have generally emphasized a multimodal approach to treatment (e.g., Jensen et al., 2001). A *multimodal approach* involves not only appropriate medication, when warranted, but also appropriate behavioral supports and behavioral interventions as well as educational interventions for children who require them, as Kevin obviously does. So far, unfortunately, Kevin's treatment has been more unimodal than multimodal. Instead, his treatment should include instructional interventions and behavioral supports (e.g., clear rules and expectations for behavior, positive reinforcement of desired behaviors, appropriate consequences for undesired behaviors), not simply medication. In fact, good educational intervention coupled with suitable behavioral supports might help to reduce or even eliminate his need for medication.

TIER I READING INSTRUCTION AND PROGRESS MONITORING

Students with MRD should continue to participate in Tier I progress monitoring, and they can benefit from participation in the Tier I literacy program. For example, like Kevin, many children with MRD can learn from classroom reading activities that involve oral discussion; like Valentina, they can often profit from classroom writing activities with differentiation of instruction to target their specific literacy needs. Similar to children with SWRD and SRCD, those with MRD require a broad, comprehensive program of literacy instruction with good integration of interventions; their participation in Tier I instruction may require certain types of supports (e.g., preteaching of vocabulary, greater scaffolding of instruction, easier texts). Children with MRD can also benefit from a range of assistive technology options, including the types of technology supports discussed in Chapters 7 and 8.

SUMMING UP

Although individual students with MRD may vary in important ways, they all share a profile of problems in word reading coupled with problems in at least one (and often multiple) core comprehension abilities or types of knowledge. For these students, good intervention therefore must address both word recognition and the specific core comprehension abilities in which individual students are weak. Because of these core comprehension weaknesses, intervention and progress monitoring for students with MRD involve the same kinds of challenges discussed at the end of Chapter 8 in relation to SRCD, such as limitations in available progress-monitoring tools and difficulties in gauging adequacy of progress. Good measures are available to monitor these students' progress in relation to word-recognition skills, however, as are generally effective ways of addressing their word-recognition difficulties.

One particularly important issue for students with MRD may involve the need to set priorities in intervention. For example, students with MRD whose word-recognition skills are especially limited may benefit from an initial emphasis on improving word recognition before an emphasis on learning comprehension strategies such as summarization, particularly in relation to applying those strategies in actual reading. Oral development of strategies and of other comprehension-related skills and knowledge such as vocabulary can and should occur in tandem with development of word-recognition skills.

Students with MRD tend to have much broader learning problems than do students with SWRD, even broader than those with SRCD. However, IQ testing is still not essential to rule out IDs in most students with MRD, unless the children evidence significant problems with adaptive functioning, such as with self-help skills (e.g., dressing themselves) and social skills. (Under IDEA 2004, children are not eligible for identification as students with an ID based only on an IQ score; they must have impairments in adaptive functioning as well.) With regard to identification of LDs, in districts using RTI criteria and no IQ–achievement discrepancy, students with MRD could potentially be eligible for services in the LD category if they showed inadequate response to research-based interventions and met exclusionary criteria. However, as discussed for Kevin and Valentina, many of these students would be much harder to qualify with the use of an IQ–achievement discrepancy because difficulties in core comprehension abilities that affect reading comprehension—such as vocabulary, language comprehension, or executive function—also tend to influence IQ test performance, yielding a lower IQ score. Of course, this means that many ELLs or children from poverty backgrounds would not be eligible with the use of an IQ–achievement discrepancy, even when they actually do have dyslexia or language-based LDs.

The children discussed in the past three chapters provide examples of some of the challenges that educators face in providing effective reading instruction to all students. Most teachers care about their students and genuinely want to help them succeed; as certain examples suggest, however, some educators are much more effective than others in doing so. The next chapter considers the knowledge and skills needed to teach not only typical readers but also children with a variety of reading difficulties to learn to read well.

10

The Role of Teacher Effectiveness in Children's Reading Achievement

When I first began my career as a teacher of reading, my classroom happened to be next door to that of a veteran educator with a sterling reputation for teaching literacy. During spare moments, operating on the theory that a good model can be worth a thousand words, I often lingered by my classroom door to observe this teacher working with her students. Happily, her reputation turned out to be well deserved. Although I had been fortunate to have good preservice preparation in reading, over time, I learned a great deal from observing this teacher's wonderful model—about how to teach explicitly and unambiguously, provide clear and constructive feedback, and engage and motivate children at different levels of achievement.

This chapter considers the knowledge and skills needed to be a successful teacher of reading as well as how schools of education might better prepare elementary-level educators to teach reading to children from a variety of backgrounds and with a range of instructional needs, including the kinds of students discussed in the past three chapters. No teacher can be maximally effective without the right supports, such as an appropriate curriculum, books, and administrative leadership; furthermore, knowledgeable, well-prepared teachers certainly will not eliminate all reading problems. However, there are good reasons why many researchers and policy makers have focused on trying to improve teacher quality. First, effective teachers matter, especially (though not only) for children with a vulnerability to reading difficulties. Moreover, unlike certain variables that may influence children's reading progress—genetic inheritance, poverty, and many disabilities—teacher quality is relatively amenable to change through teacher preparation and professional development. Research suggests that there is copious room for improvement in teacher preparation practices, improvement with the potential to help retain capable teachers in the profession and increase many students' reading achievement.

The chapter begins by reviewing research on teacher effectiveness, teacher knowledge, and teacher preparation in reading, drawing some practical implications from this research. Next, the chapter outlines the kinds of disciplinary knowledge and competencies involving reading that all elementary-level general and special educators should have as well as how knowledge about common profiles and patterns of reading difficulties can be useful in teacher education. The chapter concludes by considering how teachers could be better prepared to implement RTI/MTSS models, with some suggestions for specific educational policies that could improve preservice teacher preparation in reading.

RESEARCH ON EFFECTIVE TEACHERS OF READING

One recent line of research (e.g., Chetty et al., 2011; Heck, 2009; Hanushek & Rivkin, 2010; Nye, Konstantopoulos, & Hedges, 2004) has employed a statistical measure of teacher effectiveness termed *value-added*, an indicator of individual teachers' contributions to the achievement of their students. For example, Chetty and colleagues (2011), who studied math and reading achievement scores of Grade 4–8 students from a large urban district, first calculated predicted estimates of each student's performance based on the performance of other students with similar background characteristics and prior achievement. They then compared those predictions to students' actual performance, with differences averaged across a given teacher's students. They ranked all teachers of a particular subject (reading or math) on these average differences; high value-added teachers were in the top 5% of the teacher distribution in terms of student outcomes, and low value-added teachers were in the bottom 5%. Chetty and colleagues found that when a high value-added teacher started teaching students in a cohort, or when a low value-added teacher stopped teaching (e.g., because of naturally occurring events such as retirements), student achievement in reading improved. Conversely, achievement declined when a low value-added teacher started teaching a particular cohort of students or a high value-added teacher stopped teaching it. Similarly, the results of Nye and colleagues (2004) indicated substantial differences among teachers in the ability to promote students' reading and mathematics achievement and showed that teacher effects on achievement were especially large in schools serving students from low-SES backgrounds. Furthermore, Heck (2009) found that the effectiveness of successive teachers as well as organizational factors such as the stability of teaching staff at a school positively related to students' reading achievement, suggesting the importance of systemic factors in student outcomes.

Teacher effectiveness research has been so persuasive in showing teacher influences on achievement that some policy makers have advocated using VAM in high-stakes evaluations of individual educators—for example, in decision making about merit pay or promotion. However, the use of these measures in individual teacher evaluations is fraught with numerous technical problems as well as with the potential for unintended negative consequences (e.g., Braun, 2005; Darling-Hammond et al., 2011; David, 2010; Haertel, 2013). Technical problems include variability in results by outcome measure (e.g., the specific reading achievement test used to measure student outcomes), variability based on which students (e.g., disproportionately at risk versus not at risk) may be assigned to a given teacher, and a possible systematic bias in VAM scores based on demographics, school context, grade, or other factors. Unintended consequences include increased pressure on educators to teach to tests and less receptivity on the part of teachers to work with students who tend to score poorly. Still, even critics of VAM for teacher evaluation agree that substantial teacher effects on student achievement exist and that research studies using VAM with large groups of teachers and students can provide valuable information about these effects.

Research with VAM has focused on quantifying the contributions of teachers to student achievement, not on the specific skills needed to teach reading successfully to diverse groups of children. Other lines of research offer these more fine-grained insights. One line of work has involved systematic observations of teachers during classroom instruction as well as assessments of their students' reading progress. For example, Carlisle and her colleagues (e.g., Carlisle, Kelcey, Berebitsky, & Phelps, 2011; Carlisle, Kelcey, & Berebitsky, 2013) have studied the instructional practices of third-grade teachers in Reading First schools in relation to student achievement in reading comprehension. Carlisle, Kelcey, Berebitsky, and colleagues (2011) found that teachers who provided more teacher-directed instruction (e.g., explicit teaching and modeling) as well as more support for student learning (e.g., fostering discussion and providing feedback on student work) had students who made more reading comprehension progress during the school year, even with important confounding variables, such as students' prior achievement, accounted for. Similarly, the findings of Carlisle and colleagues (2013) showed that the amount and type of support teachers provided for their students' vocabulary learning—such as explicitly discussing word meanings and using unfamiliar words in sentences—also was positively associated with their students' gains in reading comprehension.

Teacher-directed instruction and support for student learning have often been found to be especially beneficial for at-risk students, with risk defined in relation to eligibility for free or reduced-price lunch (e.g., Connor et al., 2007; Juel & Minden-Cupp, 1999–2000). For instance, Juel and Minden-Cupp (1999–2000) studied four experienced first-grade teachers at two demographically similar schools serving primarily low-income, minority students. They found that children who entered first grade with the lowest reading-related skills did best in reading with a teacher who provided a strong dose of highly explicit, systematic phonics for the first half of the school year and more emphasis on vocabulary and discussion of text later in the year. In fact, in this teacher's classroom, all the children in the lowest reading group read on or close to end-of-first-grade level in May.

In another classroom observational research project, one involving ELLs, Graves, Gersten, and Haager (2004) and Gersten, Baker, Haager, and Graves (2005) analyzed the reading instruction of a group of first-grade teachers of ELLs using an instrument called the English Language Learners Classroom Observation Instrument (ELCOI). The ELCOI evaluated teachers' instruction on qualities such as explicitness of teaching, student engagement, provision of systematic phonemic awareness and decoding instruction, the extent to which instruction targeted the needs of low achievers, and emphasis on vocabulary development. Teachers' ratings in these areas varied greatly, with ratings significantly predicting students' gains in ORF at the end of first grade.

Overall, these observational studies suggest that primary-grade instructional practices involving explicit teaching and modeling, high levels of student engagement, clear feedback to student performance, and the use of research-based instruction all promote reading achievement, especially in children vulnerable to reading difficulties. It is also important to note that most studies in this area have been small ones focused on a particular grade level and outcome measure in reading. The characteristics of effective instruction might vary in important ways for children at different levels of development or for different areas of reading (e.g., word decoding versus comprehension).

TEACHERS' DISCIPLINARY KNOWLEDGE ABOUT READING

Yet another line of work on teacher quality involves studies of teachers' disciplinary knowledge for teaching reading (e.g., Brady et al., 2009; Carlisle, Kelcey, Rowan, & Phelps, 2011; Cunningham et al., 2004; McCutchen et al., 2009; Moats, 1994; Moats & Foorman, 2003; Piasta et al., 2009; Spear-Swerling & Brucker, 2004; Spear-Swerling et al., 2005; Spear-Swerling & Cheesman, 2012), sometimes termed *pedagogical content knowledge*. Early studies of teachers' disciplinary knowledge, following the seminal work of Moats (1994), focused on teachers' understanding of English word structure and phonics— for example, teachers' abilities to count phonemes and morphemes in words, identify phonetically irregular words, classify words by syllable type (e.g., closed, magic e, or r-controlled), or explain common spelling generalizations. More recent studies (e.g., Brady et al., 2009; Carlisle, Kelcey, Rowan, et al., 2011; Spear-Swerling & Cheesman, 2012) have attempted to use measures of teacher knowledge that encompass all five components of reading as well as classroom scenarios requiring the application of disciplinary knowledge.

The results of these studies are very worrisome. In general, they suggest that even experienced, credentialed teachers often have great difficulty with tasks measuring phonics knowledge or understanding of phonemic awareness. For example, in the studies that my colleagues and I have done, licensed teachers have repeatedly confused phonemic awareness with knowledge of letter sounds. In one study (Spear-Swerling et al., 2005), less than 10% of credentialed teachers could correctly answer the question, "What is phonemic awareness and why is it important?" In the same study, licensed teachers experienced great difficulty on a simple classification task requiring them to identify whether common words were phonetically irregular (e.g., *what, done, of*) or regular (e.g., *boy, too, at*). Educators also were frequently unfamiliar with syllable types, such as closed or magic-*e* syllables, which are useful to help children predict likely vowel sounds in words, and they could accurately count phonemes only in about 70% of words, making many errors on less transparent types of words such as *mix* (four phonemes) or *eight* (two phonemes). These findings about teachers' limited knowledge of phonemic awareness and phonics are very consistent with those of many other investigations (e.g., Brady et al., 2009; Cunningham et al., 2004, 2009; Moats, 1994; Moats & Foorman, 2003) involving varied samples of educators from different states. In part, teachers' difficulties reflect the confusion created by proficient adult readers' own automatic processing of words and knowledge of word spellings (Scarborough, Ehri, Olson, & Fowler, 1998). For example, proficient readers' knowledge of the spelling of *mix* tends to lead them to specify three, not four, phonemes in the word (/m/, /i/, /k/, /s/); they are more likely to segment a relatively transparent word such as *rocks* (/r/, /o/, /k/, /s/) correctly. Even teacher candidates with particularly strong component word-attack skills have difficulties on tasks tapping word-structure knowledge (Spear-Swerling & Brucker, 2006).

To sum up these findings, explicit knowledge about word structure is not an automatic consequence of high levels of literacy, and in order for prospective teachers to be prepared to teach phonemic awareness and phonics skills effectively, teacher educators must teach information about word structure directly, including addressing the potential confusions created by candidates' knowledge of word spellings. In addition, studies comparing licensed general and special educators (e.g., Cheesman, McGuire, Shankweiler, & Coyne, 2009; McCutchen et al., 2002) typically indicate that both groups have similar limitations in phonemic awareness and phonics knowledge. These findings are especially disquieting given that many struggling readers have difficulties centering on decoding and that the mission of special educators is to help children with the most serious reading problems; it certainly supports the need to include this information in the preparation of both groups of teachers.

Fewer studies have attempted to assess teacher knowledge in areas beyond phonemic awareness and phonics, but the existing ones are not comforting. Brady and colleagues (2009) assessed the knowledge base of 65 teachers in four areas—phonemic awareness, code concepts, fluency, and foundations of reading comprehension (including both vocabulary and oral comprehension)—with mean scores at pretest (prior to professional development) in these four areas ranging from 37% to 54% correct. Washburn, Joshi, and Binks-Cantrell (2011) surveyed elementary teachers' understanding of dyslexia, the most common LD affecting reading, and found that many teachers held antiquated views of dyslexia as caused by poor visual processing (e.g., seeing letters and words backward); few correctly understood dyslexia as a disability involving core phonological weaknesses. Spear-Swerling and Cheesman (2012) examined knowledge about the five components of reading in 142 teachers from two different states, using a multiple-choice Teacher Knowledge Survey (TKS) that included application items involving classroom scenarios. Scores on the TKS were grouped into three different subscales, involving questions about phonemic awareness and phonics; fluency, vocabulary, and comprehension; and assessment and RTI practices. Participants' mean scores for all subscales were less than 65% correct. Error rates were particularly high for questions about assessment, such as those about CBMs or those requiring participants to recognize when a child had been placed for reading in a text that was too difficult for him or her. General and special educators performed similarly on all subscales except for the one involving assessment/RTI practices on which special educators outperformed general educators; however, even on this last subscale, both groups of educators had means less than 70% correct.

One would expect teachers' disciplinary knowledge about reading to be an important foundation for effective teaching and a contributor to students' reading growth. It is difficult to imagine, for instance, that teachers can teach or assess phonemic awareness well when they themselves do not understand what phonemic awareness is and cannot count phonemes in common words correctly. Field or clinical supervision often reveals the consequences of a candidate's faulty grasp of word structure, such as the time I observed a candidate present the phonetically irregular *done* as an example of a magic-*e* word to a child. Predictably, there was much ensuing confusion on the part of the child, who then tried to decode the word to rhyme with *bone*. Candidates who lack a grasp of word structure also cannot respond appropriately and flexibly to children's errors; if a child struggles to read *done*, teacher feedback to "sound it out" (the response of the teacher candidate in the preceding example) will certainly not be helpful. Although in a supervised setting these unintentionally confusing mistakes can be corrected, the results of many studies in this area suggest that comparably faulty instruction likely occurs repeatedly, without being addressed, in the classrooms of teachers not well prepared to teach phonemic awareness or phonics skills. Indeed, Piasta and colleagues (2009) actually found an inverse relationship between teacher knowledge and time spent in explicit decoding instruction; teachers with low phonics knowledge who spent more time on decoding had students who made *less* decoding growth than if the teacher had not provided explicit decoding instruction at all, likely because of inadvertently confusing instruction. These researchers also found that the use of highly scripted, generally effective core curricula did not eliminate the need for knowledgeable teachers. Rather, both high teacher knowledge *and* time spent in explicit, research-based decoding instruction were necessary for students to make strong decoding gains.

As the findings of Piasta and colleagues (2009) indicate, relationships among teacher knowledge, effective instructional practices, and student reading growth appear to be complex. This complexity may explain why some studies have found significant relationships between individual teachers' disciplinary knowledge and their students' reading progress (e.g., McCutchen et al., 2009; Spear-Swerling & Brucker, 2004), whereas other studies have yielded nonsignificant or inconsistent relationships (e.g., Carlisle, Kelcey, Rowan, et al., 2011; Spear-Swerling, 2009). Piasta and colleagues (2009) suggest that teacher knowledge influences children's word-reading gains primarily through its impact on the quality of decoding instruction.

In line with this view, in their study of teachers' support for students' vocabulary learning, Carlisle and colleagues (2013) found that relatively knowledgeable teachers (as assessed by a multicomponent measure of teacher knowledge) tended to provide better support for students' vocabulary learning than did less knowledgeable teachers. However, teacher knowledge about reading had a stronger influence, and teachers provided more support for student vocabulary learning, in classrooms with relatively stronger reading comprehension performance at the start of the school year. Classrooms with relatively weaker reading comprehension performance tended to have relatively more challenging students, such as a higher percentage of students with disabilities and students from low-income backgrounds. Thus the researchers speculated that teachers in relatively lower-performing classes could have certain constraints on them—for example, a need to use instructional time for other purposes—that influenced how (or how much) they could apply their disciplinary knowledge in practice. In other words, even relationships between teacher knowledge and teachers' instructional practices may be quite complex. Another important issue in research examining relationships between teacher knowledge and other important variables involves problems with measurement of teacher knowledge and the need to improve the technical adequacy of these measures (Carlisle, Kelcey, Rowan, et al., 2011).

Much work remains to be done to explicate the relationships among teacher knowledge, teachers' instructional practices, and children's reading growth—for children at different developmental levels, with different learning characteristics, and for varied components of reading. However, studies yielding inconsistent relationships between teacher knowledge and student reading achievement should not be interpreted to mean that this knowledge is inconsequential for effective teaching. Teachers' knowledge about language structure, important components of reading development, research-based approaches for assessing and teaching those component areas, and common types of reading problems is fundamental knowledge akin to physicians' grasp of basic anatomy and of consensus scientific findings about common health problems. Although many kinds of knowledge and skills are important for effective medical practice, few of us would be comfortable seeing a doctor who lacked basic knowledge of anatomy or who had never heard of the germ theory of disease. Likewise, teachers' research-based disciplinary knowledge is foundational knowledge that is necessary, but certainly not sufficient, for effective teaching of reading.

PRESERVICE TEACHER PREPARATION IN READING

A consistent finding from preservice preparation studies (e.g., Spear-Swerling & Brucker, 2004) and from professional development studies (e.g., Brady et al., 2009; McCutchen et al., 2009) is that when research-based disciplinary knowledge is taught to preservice teachers or teacher candidates, they learn it. Repeated findings of inadequate knowledge in licensed teachers about some of the most fundamental, well-researched concepts needed to teach reading well point strongly to flaws in preservice teacher preparation as at least one source of these knowledge weaknesses. Tremendous variability across and even within states exists with regard to teacher preparation practices in reading, such as in course and licensure exam requirements, and there are certainly limitations in the existing database on teacher preparation (National Research Council, 2010). However, numerous studies involving a wide range of states have focused on teacher preparation in reading, and the results of these studies strongly converge with those on teachers' knowledge weaknesses. Overall, their findings suggest that many teacher preparation programs do not adequately cover the five components of reading on their course syllabi (McCombes-Tolis & Spear-Swerling, 2011; National Council on Teacher Quality [NCTQ], 2006); that textbooks popularly used in reading methods courses often provide inadequate or erroneous coverage of the five components (Joshi, Binks, Graham, et al., 2009); that teacher educators themselves may lack research-based disciplinary knowledge about reading (Joshi, Binks, Hougen, et al., 2009); and that licensure exams used for teacher credentialing often do not tap this kind of knowledge (Stotsky, 2009). Moreover, low expectations and a general lack of substance pervade too many teacher preparation programs (Levine, 2006; McCombes-Tolis & Spear-Swerling, 2011; NCTQ, 2006; Ripley, 2013).

To be sure, good teacher preparation programs do exist, and many individual, highly knowledgeable teacher educators do base their work with teachers on a solid foundation of research. However, effective teacher preparation practices are clearly not *systemic*, and they do not appear to be predictable by factors such as the cost or selectivity of the institution (NCTQ, 2006), meaning that prospective teachers who get into and pay for selective private schools are not necessarily guaranteed high-quality preparation. Currently, effective programs depend largely on the skill and knowledge of individual teacher educators who happen to be at a particular institution, and in some cases, a teacher educator who is teaching candidates erroneous information about multiple cuing systems or children who see words backward may greatly undermine the work of an outstanding colleague in the office next door. At best, this situation is likely to confuse teacher candidates, and at worst, it conveys the impression that disciplinary knowledge about reading is simply a matter of opinion, not grounded in scientific evidence. Moreover, the amount of knowledge candidates need to learn to teach reading effectively is extensive (e.g., International Dyslexia Association, 2010; International Reading Association, 2010; Moats, 1999) and continues to emerge so that even the best preservice preparation program cannot provide candidates with all the knowledge they require for a professional lifetime. In addition, both general and special educators must be prepared to assess and teach many areas besides reading. Consistent attention to foundational knowledge across preservice preparation programs is therefore essential so that all beginning teachers have at least the foundational competencies they need to teach reading well, and so that in-service professional development can emphasize advanced types of teacher competencies. In-service professional development should also support teachers' ongoing learning and application of new knowledge to specific contexts (Snow, Griffin, & Burns, 2005). In sum, teacher preparation in reading desperately needs a systemic approach, something like a comprehensive, research-based core Tier I curriculum. What should this curriculum look like?

KEY DISCIPLINARY KNOWLEDGE AND SKILLS FOR TEACHERS OF READING

Many professional groups and authorities (e.g., International Dyslexia Association, 2010; International Reading Association, 2010; Moats, 1999; Snow et al., 2005) have outlined the knowledge and skills needed to teach reading well to diverse groups of children. Although these different sources vary in important ways, substantial consensus exists among them, and along with the extensive scientific literature on reading, these professional guidelines can inform preservice teacher preparation. Drawing from this range of sources, Table 10.1 displays the kinds of important knowledge and skills that preservice preparation programs should develop in all teachers of reading at the elementary level. I use the term *teacher of reading* to refer to *any* educator responsible for reading instruction, including general educators, special educators, and reading specialists. The table is intended only as a broad overview, not an exhaustive list; readers are encouraged to consult the sources cited here for much further detail about the knowledge and skills that should be addressed by preservice preparation programs.

Core Knowledge and Skills for All Elementary-Level Teachers of Reading

As shown in Table 10.1, all prospective teachers of reading require core knowledge and skills in at least five areas: basic knowledge about typical reading development and reading problems; knowledge about the structure of language, including multiple levels of language as well as English word structure; knowledge of foundational research in reading from multiple disciplines;

Table 10.1.   Important knowledge and skills for elementary (K–6) teachers of reading

Area	Disciplinary knowledge and teaching competencies for teacher candidates
Knowledge about typical reading development, common reading difficulties, and disabilities	• Explain phases, abilities, and processes involved in typical reading development, including the five components of reading and how the importance of different components shifts during development. • Describe the influence of socioeconomic, cultural, and linguistic factors on children's reading development, including for English language learners. • Explain key abilities/knowledge involved in reading comprehension such as background knowledge, inferencing, and knowledge of text structure. • Describe common profiles and patterns of reading difficulties as well as basic features of common disabilities that affect reading (e.g., dyslexia). • Explain the most important provisions of federal and state laws for students with disabilities (e.g., free appropriate public education).
Knowledge about the structure of language	• Segment phonemes and morphemes in words, identify syllable types, and identify phonetically irregular words. • Identify common roots, prefixes, and suffixes as well as generalizations for syllabication of long words. • Explain common spelling generalizations. • Identify common morphemes, cohesive words, and semantic relationships among words. • Identify different sentence and paragraph structures. • Identify different genres and discourse structures. • Identify specific features of a text that may make comprehension difficult (e.g., complex syntax, double negatives).
Research foundations	• Explain fundamental consensus research findings about reading (e.g., skilled reading is associated with highly accurate, automatic decoding; language differences and early language delay are risk factors for reading difficulties) and their implications for educational practice. • Recognize the importance of ongoing professional development that includes reading professional journals and other sources of research.
Assessment	• Explain important concepts about the technical adequacy of tests, such as reliability and validity; interpret information about specific tests to determine if the test is technically adequate for its intended purpose. • Administer and interpret assessments for screening, progress monitoring, and evaluation of outcomes. • Administer and interpret assessments of the five components of reading, including diagnostic assessments. • Interpret multiple assessments in conjunction with each other to determine a student's overall profile or pattern of reading difficulty (e.g., recognize when a child's poor reading comprehension is due solely to decoding difficulties versus core comprehension weaknesses).

Instruction	• Provide explicit, systematic teaching of the five components of reading and of specific comprehension abilities/knowledge (e.g., inferencing, text structure, cohesive words).
	• Integrate instruction appropriately across different components, including making instructional connections between specific components of reading and specific components of writing.
	• Choose appropriate instructional examples or questions in all five component areas.
	• Provide clear, constructive feedback to children's errors and confusions for all five components.
	• Differentiate and adapt instruction for students with varied needs, including for English language learners, for students with common disabilities, and for different profiles and patterns of reading difficulties.
	• Motivate and engage students of varied achievement levels and cultural-linguistic backgrounds as well as manage groups of students.
	• Describe different text types (e.g., predictable, decodable, children's literature, informational) and how/when each is useful in instruction.
	• Place children in appropriate texts for instruction and identify when a text is too difficult / too easy for a given child.
	• Appropriately foster, monitor, and guide children's independent reading.

assessment-related knowledge and skills; and instructional knowledge and skills. In preparing teachers of reading, teacher educators should also directly address common myths, such as the idea that children from poverty backgrounds, children with disabilities, and ELLs cannot learn to read well (Snow et al., 2005).

Virtually all professional organizations and authorities in reading (e.g., Moats, 1999; Snow et al., 2005), including accrediting organizations such as the Council for the Accreditation of Educator Preparation (2010), agree that in order to develop practical teaching competencies, teacher candidates need extensive, supervised field or clinical experiences. These practical teaching experiences should be well integrated with coursework and must involve supervision by highly knowledgeable, skilled mentors. Without expert supervision, candidates will not receive the modeling, guidance, and feedback they require to learn how to teach effectively, administer assessments appropriately, engage students, and manage students' behavior. Supervision also provides teacher educators with a broad perspective on the strengths and weaknesses of individual candidates, an essential perspective given that many qualities in addition to academic competence and knowledge play a role in good teaching.

Successful implementation of the CCSS at the elementary level also hinges on the types of knowledge and competencies listed in Table 10.1. Not only do the CCSS require that educators be able to effectively teach all five components of reading as well as appropriately integrate those components with each other and with components of writing, but many of the advanced comprehension standards require teachers to have strong knowledge of language structure. For instance, in order to teach fifth graders how to "Compare and contrast the overall structure (e.g., chronology, comparison, cause/effect, problem/solution) of events, ideas, concepts, or information in two or more texts" (English/Language Arts [ELA]-Literacy.RI.5.5), teachers need to understand text and discourse structure. Effective teaching of many aspects of writing also depends heavily on teachers' knowledge of language structure, such as ELA-Literacy.W.4.2c: "Link ideas within categories of information using words and phrases (e.g., *another, for example, also, because*)." This standard requires teachers to understand the role of cohesive words in texts, an aspect of language structure that they can use to facilitate reading comprehension as well as clear, effective writing by their students.

Specialized and Advanced Knowledge and Skills for Teaching Reading

The core competencies displayed in Table 10.1 must be supplemented with other kinds of knowledge and skills for teaching reading, particularly in the case of certain professional groups. For example, teacher candidates in special education require not only the core competencies for teaching reading listed in Table 10.1 but also additional competencies. These competencies include, relative to Table 10.1, greater knowledge about disabilities, special education laws, and research foundations of special education; greater assessment knowledge and expertise; and greater instructional expertise that will enable them to teach children with the most serious, persistent reading difficulties. Special educators' teaching skills must be developed in supervised field experiences that include direct instruction of students with various disabilities. Moreover, special educators often collaborate with many other educators as well as with parents, and they must be able to modify and structure learning environments for students with disabilities (e.g., facilitating inclusion of a student with a disability in a general education class), so competencies in these areas are vital for them (Council for Exceptional Children, 2009).

Brownell, Sindelar, Kiely, and Danielson (2010) suggest using an RTI framework to rethink preparation of special educators. They argue that the extensive expertise required of special educators necessitates preparation in both general and special education coupled with extensive reforms of general as well as special education teacher preparation. If general education teacher preparation lacks a foundation in research or fails to address the types of competencies displayed in Table 10.1, then general educators will not be prepared to teach reading well and to differentiate reading instruction in Tier I, completely undermining special education reform efforts, like a growing sinkhole under the foundation of a building. Although recognizing the genuine challenges of their proposal, especially perennial teacher shortages in special education that frequently have led only to short-term, piecemeal fixes, Brownell and colleagues (2010) make a strong case for requiring dual licensure of special educators in general as well as special education. Furthermore, they point out that special education preparation can make general educators more effective teachers, even for students without disabilities; they therefore suggest that states *require dual licensure even of general educators*, with more advanced preparation in literacy (and numeracy) for special educators, and with salary scales adjusted to be commensurate with greater levels of teacher expertise.

Reading specialists and literacy coaches also require advanced knowledge and expertise (International Dyslexia Association, 2010; International Reading Association, 2010). Although the primary focus of reading specialists does not typically involve students with identified disabilities, these specialists certainly should have specialized expertise for assessing and teaching children with a variety of reading problems, including both decoding and comprehension-based types of difficulties, in culturally and linguistically diverse groups. Like special educators, reading specialists require especially strong consultative and collaborative skills because they may be involved in reading curriculum development as well as in supporting classroom teachers' professional development. Although special educators rather than reading specialists will typically deliver reading instruction for students with identified disabilities, reading specialists certainly should have strong knowledge of disabilities such as dyslexia as well as of interventions that generally work for these students and that often will benefit other poor readers, including many children to whom reading specialists may deliver tiered interventions.

All these groups of teachers require ongoing, research-based professional development in reading, with opportunities for coaching by knowledgeable mentors. Research-based knowledge surveys, classroom observations, and student achievement data should be used to target professional development efforts because different educators, or those in different schools, may have varying needs. Successful reform of preservice teacher preparation would enable in-service professional development to emphasize advanced types of teaching skills (as opposed to, e.g., what phonemic awareness is and why it is important). Conversely, however, poorly conceived professional development can weaken or even undo strong preservice preparation.

Several years ago, I visited the classroom of a teacher who had once been my student—indeed, she was one of the best students of her cohort. Although in her undergraduate special education program she had received good preparation to teach reading, during my classroom visit I was surprised and quite dismayed to find her using many inappropriate practices, such as encouraging children to guess at words instead of apply decoding skills—practices that were certainly not taught in her preservice program. It soon became apparent that 5 or 6 years of weak in-service professional development and teaching at a school with a whole language orientation had greatly undermined this educator's initial preparation. The lesson of this story is that just as a strong Tier I reading curriculum depends on good integration of instruction across grades, with later grades building on skills developed in previous grades, good integration of preservice and long-term in-service professional development is vital for effective teacher education in reading. As many authorities (e.g., Moats, 1999; Snow et al., 2005) have emphasized, teacher professional development is a career-long process; inadequate preparation at any stage of that process can lead to undesirable outcomes.

USING COMMON PROFILES AND PATTERNS OF
READING DIFFICULTIES IN TEACHER PREPARATION

Knowledge about common profiles and patterns of reading difficulties is useful for all teachers of reading at all levels of professional development. Furthermore, a model that relates reading problems to typical reading development, as discussed in Chapters 3 and 4, is very helpful for both general and special educators—for example, in highlighting the ways that at-risk readers are most likely to stray from the path to proficient reading. Especially for preservice teachers, information about profiles and patterns also provides a useful level of analysis between two extremes: "all reading problems are alike" (clearly false) and "every reading problem is different" (which implies that no generalizations about reading problems exist, also false). Profiles and patterns capture many instructionally relevant distinctions about reading problems, such as distinctions between reading comprehension problems based solely in decoding or fluency and those with a core comprehension component. They can help novice teachers integrate and interpret information from multiple assessments as well as provide practical implications for planning instructional groups, interventions, and progress monitoring.

For teachers with advanced levels of expertise, profiles and patterns provide a useful foundation for developing an increasingly nuanced understanding of reading problems. A special educator who already understands common profiles and patterns of reading difficulties has a framework for analyzing the more complex needs of certain students with disabilities, such as a child with dyslexia or with ASD who also happens to be an ELL. The teaching competencies required to address common profiles and patterns are a helpful starting point for more specialized types of intervention strategies that may be required for these students' more complex needs. Similarly, a reading specialist who is knowledgeable about common profiles and patterns of reading difficulties can use this knowledge in coaching classroom teachers and in making decisions about reading curriculum. Like special educators, reading specialists can build on this knowledge to develop a complex understanding of different reading difficulties as well as increased expertise in assessment and intervention to help them better meet the needs of a range of children.

HOW CAN TEACHERS BE BETTER PREPARED
TO IMPLEMENT RESPONSE TO INTERVENTION?

The research reviewed in this chapter suggests that, currently, many teachers, both general and special educators, are poorly prepared to implement RTI/MTSS models. Without basic knowledge of the structure of language, typical reading development, important components of reading, and research-based approaches to instruction, it seems highly unlikely that teachers can effectively differentiate classroom instruction to meet the needs of at-risk students, let alone successfully implement interventions to help the most difficult-to-teach poor readers. Limited knowledge of assessment (e.g., Spear-Swerling & Cheesman, 2012) is especially problematic for implementation of RTI because the prompt intervention at the heart of RTI depends on educators' ability to administer and interpret a range of assessments correctly.

Moreover, many teachers may be unaware of research-based instructional models and interventions that could be extremely helpful resources to them in implementing MTSS. In our study of teachers' knowledge base for implementing RTI, my colleague Elaine Cheesman and I asked participants to indicate their familiarity and experience with a list of research-based interventions widely recognized in the scientific community. "Familiar" meant that the participant had at least heard of the intervention or instructional approach, whereas "experience" meant that the participant had actual experience using it with children. Many participants indicated that they were completely unfamiliar with specific research-based interventions for multiple components of reading. For instance, 63% of participants were unfamiliar with MSL programs such as the Orton-Gillingham approach (Gillingham & Stillman, 1970) or the Wilson program (Wilson, 1988); 65% of participants were unfamiliar with specific fluency interventions such as Read Naturally (Hasbrouck et al., 1999); and 84% and 77% respectively were unfamiliar with two well-researched models for comprehension instruction: Questioning the Author (Beck & McKeown, 2006) and Reciprocal Teaching (Palincsar & Brown, 1984). A whopping 92% were unfamiliar with an extensively researched model especially useful for differentiation of core instruction and for Tier II intervention: PALS (e.g., Fuchs & Fuchs, 2005). Teachers unfamiliar with these and other specific interventions named in the study still might be able to teach poor readers well, of course. Nevertheless, these results are unsettling because well-researched, published interventions and instructional models are important resources for educators with many demands on their time. Lacking familiarity with (or access to) these resources, educators would need to develop their own, a requirement that research suggests is not realistic for many educators, especially on the wide scale demanded by RTI.

Better preparation of educators to implement RTI should begin with the types of competencies and knowledge shown in Table 10.1 but should include other competencies as well. For example, to implement RTI effectively, teachers must have at least a passing familiarity with examples of research-based interventions for different types of reading difficulties, with supervised teaching experience for educators who will actually implement interventions. For preservice candidates, placement in field and student teaching settings in which RTI is implemented well is important, as are, for in-service teachers, professional development models that include well-informed coaching (e.g., Brady et al., 2009; Carlisle, Cortina, & Katz, 2011; Moats & Foorman, 2003). Because research on RTI is ongoing, with many practical implications continuing to emerge from this work, educators' willingness and ability to keep up with this research is crucial, especially for those involved in setting district literacy policies (e.g., administrators, supervisors of special education, reading supervisors). For instance, these educators should be familiar with research on the value of two-stage screens (e.g., Fuchs, Fuchs, Compton, et al., 2012; Johnson et al., 2009) as well as with findings indicating the need to "fast-track" certain students to special education or to the most intensive level of intervention (e.g., Fuchs, Fuchs, Compton, et al., 2012; Vaughn et al., 2010).

Developing these kinds of competencies will require many reforms in preservice preparation as well as ongoing professional development for in-service educators. It should be noted, however, that many of the teacher competencies that need to be developed are important with or without the use of formal MTSS models. *All* teachers of reading should be able to identify at-risk readers early, use assessments to plan effective instruction, and deliver at least some research-based interventions to struggling students, whether or not they are in schools using RTI models.

IMPROVING PRESERVICE TEACHER PREPARATION IN READING

Here are a few specific suggestions for state departments of education, schools of education, and policy makers focused on preservice preparation, a critical foundation for all other efforts in improving teacher professional development in reading.

Require the equivalent of at least 12 credits of preparation involving reading for all candidates whose certifications will include teaching reading, with substantial integration of supervised field or clinical experiences well before student teaching. The kinds of teacher competencies displayed in Table 10.1 cannot be developed in only one or two courses, and supervised teaching experience, essential to good teacher preparation, requires considerable amounts of time as well.

Promote high expectations and substance in teacher education. Quality of preparation is as important as quantity. Not only do teacher candidates require the kinds of competencies listed in Table 10.1, but in order to teach reading well, they must also be able to serve as excellent models of literacy—as critical thinkers, good writers, and thoughtful, perceptive readers, who read widely and often. Preparation programs with minimal expectations of teacher candidates are not likely to attract or produce these kinds of educators.

Ensure that preparation in reading is delivered by faculty with the appropriate expertise. Faculty who teach reading methods courses and who supervise reading-related field experiences must have expertise that includes deep knowledge of the kind of competencies displayed in Table 10.1; as Binks-Cantrell, Washburn, Joshi, and Hougen (2012) point out, teacher educators cannot develop knowledge in their candidates that they themselves lack. Unfortunately, deep knowledge of the competencies displayed in Table 10.1 cannot be inferred merely based on whether a teacher educator has a terminal degree in "reading" or "literacy." Teacher educators with such a degree might have excellent, research-based expertise, or they might have years of preparation completely disconnected from the interdisciplinary research base on reading (see, e.g., Linn, 2012) on multiple cuing systems and whole language methods. On the other hand, a teacher educator with a terminal degree in a field other than but related to reading, such as educational psychology or special education, might have strong expertise for teaching reading methods courses to general as well as special education candidates.

Develop interdisciplinary preparation programs. Teacher candidates cannot be well prepared in programs narrowly focused on a single field—whether that field is reading, education, or special education—because the knowledge base that underlies reading is multidisciplinary. Preparation of both general and special educators therefore must include substantial content in areas such as speech-language and cognitive-developmental psychology as well as in reading, education, and special education. This content should not involve a jumble of courses picked from different departments in a university catalog; it must be well integrated into a coherent program that develops candidates' practical teaching competencies as well as their disciplinary knowledge.

Employ research-based, sufficiently detailed professional standards for teacher candidates who will teach reading. Accreditation processes for schools of education, such as those of CAEP, employ broad professional standards that reflect their accreditation of a wide range of teacher preparation programs (e.g., elementary education, secondary science, music education) in conjunction with more discipline-specific standards for different fields. As noted previously, the professional standards of different organizations with a stake in the preparation of teachers of reading (e.g., Council for Exceptional Children, 2009; International Dyslexia Association, 2010; International Reading Association, 2010) have many areas of broad consensus. However, these standards do not all provide equivalent detail about the specific knowledge and competencies that teacher candidates require in reading—and detail is essential for informing course and program design. The International Dyslexia Association (IDA; 2010) professional standards, which address important competencies for all teachers of reading, not only special educators, have this kind of explicit detail and certainly can be employed in conjunction with other standards as needed.

Adopt a research-based teacher licensure exam in reading for all initial certification candidates whose certifications include teaching reading, with a more advanced licensure exam for candidates who require more specialized or advanced knowledge (e.g., special educators, reading specialists). A research-based licensure exam that addresses disciplinary knowledge about all five components of reading as well as about other important areas, including both assessment and instruction, is essential for accountability of higher education institutions and for driving change in teacher preparation in reading. In my own state, adoption of a research-based licensure exam has not only improved accountability but also had many other benefits, such as increasing attention to research-based resources (see Spear-Swerling & Coyne, 2010). A more advanced exam for special educators and reading specialists could help to ensure that these groups of educators receive the preparation they need as well as facilitate some badly needed integration of preservice preparation and advanced levels of professional development. A sufficiently high passing score (e.g., 75%–80% of questions correct on all parts of the exam) is necessary for both the initial and advanced exam so that candidates with serious weaknesses in any area cannot obtain licensure. Retakes of exams should be permitted.

Adopt meaningful accreditation processes that require schools of education to demonstrate that they are developing research-based knowledge and competencies in their teacher candidates, with constructive review and feedback that enables programs to improve. Accreditation through organizations such as CAEP might involve this kind of meaningful accreditation process. However, if state departments of education and policy makers want to ensure adequate preparation of teachers of reading, they should not cede all oversight to any accrediting body but should have their own monitoring systems involving, for example, syllabus review by appropriate state education officials with strong, multidisciplinary, research-based expertise in reading. Accreditation and self-study processes must not be so burdensome for teacher educators that they drain disproportionate amounts of time and energy from other important responsibilities such as teaching, supervision, and scholarly activity.

Provide extensive opportunities for research-based professional development of teacher educators as well as in-service teachers. Many teacher educators are open to opportunities for ongoing professional development, and some of the other steps mentioned here may enhance their receptivity. For instance, no teacher educator wants to have students who repeatedly fail the state licensure exam. Poor teacher candidate scores on an appropriate licensure exam, one tapping candidates' knowledge about how to teach all important components of reading, can make teacher educators more aware of their students' knowledge limitations and more receptive to opportunities for professional development that could help them improve their preparation of candidates. Higher education collaboratives, which provide research-based professional development as well as other kinds of support for teacher educators (e.g., Cheesman, Hougen, & Smartt, 2010), provide one valuable model for professional development of teacher educators. Similarly, research-practice collaborations in clinical settings or through professional development schools can benefit the expertise of both teacher educators and participating schools. Other related policy steps also matter. For example, to continue their own professional development, teacher education faculty require adequate funding for travel to conferences as well as support for creative activity and service, including release time for research and for important responsibilities such as supervising field placements and accreditation processes.

Finally, policy makers and others wishing to improve teacher preparation practices in reading should seek ways to encourage new Ph.D.s with strong research backgrounds and appropriate teaching experience to pursue careers in teacher education. That recommendation might be a hard sell after the many problems in teacher preparation that I have detailed in this chapter. However, despite its frustrations and challenges, a career in teacher education can be deeply rewarding (and an academic research career has challenges and frustrations of its own). The opportunity to shape excellent teachers and to improve children's reading instruction on a broad scale, as well as the privilege of continuing to learn from these teachers and their students, is highly meaningful, important, and intellectually engaging work. Without knowledgeable, committed teacher educators as well as teachers, scientific research on reading will never have the impact on educational practice that it should.

11

Conclusions and Future Directions

S ternberg (1985) notes that one key difficulty in solving problems is deciding exactly what the problem is that needs to be solved. Unrecognized or poorly defined problems are much less likely to be addressed successfully. For example, in the 19th century, before an understanding of the germ theory of disease, cholera was thought to be due to *miasma*, or noxious air. London officials were unaware that mass dumping of human sewage into the Thames, contaminating many citizens' drinking water, was fueling the spread of cholera and other water-borne illnesses (Johnson, 2006). Until John Snow's discovery that victims of the terrible 1854 cholera epidemic had used water from the same city pump, the cholera problem was incorrectly defined as one involving bad air, and contamination of drinking water continued to lead to cholera epidemics.

One important advantage of information about common profiles and patterns of reading difficulties is that this information helps to define reading problems in educationally useful ways. Does a particular poor reader have core comprehension weaknesses, or are his or her reading problems associated entirely with word-level reading skills? If the problem involves word reading, is the child's word recognition nonalphabetic, inaccurate, or nonautomatic? If a poor reader has fluency difficulties, are those difficulties connected to word-level reading difficulties, broader language difficulties, or to both areas? Answering these kinds of questions is central to planning appropriate interventions and solving individual children's reading problems.

Similarly, RTI practices help to orient general educators, specialists, and administrators toward educationally meaningful issues. Are general education literacy curricula and instruction working well for most students, and if they are not, which specific areas need improvement? How can educators best identify at-risk readers to facilitate prompt intervention? Are most students who receive intervention making progress, and if not, how should the system of interventions be changed? Simply asking the right questions is an important start for solving educational problems, even when those problems are challenging and do not have easy answers—indeed, even when all the answers are not yet known.

This chapter sums up the case for using profiles and patterns to understand reading difficulties as well as the case for using RTI/MTSS approaches, both in general education and in identification of LDs. Moreover, the use of profiles and patterns in *conjunction* with RTI practices provides a powerful blueprint for preventing and addressing a wide variety of common difficulties in reading. The chapter concludes by considering some of the most important challenges associated with this approach to solving reading problems as well as possible ways to meet these challenges.

SUMMING UP: THE VALUE OF PROFILES AND PATTERNS

As the examples of children in this book demonstrate, information about profiles and patterns of reading difficulties is helpful in understanding many different types of reading problems, whether or not they involve disabilities. Identification of individual poor readers' profiles and patterns, by itself, certainly does not provide all the necessary information for planning instruction, because children with the same profile and pattern of reading difficulties may still vary in their specific skills and level of functioning. For example, one inaccurate word reader with SWRD may only be able to decode simple short-vowel words, whereas another inaccurate word reader may decode many one-syllable, but not two-syllable, words accurately. Poor readers with SRCD or MRD, whose problems include a core comprehension component, may differ greatly in the specific weaknesses that underlie their comprehension problems, with possible difficulties in vocabulary, background knowledge, syntactic competence, or pragmatic language—to name only a few. Furthermore, as discussed in Chapter 4, some children may not fall neatly into a particular profile or pattern because they have borderline performance near the cutoff in achievement.

Nevertheless, many poor readers do exemplify relatively clear-cut profiles and patterns of reading difficulties, such as those discussed in the case study chapters, and these profiles and patterns provide a valuable foundation for understanding reading problems and for designing successful educational interventions. Children with SWRD and MRD will usually benefit from phonics interventions, whereas those with SRCD will not, because their difficulties are not in the domain of word-level reading skills. Children with SRCD and MRD require intervention targeting their specific comprehension needs, whereas those with SWRD do not require intervention in the domain of comprehension and can usually receive their comprehension development mainly through participation in general education. Poor readers tend to require different kinds of progress monitoring in intervention, different modifications to general education instruction, and different kinds of assistive technology depending on their profile and pattern of reading difficulty.

When profiles and patterns are linked to a theoretical model for understanding typical reading development, as in the model described in Chapters 3 and 4, they are especially valuable for researchers as well as practitioners.

A comprehensive model that explains profiles and patterns of reading difficulties in relation to typical reading development is necessary for understanding why certain types of reading difficulties emerge relatively later in schooling, and others earlier. Such a model also suggests why profiles and patterns of poor reading may shift over time, as, for example, when a poor decoder with subtle, nonphonological language weaknesses, who has not had his or her decoding successfully remediated, encounters increasingly difficult reading comprehension demands in the upper grades, shifting from an SWRD to an MRD profile. (With effective decoding intervention, the shift would be from an SWRD to an SRCD profile.) The model also helps practitioners anticipate the most common sources of reading difficulty—for instance, in the early grades, problems with phonological skills and decoding, not with seeing words backward or with using multiple cuing systems—so that those areas may be better addressed in curriculum and instruction, and so that reading difficulties may be recognized more promptly. Not only is this view of reading problems helpful for both general and special educators, but it is also relevant for many others with an interest in preventing and ameliorating reading difficulties, including reading consultants, school psychologists, speech-language pathologists, and school administrators—and researchers too, of course.

SUMMING UP: WHY SCHOOLS SHOULD USE RESPONSE TO INTERVENTION PRACTICES

Although the kind of comprehensive model described here is valuable with or without RTI/MTSS practices, the use of these practices can greatly enhance the power of the model to improve instruction and intervention for children with reading problems. Equally, without a research-based model of reading development and reading problems, RTI lacks the theoretical foundations necessary to be fully effective. For instance, educators who are unaware of late-emerging SWRD, SRCD, or MRD may discontinue screening for reading problems too early or may fail to include the kinds of measures necessary to detect certain types of reading difficulties (e.g., phonological measures in the case of SWRD and nonphonological language measures in the case of SRCD).

As certain examples in this book illustrate, ample opportunities exist for RTI practices to go awry. Educators can use inadequate screening and progress-monitoring procedures, as in Kevin's case; they can let children linger too long in tiered interventions without comprehensive evaluation, as in Henry's case; or they can have poorly conceived core literacy instruction, as at Berson Elementary. Moreover, as discussed in the preceding chapter, many teachers clearly are not well prepared to implement RTI models, even in the extensively researched area of beginning reading; most educators will require professional development in order to use these approaches effectively. However, to be successful, all policies and programs rely on good implementations. Despite their many challenges, educators should not abandon RTI/MTSS approaches but should strive to implement them well, including continuing to make the improvements in them suggested by ongoing research on RTI.

The emphasis is not on any particular model of RTI, such as the three-tiered model, but rather on the effective use of the *key features* of RTI. These important features include research-based core general education literacy instruction; universal screening; prompt intervention for at-risk children as part of the general education system; the use of data to inform instruction, in relation to both individual students and to the educational system as a whole; and a systemic approach to instruction, intervention, and data collection. All schools should be using these kinds of practices, because such practices—implemented well—can greatly improve instruction for *all* children. Without research-based core literacy instruction, general education will inadvertently manufacture in some students reading problems that stem mainly from inadequate teaching, not from true learning difficulties, making reading difficulties more widespread and serious than they otherwise would be. Without appropriate universal screening and prompt intervention, educators will inevitably overlook some at-risk readers until those children's needs become severe and much more difficult to remediate. Without the use of data to inform decision making, schools cannot make the kinds of adjustments to curriculum and instruction that facilitate continuous improvement and the flexibility to deal with changes in their student populations—for example, significant increases in the number of ELLs whom they serve. And in relation to individual students receiving interventions, without data-based decision making, educators cannot know how well those interventions are working or make appropriate adjustments to interventions. Without a systemic approach, children's education cannot be maximally effective, because generally inefficient instruction within a school, or poorly informed instruction by individual teachers, will tend to compromise children's education over time, with the worst effects on the most vulnerable readers—those from poverty backgrounds, ELLs, and children with learning problems.

Years ago, long before the advent of RTI, a director of bilingual education for a large urban district, who was well known locally (and frequently in trouble for his candor), told me that he preferred to see most ELLs go to special education rather than remain in general education. He recognized that most of these children did not actually have disabilities, but he believed that special educators were more likely than were general educators to provide differentiated instruction and give ELLs the individualized help they needed. For at-risk children without disabilities, such as many language-minority students and children from poverty backgrounds, practices associated with RTI can help ensure appropriate core instruction as well as routine opportunities for extra help within the general education system. In the absence of these opportunities, children like Mateo, Alicia, or Valentina may be inappropriately classified with disabilities simply because educators see no other practical alternatives for providing them with the help they need to catch up in reading. Furthermore, even typical and high-achieving readers can benefit from an emphasis on strong core literacy instruction and data-based decision making, which may improve appropriate differentiation of instruction to meet their needs. For example, a high-achieving second grader who greatly exceeds grade benchmarks in universal screening and reads fourth-grade text fluently with good comprehension does not need second-grade phonics instruction; that instructional time could be devoted to something else more productive for the student, such as project work or independent writing. And for students with disabilities, the use of RTI practices may facilitate inclusion in general education because of RTI's emphasis on strong core instruction. These practices can also help to ensure that the reading difficulties of children classified with disabilities are not primarily due to poor teaching or an inadequate curriculum.

RECLAIMING THE IDENTITY OF SPECIAL EDUCATION

Even with the best implementations of RTI, special education has an essential role to play in serving the needs of students with the most persistent or severe types of reading difficulties, whether or not those children have or are formally classified with disabilities. Like general educators, special educators also must use practices such as research-based instruction, intensive intervention, and employing data to monitor children's progress, because children with serious, persistent reading problems—including children such as Brett and Kevin—usually cannot have their intervention needs met simply through surface adjustments to the general education program. Although appropriate access to and participation in general education are certainly important, students with serious reading difficulties also require systematic, intensive intervention that directly addresses their needs in reading (and in other academic areas) and that attempts as much as possible to close performance gaps between the children and their grade- or age-mates over time. For some of these students, especially those whose problems include core comprehension abilities or long-standing, entrenched reading difficulties, completely closing achievement gaps may not be feasible, and many children may require long-term special education support. However, educators cannot know if an individual child is capable of reaching grade expectations if they do not even aim for that goal; furthermore, children who never attain grade expectations can still have their difficulties ameliorated by intensive, research-based intervention, attaining better outcomes than they would have had without this kind of intervention.

To fulfill their roles well, special educators must be prepared to not only collaborate with general educators but also be expert interventionists, able to identify different types of literacy difficulties, deliver highly specialized instruction, and monitor individual children's progress closely. The evidence reviewed in Chapter 10 showed that, in many studies of teacher knowledge, special educators performed no better than general educators;

when the former did perform better than the latter, their performance still was often well below ceiling. This kind of evidence suggests that, currently, many special educators are not well prepared to identify and deliver specialized literacy interventions to children with the most challenging types of reading difficulties, consistent with the view of Fuchs and colleagues (2010) that the identity of special education has weakened. Reclaiming this identity and preparing special educators to serve as expert interventionists in reading will likely require extensive reforms in special as well as general educator preparation and licensure, such as those suggested by Brownell, Sindelar, and colleagues (2010), as well other reforms discussed in Chapter 10.

WHY EDUCATORS SHOULD USE RESPONSE TO INTERVENTION CRITERIA IN IDENTIFYING LEARNING DISABILITIES

As mentioned at the outset of this book, the use of RTI to identify LDs in reading entails some particularly difficult problems, even in the relatively well-researched area of elementary reading. Critics of RTI (e.g., Hale et al., 2010; Kavale et al., 2008) are correct that RTI still has a relatively limited empirical base for use in identification of LDs and that reasons other than an LD can account for a particular child's failure to respond to an intervention. It is certainly also true that poor implementations of MTSS models may undermine accurate identification of LDs when RTI criteria are used.

However, current alternatives for the identification of LDs are far more flawed than is an approach based on RTI criteria. An IQ–achievement discrepancy has all the problems detailed in Chapters 1 and 2 and described in two decades' worth of research studies and reviews (e.g., Fletcher et al., 1994, 2007; Siegel, 1988, 1989; Siegel & Himel, 1998; Spear-Swerling & Sternberg, 1996; Stanovich, 1991, 2000; Stanovich & Siegel, 1994). These problems include, but are not limited to, all those associated with the use of IQ tests as indicators of children's broad potential for learning, such as the risk of lowered academic expectations for children with modest IQs, poor validity for ELLs and children from poverty backgrounds, the fact that IQ test performance may itself be influenced by reading experience, and lack of relevance for planning reading instruction. (Consider the children whose IQ data was available in Chapters 7, 8, and 9, and ask yourself if anything essential for planning reading instruction would be lost if the IQ data were omitted. The answer is no.) Many other problems plague the IQ–achievement discrepancy, including the fact that its use makes early identification difficult and that it does not identify subgroups of poor readers with different educational needs. To sum up, there is a considerable empirical base on the use of an IQ-achievement discrepancy in identifying LDs, but these empirical studies are hardly reassuring because they strongly suggest that an IQ–achievement discrepancy should *not* be used.

Another possible alternative to the use of RTI criteria in identification of LDs involves employing listening comprehension in lieu of IQ as an indicator of a child's potential in reading. As Stanovich (1991) pointed out, this approach avoids some, but not all, the problems associated with IQ tests. Listening comprehension is indeed important in reading, and therefore assessment of listening comprehension is much more relevant to planning reading instruction than is IQ. Nonetheless, like IQ, listening comprehension is affected by reading experience and may be undermined by long-standing reading difficulties as well as by other factors such as poverty or limited experience with English. Children with LDs who have a pattern of SWRD, such as Brett and Henry in Chapter 7, can often be identified via a listening comprehension–reading comprehension discrepancy. However, children who show evidence of other profiles of poor reading, including both SRCD and MRD, would often be difficult to identify using this approach because of specific linguistic or cognitive weaknesses that may tend to result in low (or low-average) listening comprehension. There is little reason for excluding such children from special education services based solely on their lack of a listening comprehension–reading comprehension discrepancy.

Another alternative approach to identification of LDs in reading involves the pattern of strengths and weaknesses criterion suggested by Hale and colleagues (2010) and included as an option in IDEA 2004. This criterion would require that children identified with LDs demonstrate a pattern of strengths and weaknesses in cognitive-linguistic abilities along with accompanying academic impairments. Research reviewed throughout this book indicates that many poor readers do have characteristic patterns of strengths and weaknesses in specific cognitive-linguistic abilities. Indeed, some of this research is the basis for the theoretical model of reading problems in Chapter 4, and it is the reason information about certain cognitive-linguistic abilities is included in the case study chapters. Still, as the cases demonstrate, the fact that a child exemplifies a particular pattern of cognitive-linguistic weaknesses does not provide evidence that the child's learning problems are *intrinsic* as opposed to primarily influenced by instruction or experience. Therefore, a child's identification as with learning disabilities should not depend on the presence of this pattern. For example, like Brett, Alicia in Chapter 7 had weaknesses in phonological skills and decoding coupled with apparent strengths in vocabulary and broad language comprehension—but unlike Brett's difficulties, Alicia's responded quickly to intervention, with no signs of lingering problems. It would seem highly dubious to describe Alicia as dyslexic, and it certainly would make no sense to require her to receive a disability diagnosis in order to obtain extra help. Conversely, Henry in Chapter 7 had many signs of dyslexia, including persistent problems in decoding, spelling, and reading fluency despite years of appropriate intervention, as well as a family history of dyslexia. However, he did not evidence below-average performance on phonological-processing measures. Phonological-processing skills, specific cognitive-linguistic abilities generally viewed as central to dyslexia (e.g., Lyon et al., 2003), are known to have a bidirectional relationship with word decoding skills (e.g., Ehri, 2005), and it is possible that Henry had early phonemic awareness difficulties that resolved as his decoding abilities developed to some threshold level. In any case, despite lengthy intervention, Henry still had continuing reading difficulties that merited special education, and his average performance on phonological-processing measures should not exclude him from services.

In addition, as Fletcher and colleagues (2007) point out, children with the most severe reading difficulties may not show a pattern of strengths and weaknesses, and thus a requirement based on this criterion might exclude from services the very children who need them the most. Moreover, many measures of cognitive processing are not particularly useful in understanding reading difficulties or in educational planning (Fletcher, 2009), and special education has a long history of employing problematic measures of processing (Spear-Swerling & Sternberg, 1996). Scientific study of varied cognitive-linguistic processes that may play a role in reading is legitimate, of course, and may eventually yield many practical benefits. However, measures used in education must be not only scientifically well-founded and technically adequate but also practically meaningful. That is, they should add educationally useful information not already provided by other available assessments, because teachers (and students) do not have infinite amounts of time to expend in testing.

RTI criteria should not be used alone to identify LDs nor would such an approach meet the requirements of IDEA 2004. However, with the use of additional criteria, an RTI criterion involving insufficient response to research-based intervention is a much better option for identification of LDs in reading than are alternative approaches to identification. Along with RTI criteria, educators should employ exclusionary criteria and low achievement criteria as well as consider other important variables in identification of LDs, such as the child's educational history (e.g., previous need for intervention), any history of early language delay, and any significant family history of reading problems. Although any cutoff for low achievement is necessarily somewhat arbitrary, requirements for low reading achievement should avoid overly stringent cutoffs that make it difficult to identify all but the most severely impaired readers in favor of a somewhat more liberal cutoff that still designates low achievement (e.g., a standard score below 90, not 85). Use of component reading scores (e.g., reading real words, nonsense words, reading fluency) is essential, because a broad cluster score in reading can mask important weaknesses. A child's eligibility should not hinge on demonstrating a pattern of strengths and weaknesses in cognitive-linguistic abilities, but if the appropriate cognitive-linguistic abilities are assessed as part of a comprehensive evaluation, these assessments may provide useful information. As indicated in previous chapters, besides the essential measures of component reading abilities, the most helpful additional measures include those involving specific language abilities such as vocabulary and broad listening comprehension as well as, in some cases, cognitive measures involving working memory, rapid naming, and executive function. Additional language testing may sometimes be useful for children whose difficulties center on comprehension. Considered as a whole and interpreted in relation to the kind of theoretical model described in Chapters 3 and 4, these measures can help plan a comprehensive reading program as well as suggest whether a child may be at risk for certain future literacy problems (e.g., late-emerging reading comprehension difficulties).

The approach described in the preceding paragraph—and illustrated in parts of the case study chapters—involves weighing multiple criteria and making judgments. It is certainly more complex than subtracting a child's achievement standard score from his or her IQ, and it requires that educators involved in making eligibility determinations have a considerable knowledge base about reading, language, and cognition. However, it would serve children with reading difficulties far better than other approaches to the identification of LDs, because it takes seriously the need to make certain that poor readers have received appropriate instruction before consideration for an LD diagnosis while avoiding the perils of IQ testing and while also recognizing and providing for the needs of children with severe or persistent reading difficulties. In this approach, because of the use of the cutoff of 90, some identified children's difficulties may not be "severe" relative to those of the lowest poor readers, but these difficulties will still be educationally significant ones that have persisted over time despite appropriate intervention, as in Henry's case.

WHAT ABOUT THE "REAL" LEARNING DISABILITIES?

The approach I am advocating for the identification of LDs will not necessarily identify the "real" cases of dyslexia and other LDs, in the sense of identifying children who have a specific, neurobiological disorder distinct from other types of reading problems. Indeed, for the purposes of educational planning and intervention, dyslexia (for example) is *not* distinct from other types of SWRD. Children do not require completely different interventions based on whether they have a genuine case of dyslexia as opposed to SWRD that stems from, say, inadequate general education practices (although the former children may well require more intensity of intervention than the latter). However, if RTI practices are well implemented, RTI criteria for LDs do identify a subgroup of poor readers who require relatively more intensive or more long-term educational support than do other struggling readers in order to progress in reading. This type of intensity and long-term support has traditionally been the purview of special education; although the capacity of special education to provide appropriately intensive intervention may indeed need improvement, there is little reason to believe that general education is better prepared to handle this mission.

RTI criteria may not identify the "real" cases of LDs, but attempting to rule out instructional factors as the cause of children's reading problems before identifying them with disabilities surely makes sense. So does an educational system that does its best to provide high-quality core instruction and opportunities for short-term intervention to all students while still providing special education services for the subset of students needing long-term support. In addition, the use of RTI criteria in identification of LDs orients practitioners toward educationally meaningful questions when they evaluate children with reading problems. The most vital questions are not about the children's IQs, the size of the gap between individual children's IQs and their reading achievement, the presence of strengths and weaknesses in cognitive-linguistic abilities, or even whether children genuinely have dyslexia. The most important questions, educationally speaking, include those about children's profiles and patterns of reading difficulties based on component reading and language abilities; whether children's difficulties have been targeted with appropriate interventions; whether children are showing reasonable progress based on appropriate progress-monitoring measures; and how to improve interventions (or special education) for children who are not progressing. In other words, the most important questions arise from the use of RTI practices in conjunction with consideration of children's profiles and patterns of reading difficulties. Furthermore, these questions are educationally meaningful for all struggling readers, whether or not they have LDs.

KEY CHALLENGES

Preventing and solving reading problems undeniably entails many challenges. In this section, I discuss some of the most important ones and possible ways to deal with them.

Effectively Addressing Different Types of Reading Difficulties

Relatively more is known about how to identify, successfully intervene with, and monitor progress in children who have difficulties in decoding than about those whose problems center on comprehension. For poor decoders, such as children with SWRD, successful interventions are well identified, and adequate progress-monitoring tools are generally available. Regrettably, however, sometimes the appropriate interventions and progress-monitoring measures fail to be implemented in practice or core general education phonics instruction is inadequate, as was true for Brett and Valentina, contributing to decoding problems in many children. A strong phonemic awareness and phonics component to core reading curricula in the early grades is essential for avoiding and ameliorating these types of difficulties. Educators also require access to appropriate phonics interventions as well as the professional development to implement these interventions successfully with the children who need them.

     For children with comprehension-based reading difficulties, including those with SRCD and MRD, fewer good progress-monitoring tools are available, and less is known about how to gauge adequate progress or accelerate progress. In addition, because of the many factors that may influence comprehension, individual poor comprehenders' underlying instructional needs may vary greatly, and interventions may be complex, particularly for students with MRD, who have problems with word-level reading skills as well as core comprehension weaknesses. All these factors make determination of responsiveness to intervention in students with comprehension-based reading difficulties somewhat daunting. Ongoing research on the comprehension needs of different types of poor readers, such as those from language-minority backgrounds, from poverty backgrounds, or with specific disabilities such as ASD, may help to address these issues in the future. For now, these challenges underscore the importance of high-quality core reading instruction that is sensitive to the needs of the student population and that provides appropriate differentiation of instruction (e.g., a relatively greater emphasis on vocabulary and academic language for students from poverty or ELL backgrounds). Such instruction may prevent the development of reading comprehension problems or keep at-risk students from falling far behind their peers, reducing the need to deal with long-term intervention in the first place.

For students who do require comprehension interventions, especially for those with MRD, multicomponent interventions may be particularly helpful. For monitoring progress in comprehension, maze CBMs and embedded comprehension checks, such as those described in Chapters 8 and 9, may be useful, as may analysis of work products such as writing samples. In deciding whether individual students are sufficiently responsive to comprehension interventions, educators might compare the responses of poor comprehenders from similar backgrounds and with similar types of difficulties. For instance—assuming generally high-quality intervention—educators could assess the intervention responsiveness of individual primary-grade poor comprehenders who are ELLs from Spanish-speaking backgrounds by comparing each child's performance during intervention to the average performance of other Spanish-speaking ELLs receiving intervention. The least responsive students could then be considered for intensification of intervention or for comprehensive evaluation.

Developing Interdisciplinary Approaches to Assessment and Intervention

Research mapping reading development and reading difficulties has been an interdisciplinary effort; similarly, assessment and intervention for elementary students with reading difficulties should be an interdisciplinary effort capitalizing on the knowledge of professionals from general and special education, reading, speech-language pathology, school psychology, and sometimes other fields as well. In special education, the use of a multidisciplinary team in evaluation and in educational planning is standard practice, but solving all reading problems requires a multidisciplinary and interdisciplinary approach, because whether or not they have disabilities, struggling readers often have difficulties involving not only reading but also related areas such as language. Furthermore, even the best-prepared veteran practitioners typically have relatively greater expertise in some areas than others. For example, special educators who have received advanced training in behavior analysis or math interventions have valuable expertise but may not be the best specialists to deliver reading interventions. In contrast, special educators who are well trained in MSL programs and other systematic phonics interventions for poor decoders might have much better expertise for delivering decoding interventions than does a reading specialist whose training focused mainly on comprehension; however, the latter might be better prepared to deliver comprehension interventions than the former. All professionals involved in teaching reading should be well prepared, but K–12 schools also should capitalize on the specific strengths and talents of individual practitioners, which may vary from school to school, rather than assuming that reading interventions should be the purview of a single professional group.

A former graduate student of mine, an experienced special educator who had just completed her master's in special education and who had pursued many additional professional development opportunities, recently interviewed for a high-ranking supervisory position involving RTI in a large urban school district. The position, which included supervising the system of reading interventions and coaching reading interventionists, was advertised as one in general education or reading, and my former student was pessimistic about her chances of obtaining it because, although she was a licensed special educator, she did not hold a general education or reading certification. This teacher was stellar in her broad disciplinary knowledge about reading, her practical assessment and teaching skills, and her ability to collaborate well with colleagues. Furthermore, because she had a strong interest in both children with dyslexia and children with ASD, she had pursued extensive training and teaching experiences involving the types of research-based interventions often used with these students, including interventions for decoding, comprehension, and fluency. Fortunately, the school district posting the job wisely recognized that a practitioner with the expertise to assess and teach decoding, fluency, and comprehension to students with disabilities also has expertise that is highly relevant to other poor readers, even if those children do not have disabilities. My former student got the job.

Making Good Teacher Preparation Practices Systemic

In her fascinating book on countries that have achieved impressive gains in educational attainment for the overwhelming majority of students, Ripley (2013) concludes that such countries all prioritize teacher quality because they know that the quality of an educational system cannot exceed the quality of its teachers. Not only do these countries take steps to attract highly capable individuals into the teaching profession, but they also provide rigorous teacher preparation and professional development, in terms of both disciplinary knowledge and practical teaching competencies. Unfortunately, in the United States, education majors are too often undemanding, with relatively low standards for admission, graduation, or both (Levine, 2006). However, as Chapter 10 shows, and as Moats (1994, 1999) has long argued, effective teaching of reading, particularly to at-risk children, requires considerable knowledge and skill. There is plenty of important, educationally relevant, substantive content for schools of education to teach their candidates in reading—and of course, in other areas as well—if they choose to include it as part of teacher preparation.

Although excellent teacher preparation programs certainly do exist, good teacher preparation practices must become systemic if we are to prevent and address reading difficulties effectively on a large scale. First, without a systemic approach, just as is true at the K–12 level, teacher candidates' knowledge and skills depend too heavily on whether they are lucky enough to have knowledgeable teacher educators as their professors. Medical schools and medical school professors undoubtedly vary in quality, just as do education schools and teacher educators, but it is hard to imagine that we would tolerate medical training whose quality hinged heavily on whether individual physician candidates happened to take anatomy or physiology classes with particular professors. Second, without a systemic approach, long-term teacher professional development, universally recognized as essential even with the best preservice preparation, is doomed to gross inefficiency. As part of their in-service professional development for teachers, elementary schools should not have to include basic disciplinary content such as knowledge about language structure, phonemic awareness, or typical reading development; they should be able to take this knowledge for granted in any licensed teacher of reading.

Many reforms in teacher preparation are important, but in order to achieve more consistent high-quality preparation on a large scale, appropriate licensure exams, including both the more basic and advanced types of exams with sufficiently high passing scores discussed in Chapter 10, are particularly critical. Good licensure exams convey clear expectations about what candidates are expected to know at different levels of professional development, and they help to orient both candidates and teacher educators toward many fine research-based resources in reading designed specifically for educators that are currently available but too often unused in reading methods courses (Joshi, Binks, Graham, et al., 2009; NCTQ, 2006). These exams can help to ensure that candidates who lack important knowledge do not obtain a teaching license, and they create necessary accountability for teacher education programs. However, much rests on selection of the appropriate exams—for example, exams that include the kind of content listed in Table 10.1—because a bad exam will not be effective and may even drive change in the wrong direction. Nearly all states require exams for teacher licensure, but high-quality teacher preparation in reading is much less prevalent than are licensure exams, in part, because many exams do not test disciplinary knowledge about reading well (e.g., Stotsky, 2009).

Placing High-Stakes Educational Decisions in Well-Informed Hands

A friend who is a researcher in cognitive psychology at a top-tier academic institution once asked me how it could be that some schools still are not teaching phonics explicitly or systematically in the primary grades, when evidence on the importance of teaching phonics well to beginning readers has been available for decades. My answer was that high-stakes decisions about reading curriculum, instruction, assessment, and interventions frequently are in the hands of administrators or others who are unfamiliar with this research evidence, which, as discussed in Chapter 10, is often not included in teacher preparation. Lacking knowledge of the evidence, well-intended educators can easily make poor choices of assessments for universal screening and progress monitoring, of materials for core reading curriculum and instruction, or of reading interventions. These kinds of high-stakes decisions are extremely important because they affect large numbers of students, and because poor choices may totally undermine reading instruction for many children, especially those who are at risk in reading. Unfortunately, appropriate expertise for making these decisions cannot be judged solely by whether an individual has a degree in a particular field. Rather, administrators and others involved in such decision making must have, or must develop, the appropriate expertise. Decision makers can seek guidance from the work of published experts, such as those referenced in previous chapters of this book, as well as from research centers devoted to reading. Examples of such research centers include the Florida Center for Reading Research (http://www.fcrr.org), Haskins Laboratories (http://www.haskins.yale.edu), the University of Oregon Center for Teaching and Learning (http://reading.uoregon.edu), and the Vaughn Gross Center for Reading and Language Arts as well as the Meadows Center for Preventing Educational Risk at the University of Texas at Austin (http://www.meadowscenter.org/vgc). Additional examples of valuable research-based web materials for practitioners include those at the Center on Instruction (http://www.centeroninstruction.org), the Institute of Education Sciences (e.g., the practice guides at http://ies.ed.gov/ncee/wwc), and the RTI Action Network (http://www.rtinetwork.org).

Achieving the Best Possible
Implementations of Response to Intervention Practices

Implementing RTI practices well involves all the types of challenges mentioned earlier—successfully addressing different types of reading difficulties, developing interdisciplinary approaches to assessment and intervention, high-quality teacher preparation and professional development, and ensuring that high-stakes decisions central to the success of RTI efforts are made by those with the necessary expertise. Adequate access to resources, especially to appropriate instructional materials, intervention materials, and an extensive variety of children's books, also is vital.

Because research on RTI practices is continually emerging and use of these practices on a wide scale is so new, it is critical that educators who are involved in implementing RTI policy—and particularly in making key policy decisions (e.g., about district procedures for universal screening)—keep abreast of this research. For instance, as discussed in previous chapters, recent studies suggest ways that universal screening can be made more accurate, such as by supplementing initial CBM screening with monitoring of at-risk children's performance in Tier I instruction for a specific period. These studies also support "fast tracking" of certain students to more intensive levels of intervention or to special education (e.g., Fuchs, Fuchs, Compton, et al., 2012; Fuchs & Vaughn, 2012). No doubt, future studies will suggest other research-based improvements to RTI practices.

To return to Torgesen's (2006) analogy, implementing RTI practices in education in a way that is responsive to ongoing research findings may be even harder than making major repairs to an airplane while the plane is in flight; it may be more like making major in-flight repairs while the blueprint for the airplane keeps being revised. However, the effort involved in implementing RTI policies remains well worthwhile because of the many potential benefits to children—all children, but especially those at risk in reading.

THE WAY FORWARD

With or without the use of reading profiles and patterns, implementing RTI/MTSS approaches is far from easy, and effective implementation requires good guidance from states to individual school districts as well as informed leadership at the local level. However, avoiding key RTI practices such as universal screening, high-quality general education reading instruction, early intervention, and data-based decision making does nothing to prevent or address poor reading; without these practices, it is simply easier to overlook some children's difficulties, until, as for Anthony in Chapter 1, they become too big to ignore. Denial is rarely a successful solution strategy. Using RTI/MTSS approaches in conjunction with poor reader profiles is not perfect policy—in fact, it is messy, imperfect policy, fraught with challenges. Still, it is the best approach we have, by a very long way, for preventing and solving children's reading problems.

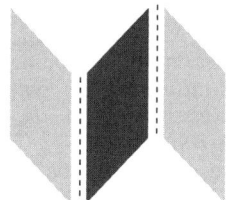

References

Aaron, P.G., Joshi, M., Gooden, R., & Bentum, K. (2008). Diagnosis and treatment of reading disabilities based on the component model of reading: An alternative to the discrepancy model of LD. *Journal of Learning Disabilities, 41,* 67–84.

Adams, G.L., & Carnine, D.W. (2003). Direct instruction. In H.L. Swanson, K.R. Harris, & S. Graham (Eds.), *Handbook of learning disabilities* (pp. 403–416). New York, NY: Guilford Press.

Adams, M.J. (1990). *Beginning to read: Thinking and learning about print.* Cambridge, MA: MIT Press.

Adams, M.J. (1998). The three-cueing system. In F. Lehr & J. Osborn (Eds.), *Literacy for all: Issues in teaching and learning* (pp. 73–99). New York, NY: Guilford Press.

Adams, M.J. (2012). On the importance of standards. *Perspectives on Language and Literacy, 38,* 11–14.

Al Otaiba, S. (2001). Children who do not respond to early literacy instruction: A longitudinal study across kindergarten and first grade. *Reading Research Quarterly, 36,* 344–346.

Algozzine, B., Wang, C., White, R., Cooke, N., Marr, M.B., Algozzine, K., . . . Duran, G. (2012). Effects of multi-tier academic and behavior instruction on difficult-to-teach students. *Exceptional Children, 79,* 45–64.

Allington, R.L., & McGill-Franzen, A. (2008). Comprehension difficulties among struggling readers. In S.E. Israel & G.G. Duffy (Eds.), *Handbook of research on reading comprehension* (pp. 551–568). New York, NY: Routledge.

Allington, R.L., McGill-Franzen, A., Camilli, G., Williams, L., Graff, J., Zeig, J., . . . Nowak, R. (2010). Addressing summer reading setback among economically disadvantaged elementary students. *Reading Psychology, 31,* 1–17.

Altemeier, L., Jones, J., Abbott, R., & Berninger, V. (2006). Executive factors in becoming writing-readers and reading-writers: Note-taking and report writing in third and fifth graders. *Developmental Neuropsychology, 29,* 161–173.

American Educational Research Association, American Psychological Association, & National Council on Measurement in Education. (1999). *Standards for educational and psychological testing.* Washington, DC: American Psychological Association.

Americans with Disabilities Act (ADA) of 1990, PL 101-336, 42 U.S.C. §§ 12101 *et seq.*

Anderson, R., Hiebert, E., Scott, J., & Wilkinson, I. (1985). *Becoming a nation of readers: The report of the Commission on Reading.* Champaign, IL: Center for the Study of Reading.

Anderson, R.C., & Nagy, W.E. (1992). The vocabulary conundrum. *The American Educator, 16,* 14–18, 44–47.

Anderson, R.C., Wilson, P.T., & Fielding, L.G. (1988). Growth in reading and how children spend their time outside of school. *Reading Research Quarterly, 23,* 285–303.

Applebee, A.N., Langer, J.A., Nystrand, M., & Gamoran, A. (2003). Discussion-based approaches to developing understanding: Classroom instruction and student performance in middle and high school English. *American Educational Research Journal, 40,* 685–730.

Appleton-Smith, L. (1997). *The sunset pond.* Lyme, NH: Flyleaf Publishing.

August, D., Carlo, M., Dressler, C., & Snow, C. (2005). The critical role of vocabulary development for English language learners. *Learning Disabilities Research & Practice, 20,* 50–57.

August, D., & Hakuta, K. (Eds.). (1998). *Educating language minority children*. Washington, DC: National Academy Press.

August, D., & Shanahan, T. (2006). *Developing literacy in second-language learners: Report of the National Literacy Panel on Language-Minority Children and Youth*. Mahwah, NJ: Erlbaum.

Ayer, E., Waterford, H., & Heck, A. (1995). *Parallel journeys*. New York: Aladdin Paperbacks.

Badian, N. (1999). Reading disability defined as a discrepancy between listening and reading comprehension. *Journal of Learning Disabilities, 32,* 138–148.

Barkley, R.A. (1997). *ADHD and the nature of self-control*. New York, NY: Guilford Press.

Barone, D.M., & Xu, S.H. (2007). *Literacy instruction for English language learners Pre-K–2*. New York, NY: Guilford Press.

Barth, A.E., Stuebing, K.K., Anthony, J.L., Denton, C.A., Mathes, P.G., Fletcher, J.M., & Francis, D.J. (2008). Agreement among response to intervention criteria for identifying responder status. *Learning and Individual Differences, 18,* 296–307.

Baum, S. (1984). Recognizing special talents in learning disabled students. *Teaching Exceptional Children, 16,* 92–98.

Beck, I.L. (2005). *Making sense of phonics: The hows and whys*. New York, NY: Guilford Press.

Beck, I.L., & McKeown, M.G. (2006). *Improving comprehension with Questioning the Author: A fresh and expanded view of a powerful approach*. New York, NY: Scholastic.

Beck, I.L., & McKeown, M.G. (2007). Increasing young low-income children's oral vocabulary repertoires through rich and focused instruction. *The Elementary School Journal, 107,* 251–271.

Beck, I.L., McKeown, M.G., & Kucan, L. (2002). *Bringing words to life: Robust vocabulary instruction*. New York, NY: Guilford Press.

Berninger, V.W., & Abbott, R.D. (1994). Redefining learning disabilities: Moving beyond aptitude-achievement discrepancies to failure to respond to validated treatment protocols. In G.R. Lyon (Ed.), *Frames of reference for the assessment of learning disabilities: New views on measurement issues* (pp. 163–183). Baltimore, MD: Paul H. Brookes Publishing Co.

Berninger, V.W., Abbott, R.D., Jones, J., Gould, L., Anderson-Youngstrom, M., Shimada, S., ... Apel, K. (2006). Early development of language by hand: Composing, reading, listening, and speaking connections; three letter-writing modes; and fast mapping in spelling. *Developmental Neuropsychology, 29,* 61–92.

Betjemann, R.S., Keenan, J.M., Olson, R.K., & DeFries, J.R. (2011). Choice of reading comprehension test influences the outcomes of genetic analyses. *Scientific Studies of Reading, 15,* 363–382.

Biemiller, A. (1999). *Language and reading success*. Cambridge, MA: Brookline Books.

Biemiller, A., & Boote, C. (2006). An effective method for building meaning vocabulary in primary grades. *Journal of Educational Psychology, 98,* 44–62.

Binks-Cantrell, E., Washburn, E.K., Joshi, R.M., & Hougen, M. (2012). Peter effect in the preparation of reading teachers. *Scientific Studies of Reading, 16,* 526–536.

Birsh, J.R. (2005). *Multisensory teaching of basic language skills* (2nd ed.). Baltimore, MD: Paul H. Brookes Publishing Co.

Bowers, L., Huisingh, R., & LoGuidice, C. (2008). *Social Language Development Test*. East Moline, IL: LinguiSystems.

Bowers, P.N., Kirby, J.R., & Deacon, S.H. (2010). The effects of morphological instruction on literacy skills: A systematic review of the literature. *Reading & Writing: An Interdisciplinary Journal, 23,* 515–537.

Bowman, M., & Treiman, R. (2008). Are young children logographic readers and spellers? *Scientific Studies of Reading, 12,* 153–170.

Boyer, N., & Ehri, L.C. (2011). Contribution of phonemic segmentation instruction with letters and articulation pictures to word reading and spelling in beginners. *Scientific Studies of Reading, 15,* 440–470.

Brady, S. (2012). Taking the Common Core Foundational Standards in reading far enough. *Perspectives on Language and Literacy, 38,* 19–30.

Brady, S., Gillis, M., Smith, T., Lavalette, M., Liss-Bronstein, L., Lowe, E., ... Wilder, T.D. (2009). First grade teachers' knowledge of phonological awareness and code concepts: Examining gains from an intensive form of professional development. *Reading and Writing: An Interdisciplinary Journal, 22,* 425–455.

Braun, H.I. (2005). *Using student progress to evaluate teachers: A primer on value-added models*. Princeton, NJ: Educational Testing Service.

Brown, K.J. (1999/2000). What kind of text— For whom and when? Textual scaffolding for beginning readers. *The Reading Teacher, 53*, 292–307.

Brown-Chidsey, R., & Steege, M. (2005). *Response to intervention: Principles and strategies for effective practice*. New York, NY: Guilford Press.

Brownell, M.T., Sindelar, P.T., Kiely, M.T., & Danielson, L.C. (2010). Special education teacher quality and preparation: Exposing foundations, constructing a new model. *Exceptional Children, 76*, 357–377.

Brownell, R. (2010a). *Expressive One-Word Picture Vocabulary Test, 4th edition*. San Antonio, TX: The Psychological Corp.

Brownell, R. (2010b). *Receptive One-Word Picture Vocabulary Test, 4th edition*. San Antonio, TX: The Psychological Corp.

Burns, P.C., & Roe, B.D. (2007). *Informal reading inventory* (7th ed.). Boston, MA: Houghton Mifflin.

Byrne, B., Samuelsson, S., Wadsworth, S., Hulslander, J., Corley, R., DeFries, J.C., . . . Olson, R. (2007). Longitudinal twin study of early literacy development: Preschool through grade 1. *Reading and Writing: An Interdisciplinary Journal, 20*, 77–102.

Cain, K., & Oakhill, J. (2008). *Children's comprehension problems in oral and written language: A cognitive perspective*. New York, NY: Guilford Press.

Carlisle, J.F. (2010). An integrative review of the effects of instruction in morphological awareness on literacy achievement. *Reading Research Quarterly, 45*, 464–487.

Carlisle, J.F., Cortina, K.S., & Katz, L.A. (2011). First-grade teachers' response to three models of professional development in reading. *Reading & Writing Quarterly, 27*, 212–238.

Carlisle, J.F., Kelcey, B., & Berebitsky, D. (2013). Teachers' support of students' vocabulary learning during literacy instruction in high poverty elementary schools. *American Educational Research Journal, 50*, 1360–1391.

Carlisle, J.F., Kelcey, B., Berebitsky, D., & Phelps, G. (2011). Embracing the complexity of instruction: A study of the effects of teachers' instruction on students' reading comprehension. *Scientific Studies of Reading, 15*, 409–439.

Carlisle, J.F., Kelcey, B., Rowan, B., & Phelps, G. (2011). Teachers' knowledge about early reading: Effects on students' gains in reading achievement. *Journal of Research on Educational Effectiveness, 4*, 289–321.

Carlisle, J., & Rice, M. (2002). *Improving reading comprehension: Research-based principles and practices*. Baltimore, MD: York Press.

Carlisle, J.F., & Stone, C.A. (2005). Exploring the role of morphemes in word reading. *Reading Research Quarterly, 40*, 428–449.

Carlo, M.S., August, D., McLaughlin, B., Snow, C.E., Dressler, C., Lippman, D.N., . . . White, C. (2004). Closing the gap: Addressing the vocabulary needs of English-language learners in bilingual and mainstream classrooms. *Reading Research Quarterly, 39*, 188–215.

Carnine, D.W., Silbert, J., Kame'enui, E.J., & Tarver, S.G. (2004). *Direct instruction reading* (4th ed.). Upper Saddle River, NJ: Pearson.

Cassar, M., & Treiman, R. (2004). Developmental variations in spelling: Comparing typical and poor spellers (pp. 627–643). In C.A. Stone, E.R. Silliman, B. Ehren, & K. Apel (Eds.), *Handbook of language and literacy: Development and disorders*. New York, NY: Guilford Press.

Catts, H.W., Adlof, S.M., & Weismer, S.E. (2006). Language deficits in poor comprehenders: A case for the simple view of reading. *Journal of Speech, Language, and Hearing Research, 49*(2), 278–293.

Catts, H.W., Compton, D.L., Tomblin, J.B., & Bridges, M.S. (2012). Prevalence and nature of late-emerging poor readers. *Journal of Educational Psychology, 104*(2), 166–181.

Chall, J. (1967). *Learning to read: The great debate*. New York, NY: McGraw-Hill.

Chall, J. (1983). *Stages of reading development*. New York, NY: McGraw-Hill.

Chard, D.J., Vaughn, S., & Tyler, B.J. (2002). A synthesis of research on effective interventions for building reading fluency with elementary students with learning disabilities. *Journal of Learning Disabilities, 35*, 386–406.

Cheesman, E.A., Hougen, M., & Smartt, S.A. (2010). Higher education collaboratives: Aligning research and practice in teacher education. *Perspectives on Language and Literacy, 36*, 27–31.

Cheesman, E.A., McGuire, J.M., Shankweiler, D., & Coyne, M. (2009). First-year teacher knowledge of phonemic awareness and its instruction. *Teacher Education and Special Education, 32*, 270–289.

Chetty, R., Friedman, J.N., & Rockoff, J.E. (2011). *The long-term impacts of teachers:*

Teacher value-added and student outcomes in adulthood (Working Paper 17699). Cambridge, MA: National Bureau of Economic Research.

Chinn, C.A., Anderson, R.C., & Waggoner, M.A. (2001). Patterns of discourse in two kinds of literature discussion. *Reading Research Quarterly, 36*, 378–411.

Christensen, C.A., & Bowey, J.A. (2005). The efficacy of orthographic rime, grapheme-phoneme correspondence, and implicit phonics approaches to teaching decoding skills. *Scientific Studies of Reading, 9*, 327–349.

Cipielewski, J., & Stanovich, K.E. (1992). Predicting growth in reading ability from children's exposure to print. *Journal of Experimental Child Psychology, 54*, 74–89.

Clarke, P.J., Snowling, M.J., Truelove, E., & Hulme, C. (2010). Ameliorating children's reading-comprehension difficulties: A randomized controlled trial. *Psychological Science, 21*, 1106–1116.

Coleman, M.R., Buysse, V., & Neitzel, J. (2006). *Recognition and response: An early intervening system for young children at risk for learning disabilities. Full report.* Chapel Hill: The University of North Carolina at Chapel Hill, Frank Porter Graham Child Development Institute.

Compton, D.L., Fuchs, D., Fuchs, L.S., Bouton, B., Gilbert, J.K., Barquero L.A., & Crouch R.C. (2010). Selecting at-risk first-grade readers for early intervention: Eliminating false positives and exploring the promise of a two-stage gated screening process. *Journal of Educational Psychology, 102*, 327–341.

Compton, D.L., Fuchs, L.S., Fuchs, D., Lambert, W., & Hamlett, C. (2011). The cognitive and academic profiles of reading and mathematics learning disabilities. *Journal of Learning Disabilities, 45*(1), 79–95.

Connor, C.M., Morrison, F.J., & Underwood, P.S. (2007). A second chance in second grade: The independent and cumulative impact of first- and second-grade reading instruction and students' letter-word reading skill growth. *Scientific Studies of Reading, 11*, 199–233.

Consortium on Reading Excellence (CORE). (2008). *CORE assessing reading: Multiple measures for kindergarten through twelfth grade* (2nd ed.). Novato, CA: Arena Press.

Cooter, R.B., Jr., Flynt, E.S., & Cooter, K.S. (2007). *Comprehensive reading inventory: Measuring reading development in regular*

and special education classrooms. Upper Saddle River, NJ: Pearson.

Council for Exceptional Children. (2009). *What every special educator must know, 6th edition.* Arlington, VA: Author.

Council for the Accreditation of Educator Preparation. (2010). *CAEP standards for accreditation of educator preparation.* Retrieved from http://www.caepsite.org/standards.html

Crowe, E.C., Connor, C.M., & Petscher, Y. (2009). Examining the core: Relations among reading curricula, poverty, and first through third grade reading achievement. *Journal of School Psychology, 47*, 187–214.

Cunningham, A.E., Perry, K.E., Stanovich, K.E., & Stanovich, P.J. (2004). Disciplinary knowledge of K–3 teachers and their knowledge calibration in the domain of early literacy. *Annals of Dyslexia, 54*, 139–167.

Cunningham, A.E., & Stanovich, K.E. (1991). Tracking the unique effects of print exposure in children: Associations with vocabulary, general knowledge, and spelling. *Journal of Educational Psychology, 83*, 264–274.

Cunningham, A.E., & Stanovich, K.E. (1997). Early reading acquisition and its relation to reading experience and ability ten years later. *Developmental Psychology, 33*, 934–945.

Cunningham, A.E., & Stanovich, K.E. (1998). What reading does for the mind. *American Educator, 22*, 8–15.

Cunningham, A.E., Zibulsky, J., Stanovich, K.E., & Stanovich, P.J. (2009). How teachers would spend their time teaching language arts: The mismatch between self-reported and best practices. *Journal of Learning Disabilities, 42*, 418–430.

Cunningham, J.W., Spadorcia, S.A., Erickson, K.A., Koppenhaver, D.A., Sturm, J.M., & Yoder, D.E. (2005). Investigating the instructional supportiveness of leveled texts. *Reading Research Quarterly, 40*, 410–417.

Cutting, L.E., Clements-Stephens, A., Pugh, K.R., Burns, S., Cao, A., Pekar, J.J., . . . Rimrodt, S.L. (2013). Not all reading disabilities are dyslexia: Distinct neurobiology of specific comprehension deficits. *Brain Connectivity, 3*, 199–211.

Cutting, L.E., Materek, A., Cole, C., Levine, T., & Mahone, E.M. (2009). Effects of fluency, oral language, and executive function on reading comprehension performance. *Annals of Dyslexia, 59*, 34–54.

Cutting, L.E., & Scarborough, H.S. (2006). Prediction of reading comprehension: Relative contributions of word recognition, language proficiency, and other cognitive skills can depend on how comprehension is measured. *Scientific Studies of Reading, 10*, 277–299.

Daneman, M., & Carpenter, P. (1980). Individual differences in working memory and reading. *Journal of Verbal Learning and Verbal Behavior, 19*, 450–466.

Darling-Hammond, L., Amrein-Beardsley, A., Haertel, E., & Rothstein, J. (2011, September 14). *Getting teacher evaluation right: A background paper for policy makers.* Capitol Hill Research Briefing, Dirksen Senate Office Building.

David, J.L. (2010). What research says about . . . / Using value-added measures to evaluate teachers. *Educational Leadership, 67*, 81–82.

Denckla, M.B. (1989). Executive function, the overlap zone between attention deficit hyperactivity disorder and learning disabilities. *International Pediatrics, 4*, 155–160.

Deno, S.L. (1985). Curriculum-based measurement: The emerging alternative. *Exceptional Children, 52*, 219–232.

Deno, S.L. (2003). Developments in curriculum-based measurement. *Journal of Special Education, 37*, 184–192.

Deno, S.L., & Fuchs, L.S. (1987). Developing curriculum-based measurement systems for data-based special education problem solving. *Focus on Exceptional Children, 19*, 1–16.

Deno, S.L., & Mirkin, P.K. (1977). *Data-based program modification: A manual.* Reston, VA: Council for Exceptional Children.

Denton, C.A., Fletcher, J.M., Anthony, J.L., & Francis, D.J. (2006). An evaluation of intensive intervention for students with persistent reading difficulties. *Journal of Learning Disabilities, 39*, 447–466.

Denton, C.A., Nimon, K., Mathes, P.G., Swanson, E.A., Kethley, C., Kurz, T.B., . . . Shih, M. (2010). Effectiveness of a supplemental early reading intervention scaled up in multiple schools. *Exceptional Children, 76*, 394–416.

Denton, C.A., Vaughn, S., & Fletcher, J.M. (2003). Bringing research-based practice in reading intervention to scale. *Learning Disabilities Research & Practice, 18*, 201–211.

Dodd, J.L., Ocampo, A., & Kennedy, K.S. (2011). Perspective-taking through narratives: An intervention for students with ASD. *Communication Disorders Quarterly, 33*, 23–33.

Duke, N.K., & Pearson, P.D. (2002). Effective practices for developing reading comprehension. In A.E. Farstrup & S.J. Samuels (Eds.), *What research has to say about reading instruction* (3rd ed., pp. 205–242). Newark, DE: International Reading Association.

Dunn, L.M., & Dunn, D.M. (2007). *Peabody Picture Vocabulary Test, 4th edition.* San Antonio, TX: The Psychological Corp.

Eason, S.H., Goldberg, L.F., Young, K.M., Geist, M.C., & Cutting, L.E. (2012). Reader–text interactions: How differential text and question types influence cognitive skills needed for reading comprehension. *Journal of Educational Psychology, 104*, 515–528.

Eason, S.H., Sabatini, J., Goldberg, L., Bruce, K., & Cutting, L.E. (2013). Examining the relationship between word reading efficiency and oral reading rate in predicting comprehension among different types of readers. *Scientific Studies of Reading, 17*, 199–223.

Eckert, M.A., Leonard, C.M., Richards, T.L., Aylward, E.H., Thomson, J., & Berninger, V.W. (2003). Anatomical correlates of dyslexia: Frontal and cerebellar findings. *Brain, 126*, 482–494.

Ehri, L.C. (1991). Learning to read and spell words. In L. Rieben & C.A. Perfetti (Eds.), *Learning to read: Basic research and its implications* (pp. 57–73). Mahwah, NJ: Erlbaum.

Ehri, L.C. (1997). Learning to read and learning to spell are one and the same, almost. In C.A. Perfetti, L. Rieben, & M. Fayol (Eds.), *Learning to spell: Research, theory, and practice across languages* (pp. 237–269). Mahwah, NJ: Erlbaum.

Ehri, L.C. (2004). Teaching phonemic awareness and phonics: An explanation of the National Reading Panel meta-analyses. In P. McCardle & V. Chhabra (Eds.), *The voice of evidence in reading research* (pp. 153–186). Baltimore, MD: Paul H. Brookes Publishing Co.

Ehri, L.C. (2005). Learning to read words: Theory, findings, and issues. *Scientific Studies of Reading, 9*, 167–188.

Eide, D. (2012). *Uncovering the logic of English: A common-sense approach to reading, spelling, and literacy.* Minneapolis, MN: Pedia Learning.

Elbaum, B., Vaughn, S., Hughes, M.T., & Moody, S.W. (1999). Grouping practices and reading outcomes for students with disabilities. *Exceptional Children, 65*, 399–415.

Elbro, C. (2004). Reading and spelling difficulties. In T. Nunes & P. Bryant (Eds.), *Handbook of children's literacy* (pp. 249–256). Dordrecht, Netherlands: Kluwer Academic Publishers.

Elkonin, D. (1973). U.S.S.R. In J. Downing (Ed.), *Comparative reading* (pp. 551–579). New York, NY: Macmillan.

Engelmann, S., & Bruner, E. (1988). *Reading mastery I*. Columbus, OH: Science Research Associates.

Erickson, K. (2013). Reading and assistive technology: Why the reader's profile matters. *Perspectives on Language and Literacy, 39*, 11–14.

Farrall, M.L. (2012). *Reading assessment: Linking language, literacy, and cognition*. Hoboken, NJ: John Wiley & Sons.

Fletcher, J.M. (2009). Dyslexia: The evolution of a scientific concept. *Journal of the International Neuropsychological Society, 15*, 501–508.

Fletcher, J.M., Lyon, G.R., Fuchs, L.S., & Barnes, M.A. (2007). *Learning disabilities: From identification to intervention*. New York, NY: Guilford Press.

Fletcher, J., Shaywitz, S., Shankweiler, D., Katz, I., Liberman, I., Steubing, K., . . . Shaywitz, B.A. (1994). Cognitive profiles of reading disability: Comparisons of discrepancy and low achievement definitions. *Journal of Educational Psychology, 86*, 6–23.

Florida Center for Reading Research. (2007). *Guidelines for reviewing a reading program*. Retrieved from http://www.doe.k12.de.us/infosuites/staff/profdev/rti_files/Guidelines%20for%20Reviewing%20a%20Reading%20Program.pdf

Fodor, J.A. (1983). *Modularity of mind*. Cambridge, MA: MIT Press.

Foorman, B.R. (2003). *Preventing and remediating reading difficulties*. Baltimore, MD: York Press.

Foorman, B.R., Francis, D.J., Fletcher, J.M., Schatschneider, C., & Mehta, P. (1998). The role of instruction in learning to read: Preventing reading disabilities in at-risk children. *Journal of Educational Psychology, 90*, 37–55.

Frith, U. (1985). Beneath the surface of developmental dyslexia. In K. Patterson, J. Marshall, & M. Coltheart (Eds.), *Surface dyslexia: Neuropsychological and cognitive studies of phonological reading* (pp. 301–330). London, England: Erlbaum.

Frith, U. (2012). Why we need cognitive explanations of autism. *Quarterly Journal of Experimental Psychology, iFirst*, 1–20.

Fuchs, D., Compton, D.L., Fuchs, L.S., Bryant, J., Hamlett, C., & Lambert, W. (2012). First-grade cognitive abilities as long-term predictors of reading comprehension and disability status. *Journal of Learning Disabilities, 45*, 217–231.

Fuchs, D., & Fuchs, L.S. (2005). Peer-assisted learning strategies: Promoting word recognition, fluency, and reading comprehension in young children. *Journal of Special Education, 39*, 34–44.

Fuchs, D., Fuchs, L.S., & Compton, D.L. (2012). Smart RTI: A next-generation approach to multilevel prevention. *Exceptional Children, 78*, 263–279.

Fuchs, D., Fuchs, L.S., & Stecker, P.M. (2010). The "blurring" of special education in a new continuum of general education placements and services. *Exceptional Children, 76*, 301–323.

Fuchs, L.S., Deno, S.L., & Mirkin, P. (1984). Effects of frequent curriculum-based measurement and evaluation on pedagogy, student achievement, and student awareness of learning. *American Educational Research Journal, 21*, 449–460.

Fuchs, L.S., & Vaughn, S. (2012). Responsiveness to intervention: A decade later. *Journal of Learning Disabilities, 45*, 195–203.

Gallistel, E., & Ellis, K. (1974). *Gallistel-Ellis Test of Coding Skills*. Hamden, CT: Montage Press.

Gamson, D.A., Lu, X., & Eckert, S.A. (2013). Challenging the research base of the Common Core State Standards: A historical reanalysis of text complexity. *Educational Researcher, 42*, 381–391.

Garan, E. (2001). Beyond the smoke and mirrors: A critique of the National Reading Panel report on phonics. *Phi Delta Kappan, 82*, 500–506.

Gawande, A. (2011, January 24). The hot spotters: Can we lower medical costs by giving the neediest patients better care? *The New Yorker*, 1–17.

Gelzheiser, L.M., Scanlon, D., Vellutino, F., Hallgren-Flynn, L., & Schatschneider, C. (2011). Effects of the Interactive Strategies approach—extended: A response and comprehensive intervention for intermediate-grade struggling readers. *The Elementary School Journal, 112*, 280–306.

Genesee, F., Paradis, J., & Crago, M. (2004). *Dual language development & disorders: A handbook on bilingualism & second language learning.* Baltimore, MD: Paul H. Brookes Publishing Co.

Gerber, M.M., & Durgunoglu, A.Y. (Guest Eds.). (2004). Reading risk and intervention for young English learners (special series). *Learning Disabilities Research and Practice, 19,* 199–272.

Gernsbacher, M.A. (1990). *Language comprehension as structure building.* Hillsdale, NJ: Erlbaum.

Gersten, R., Baker, S.K., Haager, D., & Graves, A. (2005). Exploring the role of teacher quality in predicting reading outcomes for first-grade English learners: An observational study. *Remedial and Special Education, 26,* 197–206.

Gersten, R., Baker, S.K., Shanahan, T., Linan-Thompson, S., Collins, P., & Scarcella, R. (2007). *Effective literacy and English language instruction for English learners in the elementary grades: A practice guide* (National Center for Education Evaluation [NCEE] 2007-4011). Washington, DC: NCEE, Institute of Education Sciences, U.S. Department of Education. Retrieved from http://ies.ed.gov/ncee

Gersten, R., Beckmann, S., Clarke, B., Foegen, A., Marsh, L., Star, J.R., . . . Witzel, B. (2009). *Assisting students struggling with mathematics: Response to Intervention (RtI) for elementary and middle schools* (NCEE 2009-4060). Washington, DC: National Center for Education Evaluation and Regional Assistance, Institute of Education Sciences, U.S. Department of Education. Retrieved from http://ies.ed.gov/ncee/wwc/publications/practiceguides

Gersten, R., Fuchs, L.S., Williams, J.P., & Baker, S. (2001). Teaching reading-comprehension strategies to students with learning disabilities: A review of research. *Review of Educational Research, 71,* 279–320.

Gillingham, A., & Stillman, B. (1970). *Remedial training for children with specific language disability.* Cambridge, MA: Educators' Publishing Service.

Goldberg, R.J., Higgins, E.L., Raskind, M.H., & Herman, K.L. (2003). Predictors of success in individuals with learning disabilities: A qualitative analysis of a 20-year longitudinal study. *Learning Disabilities Research & Practice, 18,* 222–236.

Good, R.H., & Kaminski, R.A. (with Cummings, K., Dufour-Martel, C., Petersen, K., Powell-Smith, K., Stollar, S., & Wallin, J.). (2011). *DIBELS Next assessment manual.* Eugene, OR: Dynamic Measurement Group. Retrieved from https://dibels.org

Goodman, K.S. (1976). Reading: A psycholinguistic guessing game. In H. Singer & R. Ruddell (Eds.), *Theoretical models and processes of reading* (pp. 497–508). Newark, DE: International Reading Association.

Goodwin, A.P., & Ahn, S. (2013). A meta-analysis of morphological interventions in English: Effects on literacy outcomes for school-age children. *Scientific Studies of Reading, 17,* 257–285.

Goodwin, A.P., Gilbert, J., & Cho, S. (2013). Morphological contributions to adolescent word reading: An item response approach. *Reading Research Quarterly, 48,* 39–60.

Goral, M., & Conner, P.S. (2013). Language disorders in multilingual and multicultural populations. *Annual Review of Applied Linguistics, 33,* 128–161.

Gough, P.B., & Tunmer, W.E. (1986). Decoding, reading, and reading disability. *Remedial and Special Education, 7,* 6–10.

Graham, S., Harris, K., & Fink, B. (2000). Is handwriting causally related to learning to write? Treatment of handwriting problems in beginning writers. *Journal of Educational Psychology, 92,* 620–633.

Graham, S., & Hebert, M.A. (2010). *Writing to read: Evidence for how writing can improve reading. A Carnegie Corporation Time to Act report.* Washington, DC: Alliance for Excellent Education.

Graves, A., Gersten, R., & Haager, D. (2004). Literacy instruction in multiple-language first-grade classrooms: Linking student outcomes to observed instructional practice. *Learning Disabilities Research and Practice, 19,* 262–272.

Graves, M.F. (2006). *The vocabulary book: Learning and instruction.* Newark, DE: International Reading Association.

Gresham, F.M., & Vellutino, F.R. (2010). What is the role of intelligence in the identification of specific learning disabilities? Issues and clarifications. *Learning Disabilities Research & Practice, 25,* 194–206.

Grigorenko, E.L. (2005). A conservative meta-analysis of linkage and linkage-association studies of developmental dyslexia. *Scientific Studies of Reading, 9,* 285–316.

Gunderson, L., & Siegel, L.S. (2001). The evils of the use of IQ tests to define learning disabilities in first- and second-language learners. *The Reading Teacher, 55,* 48–55.

Guthrie, J.T., Wigfield, A., Barbosa, P., Perencevich, K.C., Taboada, A., Davis, M.H., . . . Tonks, S. (2004). Increasing reading comprehension and engagement through concept-oriented reading instruction. *Journal of Educational Psychology, 96*, 403–423.

Guthrie, J.T., Wigfield, A., Metsala, J.L., & Cox, K.E. (1999). Motivational and cognitive predictors of text comprehension and reading amount. *Scientific Studies of Reading, 3*, 231–256.

Haager, D., & Vaughn, S. (2013). The Common Core State Standards and reading: Interpretations and implications for elementary students with learning disabilities. *Learning Disabilities Research & Practice, 28*, 5–16.

Haertel, E.H. (2013). *Reliability and validity of inferences about teachers based on student test scores.* Princeton, NJ: Educational Testing Service.

Hale, J., Alfonso, V., Berninger, V., Bracken, B., Christo, C., Clark, E., . . . Yalof, J. (2010). Critical issues in response-to-intervention, comprehensive evaluation, and specific learning disabilities identification and intervention: An expert white paper consensus. *Learning Disability Quarterly, 33*, 223–236.

Hallahan, D.P., & Mock, D.R. (2003). A brief history of the field of learning disabilities. In H.L. Swanson, K.R. Harris, & S. Graham (Eds.), *Handbook of learning disabilities* (pp. 16–29). New York, NY: Guilford Press.

Hammill, D.D., & Larsen, S.C. (2009). *Test of Written Language, 4th edition.* Austin, TX: Pro-Ed.

Hanushek, E., & Rivkin, S.G. (2010). Generalizations about using value-added measures of teacher quality. *The American Economic Review, 100*, 267–271.

Hanushek, E., & Woessman, L. (2009). *Do better schools lead to more growth? Cognitive skills, economic outcomes, and causation.* NBER Working Paper No. 14633, National Bureau of Economic Research, Cambridge, MA.

Hart, B., & Risley, T.R. (1995). *Meaningful differences in the everyday experience of young American children.* Baltimore, MD: Paul H. Brookes Publishing Co.

Hasbrouck, J., Ihnot, C., & Rogers, G. (1999). Read naturally: A strategy to increase oral reading fluency. *Reading Research and Instruction, 39*, 27–37.

Hasbrouck, J., & Tindal, G. (2006). Oral reading fluency norms: A valuable assessment tool for reading teachers. *The Reading Teacher, 59*, 636–644.

Hayes, D.P., & Ahrens, M. (1988). Vocabulary simplification for children: A special case of "motherese." *Journal of Child Language, 15*, 395–410.

Heck, R.H. (2009). Teacher effectiveness and student achievement: Investigating a multilevel cross-classified model. *Journal of Educational Administration, 47*, 227–249.

Henry, M.K. (2010). *Unlocking literacy: Effective decoding and spelling instruction* (2nd ed.). Baltimore, MD: Paul H. Brookes Publishing Co.

Hensler, B.S., Schatschneider, C., Taylor, J., & Wagner, R.K. (2010). Behavioral genetic approach to the study of dyslexia. *Journal of Developmental & Behavioral Pediatrics, 31*, 525–532.

Hiebert, E.H. (2012a). The Common Core's staircase of text complexity: Getting the size of the first step right. *Reading Today, 29*, 26–27.

Hiebert, E.H. (2012b). The Common Core State Standards and text complexity. In M.C. Hougen & S.M. Smartt (Eds.), *Fundamentals of literacy instruction & assessment, pre-K–6* (pp. 111–120). Baltimore, MD: Paul H. Brookes Publishing Co.

Hiebert, E.H., & Mesmer, H.A. (2013). Upping the ante of text complexity in the Common Core State Standards: Examining its potential impact on young readers. *Educational Researcher, 42*, 44–51.

Hoover, W.A., & Gough, P.B. (1990). The simple view of reading. *Reading and Writing: An Interdisciplinary Journal, 2*, 127–160.

Huemer, S.V., & Mann, V. (2010). A comprehensive profile of decoding and comprehension in autism spectrum disorders. *Journal of Autism and Developmental Disorders, 40*, 485–493.

Hulme, C., & Snowling, M. (2011). Children's reading comprehension difficulties: Nature, causes, and treatments. *Current Directions in Psychological Science, 20*, 139–142.

International Dyslexia Association. (2010). *Knowledge and practice standards for teachers of reading.* Baltimore, MD: Author.

International Reading Association. (2010). *Standards for reading professionals—revised.* Newark, DE: Author.

Iversen, S., Tunmer, W.E., & Chapman, J.W. (2005). The effects of varying group size on the Reading Recovery approach to preventative early intervention. *Journal of Learning Disabilities, 38*, 456–472.

Jenkins, J.R., Johnson, E., & Hileman, J. (2004). When is reading also writing: Sources of individual differences on the new reading performance assessments. *Scientific Studies of Reading, 8*, 125–152.

Jensen, P.S., Hinshaw, S.P., Swanson, J.M., Greenhill, L.L., Conners, C.K., Arnold, L.E., …Wigal, T. (2001). Findings from the NIMH multimodal treatment study of ADHD (MTA): Implications and applications for primary care providers. *Developmental and Behavioral Pediatrics, 22*, 60–73.

Johns, J.L. (2005). *Basic reading inventory* (9th ed.). Dubuque, IA: Kendall/Hunt.

Johnson, E.S., Jenkins, J.R., Petscher, Y., & Catts, H.W. (2009). How can we improve the accuracy of screening instruments? *Learning Disabilities Research & Practice, 24*, 174–185.

Johnson, S.B. (2006). *The ghost map: The story of London's most terrifying epidemic—and how it changed science, cities, and the modern world*. New York, NY: Riverhead.

Johnston, P., & Rogers, R. (2002). Early literacy development: The case for "informed assessment." In S.B. Neuman & D.K. Dickinson, *Handbook of early literacy research* (pp. 377–389). New York, NY: Guilford Press.

Joshi, R.M., Binks, E., Graham, L., Ocker-Dean, E., Smith, D., & Boulware-Gooden, R. (2009). Do textbooks used in university reading education courses conform to the instructional recommendations of the National Reading Panel? *Journal of Learning Disabilities, 42*, 458–463.

Joshi, R.M., Binks, E., Hougen, M., Dahlgren, M., Ocker-Dean, E., & Smith, D. (2009). Why elementary teachers might be inadequately prepared to teach reading. *Journal of Learning Disabilities, 42*, 392–402.

Joshi, R.M., Treiman, R., Carreker, S., & Moats, L. (2008–2009, Winter). How words cast their spell. *American Educator, 6–16*, 42–43.

Juel, C., & Minden-Cupp, C. (1999–2000). One down and 80,000 to go: Word recognition instruction in the primary grades. *The Reading Teacher, 53*, 332–335.

Just, M.A., & Carpenter, P. (1992). A capacity theory of comprehension: Individual differences in working memory. *Psychological Review, 99*, 122–149.

Kame'enui, E., Fuchs, L., Francis, D.J., Good, R., O'Connor, R., Simmons, D.C., … Torgesen, J.K. (2006). The adequacy of tools for assessing reading competence: A framework and review. *Educational Researcher, 35*, 3–11.

Kamps, D.M., Barbetta, P.M., Leonard, B.R., & Delquadri, J. (1994). Classwide peer tutoring: An integration strategy to improve reading skills and promote peer interactions among students with autism and general education peers. *Journal of Applied Behavior Analysis, 27*, 49–61.

Kaufman, A.S., & Kaufman, N.L. (2004). *Kaufman Test of Educational Achievement, 2nd edition*. San Antonio, TX: The Psychological Corp.

Kavale, K.A., Kauffman, J.M., Bachmeier, R.J., & LeFever, G.B. (2008). Response-to-intervention: Separating the rhetoric of self-congratulation from the reality of specific learning disability identification. *Learning Disability Quarterly, 31*, 135–150.

Keenan, J.M., & Betjemann, R.S. (2006). Comprehending the Gray Oral Reading Test without reading it: Why comprehension tests should not include passage-independent items. *Scientific Studies of Reading, 10*, 363–380.

Keenan, J.M., Betjemann, R.S., & Olson, R.K. (2008). Reading comprehension tests vary in the skills they assess: Differential dependence on decoding and oral comprehension. *Scientific Studies of Reading, 12*, 281–300.

Keenan, J.M., Betjemann, R., Wadsworth, S.J., DeFries, J.C., & Olson, R.K. (2006). Genetic and environmental influences on reading and listening comprehension. *Journal of Research in Reading, 29*, 75–91.

Kieffer, M.J. (2010). Socioeconomic status, English proficiency, and late-emerging reading difficulties. *Educational Researcher, 39*, 484–486.

Kirby, J.R., Georgiou, G.K., Martinussen, R., & Parrila, R. (2010). Naming speed and reading: From prediction to instruction. *Reading Research Quarterly, 45*, 341–362.

Kirby, J., Parrila, R., & Pfeiffer, S. (2003). Naming speed and phonological awareness as predictors of reading development. *Journal of Educational Psychology, 95*, 453–464.

Kuhn, M.R., Schwanenflugel, P.J., & Meisinger, E.B. (2010). Aligning theory and assessment of reading fluency: Automaticity, prosody, and definitions of fluency. *Reading Research Quarterly, 45*, 230–251.

Kuhn, M.R., & Stahl, S.A. (2003). Fluency: A review of developmental and remedial practices. *Journal of Educational Psychology, 95*, 3–21.

Leach, J.M., Scarborough, H.S., & Rescorla, L. (2003). Late-emerging reading disabilities. *Journal of Educational Psychology, 95,* 211–224.

Lesaux, N.K., & Kieffer, M.J. (2010). Exploring sources of reading comprehension difficulties among language minority learners and their classmates in early adolescence. *American Educational Research Journal, 47,* 596–632.

Lesaux, N.K., Kieffer, M.J., Faller, S.E., & Kelley, J.G. (2010). The effectiveness and ease of implementation of an academic vocabulary intervention for linguistically diverse students in urban middle schools. *Reading Research Quarterly, 45,* 196–228.

Leslie, L., & Caldwell, J. (2006). *Qualitative Reading Inventory-4.* Upper Saddle River, NJ: Pearson Education.

Levine, A. (2006). *Educating school teachers.* Washington, DC: Education Schools Project.

Liberman, I.Y., & Liberman, A.M. (1990). Whole language versus code emphasis: Underlying assumptions and their implications for reading instruction. *Annals of Dyslexia, 40,* 51–76.

Lindamood, P., & Lindamood, P. (1998). *The Lindamood Phoneme Sequencing Program for Reading, Spelling, and Speech.* Austin, TX: Pro-Ed.

Linn, B.M. (2012). *In the wake of the reading wars: Cognitive psychologists' and teacher educators' familiarity with and evaluation of cognitive reading research.* Doctoral dissertation, Department of Educational and Counselling Psychology and Department of Integrated Studies in Education, McGill University. Retrieved from http://digitool.library.mcgill.ca/web client/StreamGate?folder_id=0&dvs=13854 98849767~642

Lipka, O., Lesaux, N., & Siegel, L. (2006). Retrospective analyses of the reading development of grade 4 students with reading disabilities: Risk status and profiles over 5 years. *Journal of Learning Disabilities, 39,* 364–378.

Lipson, M.Y., & Wixson, K.K. (1986). Reading disability research: An interactionist perspective. *Review of Educational Research, 56,* 111–136.

Loftus, S.M., Coyne, M.D., McCoach, B., Zipoli, R., & Pullen, P.C. (2010). Effects of a supplemental vocabulary intervention on the word knowledge of kindergarten students at risk for language and literacy difficulties. *Learning Disabilities Research & Practice, 25,* 124–136.

Lovett, M.W., Barron, R.W., & Benson, N.J. (2003). Effective remediation of word identification and decoding difficulties in school-age children with reading disabilities. In H.L. Swanson, K.R. Harris, & S. Graham (Eds.), *Handbook of learning disabilities* (pp. 273–292). New York, NY: Guilford Press.

Lovett, M.W., Lacerenza, L., Borden, S.L., Frijters, J.C., Steinbach, K.A., & DePalma, M. (2000). Components of effective remediation for developmental reading disabilities: Combining phonological and strategy-based instruction to improve outcomes. *Journal of Educational Psychology, 92,* 263–283.

Lyon, G.R., Shaywitz, S.E., & Shaywitz, B.A. (2003). A definition of dyslexia. *Annals of Dyslexia, 53,* 1–14.

MacArthur, C.A. (2013). Technology applications for improving literacy: A review of research. In H.L. Swanson, K. Harris, & S. Graham (Eds.), *Handbook of learning disabilities, 2nd edition* (pp. 565–592.). New York, NY: Guilford Press.

Martin, J.L. (2013). *Understanding the modern menu of public education services for struggling learners: RTI programs, Section 504, and special education.* Retrieved from http://www.rtinetwork.org/learn/ld/understanding-the-modern-menu-of-public-education-services-for-struggling-learners-rti-programs-section-504-and-special-education

Mathes, P.G., Denton, C.A., Fletcher, J.M., Anthony, J.L., Francis, D.J., & Schatschneider, C. (2005). The effects of theoretically different instruction and student characteristics on the skills of struggling readers. *Reading Research Quarterly, 40,* 148–182.

McCandliss, B., Beck, I.L., Sandak, R., & Perfetti, C. (2003). Focusing attention on decoding for children with poor reading skills: Design and preliminary tests of the word building intervention. *Scientific Studies of Reading, 7,* 75–104.

McCardle, P., Mele-McCarthy, J., Cutting, L., & Leos, K. (Guest Eds.). (2005). Learning disabilities in English language learners: Research issues and future directions (special series). *Learning Disabilities Research and Practice, 20,* 1–78.

McCombes-Tolis, J., & Spear-Swerling, L. (2011). The preparation of pre-service elementary educators in understanding and

applying the terms, concepts, and practices associated with response to intervention in early reading contexts. *Journal
of School Leadership, 21*, 360–389.

McCutchen, D. (2000). Knowledge, processing, and working memory: Implications
for a theory of writing. *Educational Psychologist, 35*, 13–23.

McCutchen, D., Green, L., Abbott, R.D., &
Sanders, E.A. (2009). Further evidence
for teacher knowledge: Supporting strug-
gling readers in grades three through five.
*Reading and Writing: An Interdisciplinary
Journal, 22*, 401–423.

McCutchen, D., Harry, D.R., Cunningham,
A.E., Cox. S., Sidman, S., & Covill, A.E.
(2002). Reading teachers' knowledge of
children's literature and English phonology. *Annals of Dyslexia, 52*, 207–228.

McKeown, M.G., Beck, I.L., & Blake, R. (2009).
Rethinking reading comprehension
instruction: A comparison of instruction
for strategies and content approaches.
Reading Research Quarterly, 44, 218–253.

McMaster, K.L., Fuchs, D., & Fuchs, L.S.
(2006). Research on peer-assisted learning
strategies: The promise and limitations of
peer-mediated instruction. *Reading & Writing Quarterly, 22*, 5–25.

Meltzer, L. (2010). *Promoting executive function in the classroom*. New York, NY: Guilford Press.

Menon, S., & Hiebert, E. (2005). A comparison
of first graders' reading with little books or
literature-based basal anthologies. *Reading Research Quarterly, 40*, 12–38.

Mesmer, H.A., Cunningham, J.W., & Hiebert,
E.H. (2012). Toward a theoretical model
of text complexity for the early grades:
Learning from the past, anticipating the
future. *Reading Research Quarterly, 47*,
235–258.

Meyer, M.S., & Felton, R.H. (1999). Repeated
reading to enhance fluency: Old approaches
and new directions. *Annals of Dyslexia, 49*,
283–306.

Moats, L.C. (1994). The missing foundation
in teacher education: Knowledge of the
structure of spoken and written language.
Annals of Dyslexia, 44, 81–102.

Moats, L.C. (1999). *Teaching reading is rocket
science: What expert teachers of reading
should know and be able to do*. Washington,
DC: American Federation of Teachers.

Moats, L.C. (2012). Reconciling the Common Core State Standards with reading

research. *Perspectives on Language and
Literacy, 38*, 15–18.

Moats, L.C., & Foorman, B.R. (2003). Measuring teachers' content knowledge of language and reading. *Annals of Dyslexia, 53*,
23–45.

Moats, L.C., & Lyon, G.R. (1993). Learning
disabilities in the United States: Advocacy,
science, and the future of the field. *Journal
of Learning Disabilities, 26*, 282–294.

Mol, S.E., & Bus, A.G. (2011). To read or not
to read: A meta-analysis of print exposure
from infancy to early adulthood. *Psychological Bulletin, 137*, 267–296.

Morgan, P.L., Farkas, G., & Wu, Q. (2012). Do
poor readers feel angry, sad, and unpop-
ular? *Scientific Studies of Reading, 16*,
360–381.

Morris, D. (2014). *Diagnosis and correction of
reading problems* (2nd ed.). New York, NY:
Guilford Press.

Nagy, W., & Scott, J. (2000). Vocabulary processes. In M. Kamil, P. Mosenthal, P.D. Pearson, & R. Barr (Eds.), *Handbook of reading
research* (Vol. 3). Mahwah, NJ: Erlbaum.

Nation, K. (2005). Children's reading comprehension difficulties. In M.J. Snowling &
C. Hulme (Eds.), *The science of reading: A
handbook* (pp. 248–266). Oxford, England:
Blackwell.

Nation, K., Clarke, P., Wright, B., & Williams,
C. (2006). Patterns of reading ability in
children with autism spectrum disorder.
*Journal of Autism and Developmental Disor-
ders, 36*, 911–919.

Nation, K., & Snowling, M. (1997). Assessing
reading difficulties: The validity and utility of current measures of reading skill.
*British Journal of Educational Psychology,
67*, 359–370.

National Council on Teacher Quality (NCTQ).
(2006). *What education schools aren't
teaching about reading and what elementary teachers aren't learning*. Washington,
DC: Author.

National Governors Association Center for
Best Practices & Council of Chief State
School Officers. (2010). *Common Core
State Standards for English language arts
and literacy in history/social studies, sci-
ence, and technical subjects*. Washington,
DC: Authors.

National Reading Panel (NRP). (2000).
*Teaching children to read: An evidence-
based assessment of the scientific research
literature on reading and its implications*

for reading instruction. Washington, DC: National Institutes of Health.

National Research Council. (1998). *Preventing reading difficulties in young children.* Washington, DC: National Academies Press.

National Research Council. (2010). *Preparing teachers: Building evidence for sound policy.* Washington, DC: National Academies Press.

Neuman, S.B., & Celano, D. (2001). Access to print in middle- and low-income communities: An ecological study of four neighborhoods. *Reading Research Quarterly, 36,* 8–26.

Neuman, S.B., & Celano, D. (2006). The knowledge gap: Implications of leveling the playing field on low- and middle-income children. *Reading Research Quarterly, 41,* 35–70.

Nisbett, R.E., Aronson, J., Blair, C., Dickens, W., Flynn, J., Halpern, D.F., . . . Turkheimer, E. (2012). Intelligence: New findings and theoretical developments. *American Psychologist, 67,* 130–159.

Nolen, P.A., McCutchen, D., & Berninger, V. (1990). Ensuring tomorrow's literacy: A shared responsibility. *Journal of Teacher Education, 41,* 63–72.

Norbury, C., & Nation, K. (2011). Understanding variability in reading comprehension in adolescents with autism spectrum disorders: Interactions with language status and decoding skill. *Scientific Studies of Reading, 15,* 191–210.

Norton, E.S., & Wolf, M. (2012). Rapid automatized naming (RAN) and reading fluency: Implications for understanding and treatment of reading disabilities. *Annual Review of Psychology, 63,* 427–452.

Nunes, T., Bryant, P., Pretzlik, U., Burman, D., Bell, D., & Gardner, S. (2006). An intervention program for classroom teaching about morphemes: Effects on the children's vocabulary. In T. Nunes & P. Bryant (Eds.), *Improving literacy by teaching morphemes* (pp. 121–134). London, England: Routledge.

Nye, B., Konstantopoulos, S., & Hedges, L.V. (2004). How large are teacher effects? *Educational Evaluation and Policy Analysis, 26,* 237–57.

O'Connor, I., & Klein, P. (2004). Explorations of strategies for facilitating the reading comprehension of high-functioning students with autism spectrum disorders. *Journal of Autism and Developmental Disorders, 34,* 115–127.

O'Connor, R.E. (2011). Phoneme awareness and the alphabetic principle. In R.E. O'Connor & P.F. Vadasy (Eds.), *Handbook of reading interventions* (pp. 9–26). New York, NY: Guilford Press.

O'Connor, R.E., White, A., & Swanson, H.L. (2007). Repeated reading versus continuous reading: Influences on reading fluency and comprehension. *Exceptional Children, 74,* 31–46.

Olson, R.K., & Byrne, B. (2005). Genetic and environmental influences on reading and language ability and disability. In H. Catts & A. Kamhi (Eds.), *The connections between language and reading disabilities* (pp. 173–200). Mahwah, NJ: Laurence Erlbaum Associates.

Olson, R.K., Keenan, J.M., Byrne, B., Samuelsson, S. Coventry, W., Corley, R., . . . Hulslander, J. (2011). Genetic and environmental influences on vocabulary and reading development. *Scientific Studies of Reading, 15,* 26–46.

Palincsar, A.S., & Brown, A.L. (1984). Reciprocal teaching of comprehension-fostering and comprehension-monitoring activities. *Cognition and Instruction, 1,* 117–175.

Pearson, P.D., Hiebert, E.H., & Kamil, M.L. (2007). Vocabulary assessment: What we know and what we need to learn. *Reading Research Quarterly, 42,* 282–296.

Perfetti, C.A. (1992). The representation problem in reading acquisition. In P.B. Gough, L.C. Ehri, & R. Treiman (Eds.), *Reading acquisition* (pp. 145–174). Hillsdale, NJ: Erlbaum.

Perfetti, C.A., Landi, N., & Oakhill, J. (2005). The acquisition of reading comprehension skill. In M.J. Snowling & C. Hulme (Eds.), *The science of reading: A handbook* (pp. 227–253). Oxford, England: Blackwell.

Phelps-Terasaki, D., & Phelps-Gunn, T. (2007). *Test of Pragmatic Language, 2nd edition.* Austin, TX: Pro-Ed.

Piasta, S.B., Connor, C.M., Fishman, B.J., & Morrison, F.J. (2009). Teachers' knowledge of literacy concepts, classroom practices, and student reading growth. *Scientific Studies of Reading, 13,* 224–248.

Podhajski, B., Mather, N., Nathan, J., & Sammons, J. (2009). Professional development in scientifically based reading instruction: Teacher knowledge and reading outcomes. *Journal of Learning Disabilities, 42,* 403–417.

Pressley, M.P., Dolezal, S., Roehrig, A.D., & Hilden, K. (2002). Why the National Reading Panel's recommendations are not enough. In R.L. Allington (Ed.), *Big brother and the National Reading Curriculum: How ideology trumped evidence* (pp. 75–89). Portsmouth, NH: Heinemann.

Pressley, M., El-Dinary, P.B., Gaskins, I., Schuder, T., Bergman, J.L., Almasi, J., ... Brown, R. (1992). Beyond direct explanation: Transactional instruction of reading comprehension strategies. *The Elementary School Journal, 92,* 513–555.

Pugh, K.R., & McCardle, P. (2009). *How children learn to read: Current issues and new directions in the integration of cognition, neurobiology and genetics of reading and dyslexia research and practice.* New York, NY: Psychology Press.

Pullen, P.C., Tuckwiller, E.D., Konold, T.R., Maynard, K.L., & Coyne, M.D. (2010). A tiered intervention model for early vocabulary instruction: The effects of tiered instruction for young students at risk for reading disability. *Learning Disabilities Research & Practice, 25,* 110–123.

Rack, J.P., Snowling, M.J., & Olson, R.K. (1992). The nonword reading deficit in developmental dyslexia: A review. *Reading Research Quarterly, 27,* 28–53.

Rand Reading Study Group. (2002). *Reading for understanding: Toward an R&D program in reading comprehension.* Santa Monica, CA: Rand.

Richlan, F., Kronbichler, M., & Wimmer, H. (2009). Functional abnormalities in the dyslexic brain: A quantitative meta-analysis of neuroimaging studies. *Human Brain Mapping, 30,* 3299–3308.

Riedel, B.W. (2007). The relation between DIBELS, reading comprehension, and vocabulary in urban first-grade students. *Reading Research Quarterly, 42,* 546–567.

Ripley, A. (2013). *The smartest kids in the world—and how they got that way.* New York, NY: Simon & Schuster.

Rivera, M.O., Moughamian, A.C., Lesaux, N.K., & Francis, D.J. (2008). *Language and reading interventions for English language learners and English language learners with disabilities.* Portsmouth, NH: RMC Research Corporation, Center on Instruction.

Robertson, C., & Salter, W. (2007). *Phonological Awareness Test 2.* East Moline, IL: LinguiSystems.

Roid, G.H. (2003). *Stanford-Binet Intelligence Scales, 5th edition.* Rolling Meadows, IL: Riverside.

Salvia, J., Ysseldyke, J.E., & Bolt, S. (2013). *Assessment in special and inclusive education*

(12th ed.). Belmont, CA: Wadsworth, Cengage Learning.

Scarborough, H.S. (1998). Early identification of children at risk for reading disabilities: Phonological awareness and some other promising predictors. In B.K. Shapiro, P.J. Accardo, & A.J. Capute (Eds.), *Specific reading disability: A view of the spectrum* (pp. 75–119). Timonium, MD: York Press.

Scarborough, H.S. (2002). Connecting early language and literacy to later reading (dis)abilities: Evidence, theory, and practice. In S.B. Neuman & D.K. Dickinson (Eds.), *Handbook of early literacy research* (pp. 97–125). New York, NY: Guilford Press.

Scarborough, H.S. (2005). Developmental relationships between language and reading: Reconciling a beautiful hypothesis with some ugly facts. In H.W. Catts & A. Kamhi (Eds.), *The connections between language and reading disabilities* (pp. 3–24). Mahwah, NJ: Erlbaum.

Scarborough, H.S., & Brady, S.A. (2002). Toward a common terminology for talking about speech and reading: A glossary of the "phon" words and some related terms. *Journal of Literacy Research, 34,* 299–334.

Scarborough, H.S., & Dobrich, W. (1994). On the efficacy of reading to preschoolers. *Developmental Review, 14,* 245–302.

Scarborough, H.S., Ehri, L.C., Olson, R.K., & Fowler, A.E. (1998). The fate of phonemic awareness beyond the elementary school years. *Scientific Studies of Reading, 2,* 115–142.

Seidenberg, M.S. (2005). Connectionist models of word reading. *Current Directions in Psychological Science, 14,* 238–242.

Semel, E., Wiig, E.H., & Secord, W.A. (2013). *Clinical Evaluation of Language Fundamentals, 5th edition.* San Antonio, TX: The Psychological Corp.

Sesma, H.W., Mahone, E.M., Levine, T., Eason, S.H., & Cutting, L.E. (2009). The contribution of executive skills to reading comprehension. *Child Neuropsychology, 15,* 232–246.

Seymour, P.H.K. (1997). Foundations of orthographic development. In C.A. Perfetti, L. Rieben, & M. Fayol (Eds.), *Learning to spell: Research, theory, and practice among languages* (pp. 319–337). Hillsdale, NJ: Erlbaum.

Shanahan, T. (2004). Critiques of the National Reading Panel report: Their implications for research, policy, and practice. In P. McCardle & V. Chhabra (Eds.), *The voice of evidence in reading research* (pp. 235–265). Baltimore, MD: Paul H. Brookes Publishing Co.

Shanahan, T. (2013). Letting the text take center stage: How the Common Core State Standards will transform English language arts instruction. *American Educator, 4–11,* 43.

Share, D.L. (2008). On the Anglocentricities of current reading research and practice: The perils of overreliance on an "outlier" orthography. *Psychological Bulletin, 134,* 584–615.

Shaywitz, B., Shaywitz, S., Blachman, B., Pugh, K., Fulbright, R., Skudlarski, P., . . . Gore, J.C. (2004). Development of left occipito-temporal systems for skilled reading in children after a phonologically-based intervention. *Biological Psychiatry, 55,* 926–933.

Shaywitz, S. (2003). *Overcoming dyslexia: A new and complete science-based program for reading problems at any level.* New York, NY: Knopf.

Shepard, L.A. (2000). The role of assessment in a learning culture. *Educational Researcher, 29,* 4–14.

Shinn, M.R. (2008). Best practices in using curriculum-based measurement in a problem-solving model. In A. Thomas & J. Grimes (Eds.), *Best practices in school psychology* (pp. 671–697). Bethesda, MD: National Association of School Psychologists.

Siegel, L.S. (1988). Evidence that IQ scores are irrelevant to the definition and analysis of reading disability. *Canadian Journal of Psychology, 42,* 201–215.

Siegel, L.S. (1989). IQ is irrelevant to the definition of learning disabilities. *Journal of Learning Disabilities, 22,* 469–478.

Siegel, L.S. (1999). Learning disabilities: The roads we have traveled and the path to the future. In R.J. Sternberg & L. Spear-Swerling (Eds.), *Perspectives on learning disabilities: Biological, cognitive, contextual* (pp. 159–175). Boulder, CO: Westview Press.

Siegel, L.S., & Himel, N. (1998). Socioeconomic status, age, and the classification of dyslexics and poor readers: The dangers of using IQ scores in the definition of reading disability. *Dyslexia, 4,* 90–104.

Simmons, D.C., Coyne, M.D., Hagan-Burke, S., Kwok, O., Simmons, L., Johnson, C., . . . Crevecoeur, Y.C. (2011). Effects of supplemental reading interventions in authentic contexts: A comparison of kindergartners' response. *Exceptional Children, 77,* 207–228.

Simmons, D.C., & Kame'enui, K.J. (2003). *A consumer's guide to evaluating a core reading program Grades K–3: A critical elements analysis.* Retrieved from http://reading.uoregon.edu/cia/curricula/con_guide.php

Smith, L.E., Borkowski, J.G., & Whitman, T.L. (2008). From reading readiness to reading competence: The role of self-regulation in at-risk children. *Scientific Studies of Reading, 12,* 131–152.

Snow, C.E. (2013). Cold versus warm close reading: Building students' stamina for struggling with text. *Reading Today, 30,* 18–19.

Snow, C.E., Griffin, P., & Burns, M.S. (2005). *Knowledge to support the teaching of reading: Preparing teachers for a changing world.* San Francisco, CA: Jossey-Bass.

Spear-Swerling, L. (2004a). A road map for understanding reading disability and other reading problems: Origins, intervention, and prevention. In R. Ruddell & N. Unrau (Eds.), *Theoretical models and processes of reading* (Vol. 5). Newark, DE: International Reading Association.

Spear-Swerling, L. (2004b). Fourth-graders' performance on a state-mandated assessment involving two different measures of reading comprehension. *Reading Psychology, 25,* 121–148.

Spear-Swerling, L. (2009). A literacy tutoring experience for prospective special educators and struggling second graders. *Journal of Learning Disabilities, 42,* 431–443.

Spear-Swerling, L. (2011a). Patterns of reading disabilities across development. In R. Allington & A. McGill-Franzen (Eds.), *Handbook of research on reading disabilities* (pp. 149–161). New York, NY: Routledge.

Spear-Swerling, L. (2011b). Phases in reading words and phonics interventions. In R. O'Connor and P. Vadasy (Eds.), *Handbook of reading interventions* (pp. 63–87). New York, NY: Guilford Press.

Spear-Swerling, L. (2013). A road map for understanding reading disabilities and other reading problems, redux. In D.E. Alvermann, N.J. Unrau, & R.B. Ruddell (Eds.), *Theoretical models and processes of reading* (Vol. 6, pp. 412–436). Newark, DE: International Reading Association.

Spear-Swerling, L., & Brucker, P. (2004). Preparing novice teachers to develop basic reading and spelling skills in children. *Annals of Dyslexia, 54*, 332–364.

Spear-Swerling, L., & Brucker, P. (2006). Teacher-education students' reading abilities and their knowledge about word structure. *Teacher Education and Special Education, 29*, 113–123.

Spear-Swerling, L., Brucker, P., & Alfano, M. (2005). Teachers' literacy-related knowledge and self-perceptions in relation to preparation and experience. *Annals of Dyslexia, 55*, 266–293.

Spear-Swerling, L., & Cheesman, E. (2012). Teachers' knowledge base for implementing response-to-intervention models in reading. *Reading & Writing: An Interdisciplinary Journal, 25*, 1691–1723.

Spear-Swerling, L., & Coyne, M. (2010). How research-based licensure exams can improve teacher preparation in reading: Lessons from Connecticut. *Perspectives on Language and Literacy, 36*, 18–21.

Spear-Swerling, L., & Sternberg, R.J. (1994). The road not taken: An integrative theoretical model of reading disability. *Journal of Learning Disabilities, 27*, 91–103, 122.

Spear-Swerling, L., & Sternberg, R.J. (1996). *Off track: When poor readers become "learning disabled."* Boulder, CO: Westview Press.

Spear-Swerling, L., & Zibulsky, J. (in press). Making time for literacy: Teacher knowledge and time allocation in instructional planning. *Reading and Writing: An Interdisciplinary Journal.*

Spector, J.E. (2005). How reliable are informal reading inventories? *Psychology in the Schools, 42*, 593–603.

Speece, D.L., Case, L.P., & Molloy, D.W. (2003). Responsiveness to general education instruction as the first gate to learning disabilities identification. *Learning Disabilities Research and Practice, 18*, 147–156.

Stahl, S.A. (2004). What do we know about fluency? Findings of the National Reading Panel. In P. McCardle & V. Chhabra (Eds.), *The voice of evidence in reading research* (pp. 187–211). Baltimore, MD: Paul H. Brookes Publishing Co.

Stahl, S.A., & Nagy, W.E. (2006). *Teaching word meanings.* Mahwah, NJ: Erlbaum.

Stanovich, K.E. (1986). Matthew effects in reading: Some consequences of individual differences in the acquisition of literacy. *Reading Research Quarterly, 21*, 36–406.

Stanovich, K.E. (1991). Discrepancy definitions of reading disability: Has intelligence led us astray? *Reading Research Quarterly, 26*, 7–29.

Stanovich, K.E. (2000). *Progress in understanding reading: Scientific foundations and new frontiers.* New York, NY: Guilford Press.

Stanovich, K.E. (2009). *What intelligence tests miss: The psychology of rational thought.* New Haven, CT: Yale University Press.

Stanovich, K., & Siegel, L. (1994). The phenotypic performance profile of reading-disabled children: A regression-based test of the phonological-core-variable-difference model. *Journal of Educational Psychology, 86*, 24–53.

Steele, C.M., & Aronson, J. (1995). Stereotype threat and the intellectual test performance of African Americans. *Journal of Personality and Social Psychology, 69*, 797–811.

Sternberg, R.J. (1985). *Beyond IQ: A triarchic theory of intelligence.* New York, NY: Cambridge University Press.

Stotsky, S. (2009). Licensure tests for special education teachers: How well they assess knowledge of reading instruction and mathematics. *Journal of Learning Disabilities, 42*, 464–474.

Sugai, G., & Horner, R.H. (2005). School-wide positive behavior supports: Achieving and sustaining effective learning environments for all students. In W.H. Heward (Ed.), *Focus on behavior analysis in education: Achievements, challenges, and opportunities* (pp. 90–102). Upper Saddle River, NJ: Pearson Prentice-Hall.

Templeton, S., & Morris, D. (2000). Spelling. In M.L. Kamil, P.B. Mosenthal, P.D. Pearson, & R. Barr, *Handbook of reading research* (pp. 525–543). Mahwah, NJ: Erlbaum.

Tilstra, J., McMaster, K., van den Broek, P., Kendeou, P., & Rapp, D. (2009). Simple but complex: Components of the simple view of reading across grade levels. *Journal of Research in Reading, 32*, 383–401.

Torgesen, J.K. (2004). Lessons learned from research on interventions for students who have difficulty learning to read. In P. McCardle & V. Chhabra (Eds.), *The voice of evidence in reading research* (pp. 355–381). Baltimore, MD: Paul H. Brookes Publishing Co.

Torgesen, J.K. (2006). *Preventing reading difficulties in very large numbers of students: The Reading First initiative.* Paper presented at the Annual Meeting of the

International Dyslexia Association, Indianapolis, IN.

Torgesen, J.K., Alexander, A., Wagner, R.K., Rashotte, C., Voeller, K., & Conway, T. (2001). Intensive remedial instruction for children with severe reading disabilities: Immediate and long-term outcomes from two instructional approaches. *Journal of Learning Disabilities, 34*(1), 33–58.

Torgesen, J.K., Wagner, R.K., & Rashotte, C.A. (1994). Longitudinal studies of phonological processing and reading. *Journal of learning Disabilities, 27,* 276–286.

Torgesen, J.K., Wagner, R.K., & Rashotte, C.A. (2012). *Test of Word Reading Efficiency, 2nd edition.* San Antonio, TX: Pearson.

Vadasy, P.F., Sanders, E.A., & Peyton, J.A. (2005). Contributions of reading practice to first-grade supplemental tutoring: How text matters. *Journal of Learning Disabilities, 38,* 364–380.

Valencia, S.W. (2011). Reader profiles and reading disabilities. In R. Allington & A. McGill-Franzen (Eds.), *Handbook of research on reading disabilities* (pp. 25–35). New York, NY: Routledge.

Valencia, S.W., Smith, A.T., Reece, A.M., Li, M., Wixson, K.K., & Newman, H. (2010). Oral reading fluency assessment: Issues of construct, criterion, and consequential validity. *Reading Research Quarterly, 45,* 270–291.

Vaughn, S., Denton, C.A., & Fletcher, J.M. (2010). Why intensive interventions are necessary for students with severe reading difficulties. *Psychology in the Schools, 47,* 432–444.

Vaughn, S., Wanzek, J., Woodruff, A.L., & Thompson, S. (2007). Prevention and early identification of students with reading disabilities. In D.H. Haager, S. Vaughn, & J.K. Klingner (Eds.), *Evidence-based reading practices for response to intervention* (pp. 11–27). Baltimore, MD: Paul H. Brookes Publishing Co.

Vaughn, S., Wexler, J., Roberts, G., Barth, A.A., Cirino, P.T., Romain, M.A., . . . Denton, C.A. (2011). Effects of individualized and standardized interventions on middle school students with reading disabilities. *Exceptional Children, 77,* 391–407.

Vellutino, F.R. (1979). *Dyslexia: Theory and research.* Cambridge, MA: MIT Press.

Vellutino, F.R., & Scanlon, D.M. (2002). Emergent literacy skills, early instruction, and individual differences as determinants of difficulties in learning to read: The case for early intervention. In S.B. Neuman &
D.K. Dickinson (Eds.), *Handbook of early literacy research* (pp. 295–321). New York, NY: Guilford Press.

Vellutino, F.R., Scanlon, D.M., Sipay, E.R., Small, S.G., Pratt, A., Chen, R., . . . Denckla, M.B. (1996). Cognitive profiles of difficult-to-remediate and readily remediated poor readers: Early intervention as a vehicle for distinguishing between cognitive and experiential deficits as basic causes of specific reading disability. *Journal of Educational Psychology, 88,* 601–638.

Vukovic, R.K., & Siegel, L.S. (2006). The double deficit hypothesis: A comprehensive review of the evidence. *Journal of Learning Disabilities, 39,* 25–47.

Waesche, J.S.B., Schatschneider, C., Maner, J.K., Ahmed, Y., & Wagner, R.K. (2011). Examining agreement and longitudinal stability among traditional and response-to-intervention-based definitions of reading disability using the affected-status agreement statistic. *Journal of Learning Disabilities, 44,* 296–307.

Wagner, R.K., Torgesen, J.K., Rashotte, C.A., & Pearson, N.A. (2013). *Comprehensive Test of Phonological Processing, 2nd edition.* Austin, TX: Pro-Ed.

Walberg, H.J., & Tsai, S. (1983). Matthew effects in education. *American Educational Research Journal, 20,* 359–373.

Walley, A.C., Metsala, J.L., & Garlock, V.M. (2003). Spoken vocabulary growth: Its role in the development of phoneme awareness and early reading ability. *Reading & Writing: An Interdisciplinary Journal, 16,* 5–20.

Walton, G.M., & Spencer, S.J. (2009). Latent ability: Grades and test scores systematically underestimate the intellectual ability of negatively stereotyped students. *Psychological Science, 20,* 1132–1139.

Washburn, E.K., Joshi, R.M., & Binks-Cantrell, E.S. (2011). Teacher knowledge of basic language concepts and dyslexia. *Dyslexia, 17,* 165–183.

Wechsler, D. (1999). *Wechsler Abbreviated Scale of Intelligence (WASI).* San Antonio, TX: The Psychological Corp.

Wechsler, D. (2003). *Wechsler Intelligence Scale for Children, 4th edition (WISC-IV).* San Antonio, TX: Pearson.

Wechsler, D. (2005). *Wechsler Individual Achievement Test, 2nd edition (WIAT II).* London, England: The Psychological Corp.

Wechsler, D. (2009). *Wechsler Individual Achievement Test, 3rd edition (WIAT III).* San Antonio, TX: Pearson.

Wexler, J., Vaughn, S., Roberts, G., & Denton, C. (2010). The efficacy of repeated reading and wide reading practice for high school students with severe reading disabilities. *Learning Disabilities Research & Practice, 25*, 2–10.

Whalon, K.J., Al Otaiba, S., & Delano, M.E. (2009). Evidence-based reading instruction for individuals with autism spectrum disorders. *Focus on Autism and Other Developmental Disabilities, 24*, 3–16.

Whalon, K.J., & Hanline, M.F. (2008). Effects of a reciprocal questioning intervention on the question generation and responding of children with autism spectrum disorder. *Education and Training in Developmental Disabilities, 432*, 367–387.

Whitehurst, G.J., & Lonigan, C.J. (2002). Emergent literacy: Development from pre-readers to readers. In S.B. Neuman & D.K. Dickinson (Eds.), *Handbook of early literacy research* (pp. 11–29). New York, NY: Guilford Press.

Wiederholt, J.L., & Bryant, B.R. (2012). *Gray Oral Reading Test, 5th edition.* Austin, TX: Pro-Ed.

Willcutt, E.G., Pennington, B.F., Duncan, L., Smith, S.D., Keenan, J.M., Wadsworth, S., . . . Olson, R.K. (2010). Understanding the complex etiologies of developmental disorders: Behavioral and molecular genetic approaches. *Journal of Developmental & Behavioral Pediatrics, 31*, 533–544.

Williamson, G.L., Fitzgerald, J., & Stenner, A.J. (2013). The Common Core State Standards' quantitative text complexity trajectory: Figuring out how much complexity is enough. *Educational Researcher, 42*, 59–69.

Willingham, D.T. (2006–2007, Winter). The usefulness of *brief* instruction in reading comprehension strategies. *American Educator, 39–45,* 50.

Wilson, B.A. (1988). *Wilson reading system.* Oxford, MA: Wilson Language Training Corporation.

Wolf, M. (2007). *Proust and the squid: The story and science of the reading brain.* New York, NY: HarperCollins.

Wolf, M., & Bowers, P. (1999). The double-deficit hypothesis for the developmental dyslexias. *Journal of Educational Psychology, 91*, 415–438.

Woodcock, R.W., McGrew, K.S., & Mather, N. (2007). *Woodcock-Johnson Tests of Achievement.* Rolling Meadows, IL: Riverside.

Yatvin, J. (2000). Minority view. In *Report of the National Reading Panel: Teaching children to read: An evidence-based assessment of the scientific research literature on reading and its implications for reading instruction* (pp. 1–6). Washington, DC: National Institutes of Health.

Yoon, K.S., Duncan, T., Lee, S.W.-Y., Scarloss, B., & Shapley, K. (2007). *Reviewing the evidence on how teacher professional development affects student achievement* (Issues & Answers Report, Regional Educational Laboratory [REL] 2007-No. 033). Washington, DC: U.S. Department of Education, Institute of Education Sciences, National Center for Education Evaluation and Regional Assistance, Regional Educational Laboratory Southwest. Retrieved from http://ies.ed.gov/ncee/edlabs

Youman, M., & Mather, N. (2013). Dyslexia laws in the USA. *Annals of Dyslexia, 63*, 133–153.

Yuill, N., & Oakhill, J. (1991). *Children's problems in text comprehension.* Cambridge, MA: Cambridge University Press.

Zirkel, P.A. (2011). State laws and guidelines for RTI: Additional implementation features. *Communique Online, 39.* Retrieved from http://www.nasponline.org/publications/cq/39/7/professional-practice-state-laws.aspx

Zirkel, P.A., & Thomas, L.B. (2010). State laws and guidelines for implementing RTI. *Teaching Exceptional Children, 43*, 60–73.

Index

Tables and figures are indicated by *t* and *f*, respectively.

LDs, *see* Learning disabilities
Leadership, for implementation of response to intervention (RTI), 15
Learning disabilities (LDs), 2, 122, 132, 170, 177–178
    identification of, 15–16, 36–39, 94–95, 206–210
    see also Accommodations; Special education
Licensure exams, 198, 213–214
Listening comprehension, 29–30, 43–44, 52, 206–207
Listening comprehension–reading comprehension (LC-RC) discrepancy, 35–36
Literacy skills, higher order, 106
Low-income backgrounds, students from, 1–3, 33, 124

Matthew effects, 69–70
Mental model, 24–25
Mixed reading difficulties (MRD), 63, 68, 113, 159–179
Morphemes, 45
Morphological development, 44–46
Morphology
    early instruction, 102
    explicit teaching of, 165, 171
Motivating texts, 156
MRD, *see* Mixed reading difficulties
MTSS, *see* Multi-tiered systems of support
Multiple comprehension tasks, 89
Multisensory activities, 109
Multistage screening, 86
Multisyllabic words
    decoding, 57
    syllabication and structural analysis, 101–102
Multi-tiered systems of support (MTSS), 4, 6–11, 34–36, 195

National Reading Panel (NRP), 10, 20–23, 34, 100, 104
Native language assessments, 84
Nonalphabetic word readers, 66, 127
Nonautomatic word readers, 67, 131, 133, 163–164
Nonresponders, 11
Nonsense Word Fluency (NWF), 126
Nonstrategic comprehenders, 67–68, 142, 148, 164, 175–176
NRP, *see* National Reading Panel
NWF, *see* Nonsense Word Fluency

Onset-rime approach, to phonics instruction, 101
Oral language, 29–30, 105, 112–113, 165, 175–176
Oral reading fluency (ORF), 85–87, 148
Oral reading of text, 103, 144, 177
ORF, *see* Oral reading fluency
Out-of-context word reading, 168

Partial alphabetic reading, 49
Partial letter cues, in conjunction with context, 42–43
Passage-independent questions, 88
Pattern of strengths and weaknesses, 37
    identification of learning disabilities (LDs), 207–208
Phoneme Segmentation Fluency (PSF), 126
Phonemic awareness, 21–22, 166
    instruction, 100–102
Phonetic regularity, continuum of, 53
Phonetic-cue word recognition, 49
Phonics, 19, 22, 137
    application of skills, 110
    instruction, 97, 100–102
    interventions, 123, 170, 177
    synthetic, 100–101
Phonological awareness, 22, 126
Phonological skills, 41, 110, 119, 173, 175
PL 94-142, *see* Education for All Handicapped Children Act
PL 101-336, *see* Americans with Disabilities Act (ADA) of 1990
Pragmatic language, 28, 163
Prealphabetic phase, 49
Predictable texts, 102
Prerequisite abilities, development of, 74
Problem-solving approaches, to interventions, 14
Professional development, 33, 188–213
Proficient reading, 51–52
Profiles
    necessity for interventions, 73
    patterns of difficulties, 65–68
    of reading difficulties, 4, 17–18, 57–75, 60t–61t, 91–93
    use in teacher preparation, 194
    value of, 202–203
Progress monitoring, 79, 151, 165
Prosody of reading, 93
PSF, *see* Phoneme Segmentation Fluency

Question-answering measures, of reading comprehension, 87